I0084760

The
Constitution
of Interests

ADVANCE PRAISE FOR THE BOOK

"*The Constitution of Interests* addresses important issues within the politics of law. More specifically it is concerned to focus attention upon the pervasive institutional reality of legal relations upon the plethora of laws that constitute the politics of the public sphere. John Brigham argues persuasively that law should be understood by reference to the diverse political communities, both radical and conservative which interpret and reproduce its rule."

—Peter Goodrich, University of London

"A brilliant theory of law, rhetoric, and movement politics. An extremely important book."

—Susan Burgess, University of Wisconsin, Milwaukee

"Socio-legal scholars with a post-modern sensibility have been developing constitutive conceptions of the law and of legal research for at least the last decade. John Brigham's book moves the constitutive enterprise a significant step forward and may indeed have provided it with a founding document. Brigham demonstrates that the constitutive force of the law is both pervasive and contingent. In so doing, he breathes new life into E. P. Thompson's seminal admonition to abandon notions of the law as exclusively a site of domination (or of resistance) and to think instead of law as a contingent arena of conflict."

—Stuart A. Scheingold, author of *The Politics of Rights*

The
Constitution
of Interests

Beyond the
Politics of Rights

John Brigham

NEW YORK UNIVERSITY
New York and London

NEW YORK UNIVERSITY PRESS
New York and London

©1996 by New York University

All rights reserved

Library of Congress Cataloging-in-Publication Data
Brigham, John, 1945–
The constitution of interests: beyond the politics of rights /
John Brigham.
p. cm.
Includes bibliographical references and index.
ISBN 0-8147-1285-1 (alk. paper)
1. Law—United States. 2. Jurisprudence—United States.
3. Law—United States—Philosophy. 4. Law and politics.
5. Civil rights—United States. I. Title.
KF384.B75 1996
349.73—dc20   96-25301
[347.3]   CIP

New York University Press books are printed on acid-free paper,
and their binding materials are chosen for strength and durability.

Manufactured in the United States of America

10 9 8 7 6 5 4 3 2 1

This book is dedicated to
Christine B. Harrington
Professor, student of the
constitutive, activist, mother,
and partner.

Contents

Preface

*T*he *Constitution of Interests* sets forth a theory of law, rhetoric, and movement politics and applies it to various instances when Americans have organized in the shadow of the law. The interests developed in the following chapters concern gay rights, realism in the legal academy, the remedial response to law called "informalism," and the radical feminist antipornography campaign. Each case illustrates the constitutive power of law. The events on which I focus here, such as the closing of the gay baths in San Francisco and the early antipornography movement, transpired roughly ten years ago. The debates about how to understand them continue to occupy social scientists up to the present moment.

This book tries to engage law and politics at the ideological and epistemological levels. The relationship between the two, and their influence on public authority, has been one of my professional preoccupations. Law derives its power from positivism both in jurisprudence and in philosophy. How Americans know what is law and what is politics goes a long way toward determining the structure of authority in this country. Law consists of pronouncements from the sovereign—such as the protection for abortion emanating from *Roe v. Wade.* Law is also what we think about the subjects covered by those pronouncements—for example, that abortion is either a choice or that it is murder. Law is formed in the dynamic tension between official pronouncements and their reception at least as much as it is formed in legislatures and courts.

Liberal legal and political theory typically downplays the power of the law to constitute social relations, including identity, movement politics, and categories of scholarship. As Susan Burgess has said, "When scholars base their study of the law on liberal concepts and categories such as pluralism and individual interest, they inevitably fail to see the way that law creates and maintains hierarchy and dominance in society."[1] In addition, when political activists fail to note the power of conventional legal forms, they cannot understand the power of law to shape their interests.

The constitutive approach incorporates the two poles at which most legal theory is situated: the formalist, which assumes that law determines the shape of social life, and the realist, which sees politics and interests driving society. The law may be what the judge says it is. The politics and behavior of judges are certainly central features of law. But we can no more understand the meaning of judicial politics without law than assess judicial behavior without a bench. Law does not need to determine every aspect of life to have a constitutive effect. Law constitutes along with other social forces, like religion, family, and entertainment. The law we find in society we call constitutive. Hence, constitutive work is a level of analysis. By breaking out of the dichotomy between "legal" and "political" or between "law" and "social life," we hope to offer a new perspective on politics—one that looks at the places where law matters.

In my work, the law takes a different form for each of the groups examined. There are multiple forms for law, a plurality. These forms depend on perception, which is manifested in social life. At the same time, and unlike some traditional pluralists, I recognize a centrifugal influence in the forms produced by governing institutions. By beginning with "rights" and ending with radicalism or "rage," I have organized the chapters to highlight both the most common conceptions of law and the polar responses to it. In this sense, the constitution of interests takes us beyond a politics of rights. Gays in the first instance and radical feminists in the second each see law as a powerful force in society. Law professors, who profess versions of legal realism, and reformers, who built a network of "informal" institutions, manipulate the forms of law more instrumentally.

The examples in this book show a mutually constitutive process by which groups seeking to influence the law are themselves influenced by the way they understand it. Law and legal forms constitute social relations and political practice by delineating possible movement action and determining movement practice. For instance, gays who saw themselves in terms of rights turned to this form of law in response to public health measures during the early years of the AIDS epidemic. I demonstrate this constitutive dimension of law through speeches and writings of activists in each movement, under the premise that intelligible communication depends on shared practices. Additionally, linguistic activity depends on a context within which it is possible to delineate who is engaging in the activity and who is not.

Each of these movements is of interest on its own. Each has fascinating characters, interesting dynamics, and important consequences for American law and politics. Some, like the campaign for gay rights and radical feminism, are identity and life style movements that are commonly seen as "new." The influence on identity that law exerts when it encourages gays to see themselves as oppressed minorities or radical feminists to see themselves as outside mainstream society is very important to understanding the constitutive consequences of law for social relations. Law-school realists and informalists often fail to recognize their own activities as movements at all. I argue that this is because the movement qualities have been hidden within institutional and professional practices, such as old law school ties or bar association economic support, that are crucial in defining social relations for these movements. Together, the four areas I will examine are instructive in revealing how law influences social life. Law is not as prominent in some of these contexts as it is in, say, elections, where laws provide for PACS or set no limits on private contributions candidates can make to their own campaigns, but interests examined are all important for what they show about the influences of law that go unnoticed.

This book moves gingerly around the notion "empirical." Except for the occasional slip, my presentation of movement politics avoids the word as well as the claim that reality is something that exists in an untheorized "outer" space. Some of my colleagues are still wedded to the notion that the world is divided between facts and values. They would put the aspiration to rid the country of pornography on one side—as a value—and describe constitutional protection for pornographers as a fact. Often they know that this is not actually so, or at least that fashionable scholars no longer see things that way, but the notion is kept alive by language that speaks of empirical research and empiricism, critical or otherwise.[2]

The problem of this recalcitrant, lingering positivism becomes acute when we examine political practices. Ordinarily people do not make a distinction between the world they live in and theories about it. I will try to avoid that distinction as well. I will not speak of "empirical findings" or of "data" in the traditional way, because the distinction between facts and theory, between the "real" world and the ideas of the academy, does more harm than good. Indeed, my whole argument rests on the recognition that *all* our judgments—"Pornography is violence against women," "Legal academics tend to be realists"—are judgments both of fact and of value; the "real" and the "ideal" are inextricably combined in them.

Of course, where my argument is not convincing, it might be for lack of decent evidence rather than confusion about what the evidence means. I have visited the sites, spoken with participants, read what scholars and journalists have said, and often participated in the movements discussed, but there will always be other evidence. The distinction between evidence and theory is an aspect of modern intellectual life. Here, rather than attempting to dominate through virtuosity in either the world of data or theory, my effort has been to say some things that are true and perhaps somewhat illuminating, while using whatever sources and rhetorical forms it takes to accomplish that today. Although I accept many of the constraints conventionally associated with science, such as the need to be careful and rigorous, the need for validity (as against varieties of experience), and the pursuit of truth, I do not think scientific research must be plodding.

I wrote this book for professional political scientists and students of law, some of whom might be legal academics. Having worked in this field for a while, I have some sense of the challenge of interdisciplinary publishing. Law is a literate giant whose practitioners do not read widely outside professional texts. My primary audience will not be legal intellectuals but those with a broader interest in the field now often called "law and society." This includes social scientists, along with some law school teachers and philosophers. My secondary audience is in political science and includes scholars of movements and of law. It is my hope that at least a substantial segment of scholars in political science and law—fields that overlap in various ways with my own—will come to take this work seriously in the way that reviewers such as Michael Musheno, Susan Burgess, Howard Gillman, and Girardeau Spann have.

The position I offer here was initially presented to the Western Political Science Meetings held at Eugene, Oregon, in 1986 and comments by Stuart Scheingold, Jim Foster, and Susan Leeson helped refine the argument. Later, the paper was discussed in Paris, where Yves Dezalay and Boa de Sousa Santos added depth, particularly with regard to the analysis of social movements. That same year, the Amherst Seminar put on a mini-conference, where comments by the Seminar and by Duncan Kennedy, Carol Smart, and David Sugarman helped further focus the position. A related paper entitled "Right, Rage and Remedy" was published in 1988 by *Studies in American Political Development,* and the editor, Stephen Skowronek, made very helpful refinements. In the process of preparing this article, his editorial colleague Karen Orren made perhaps the simplest and most challenging comment of all when she described what I was doing as "making *law* the independent variable." Since I don't think in terms of variables very often, I was at first perplexed by her remark, but when I learned what she meant, the proposition provided a great deal of pleasure.

Some of the materials included here have been presented or published elsewhere and have benefited from the critical contributions of scholars in the fields of political science and law and society. The discussion of rights and AIDS was presented on the panel "Legalbodies I" at the Annual Meeting of the Law and Society Association in Philadelphia in 1992. The discussion of consciousness and the feminist antipornography movement was presented to Christine Harrington's seminar at New York University in the summer of 1989 and benefited from the contributions of Nan Hunter and Sandra Goodman. Versions of this study have appeared in the *Review of Politics*, *Polity* and the *Legal Studies Forum*. My thanks to editors David Papke and Dennis William Moran for the intense collegial involvement that great editing can bring.

Sally Merry and Christine Harrington kept the idea of legal forms alive by citing "Right, Rage and Remedy."[3] It is one thing to have an idea, get it into print, and have it meet with favorable comment, quite another to get a substantial body of people to pay attention to it. In a sense, this book is about attention—people responding to my work and people responding to the social phenomenon we call *law*. It is also about the consequences of people understanding the rule of law in various ways. There really is no such thing as "the law." Although many of my colleagues want to believe something of this sort, paying lip service to the diversity of legal forms, few are able consistently to avoid playing along with the idea. The legal forms in politics about which the title speaks are ideas in living or social worlds. Ideas only matter when people pay attention. This attention determines the operative clout of such otherwise seemingly objective considerations as validity and some obviously subjective ones, like influence.

Beyond all of this or as a foundation for it, I live a life that is very heavily engaged with the politics of law. For a social scientist with an eye on the courts, doctrine, and legal practice, Amherst offers a great deal: students like Phyllis Rippey, Joyce O'Connor, Rosalie Young, Tim Carrier, Bill Rose, and Alan Gaitenby; colleagues like Austin Sarat,

Kristin Bumiller, Sheldon Goldman, and Barbara Yngvesson; and the Amherst Seminar. My discipline, ever striving to develop a distinctive political science of law, has provided me with valued colleagues from many different venues, including Walter Murphy, D. Marie Provine, Karen O'Connor, Martin Shapiro, Lief Carter, Michael McCann, Howard Gillman, Susan Burgess, and Stuart Scheingold. This would all be sufficient inspiration and support, but Christine Harrington has given me yet more. She introduced me to the problems with dispute resolution; she has been an active link to the community of international scholars whose insights I have drawn from; we have coauthored work on how laws constitute social relations; and together we are parents. Christine has also shared her resources and her enthusiasm for this work. In gratitude for her generosity, I dedicate *The Constitution of Interests* to her.

Legal Forms
Toward a Constitutive Theory

Chapter 1

Men wanted national
independence largely
for economic reasons,
but they said they
wanted it because their
rights were invaded.
Since the pressures
they fought against
were first imposed by
law, it was a natural
way to express
their resistance.

—James Willard Hurst,
*The Growth of
American Law*

Distinctive legal forms have defined various interests in American history. A constitutional confederacy bound the Six Nations of the Iroquois. The compact drawn up by the Pilgrims on the *Mayflower* was the basis for their short-lived community at Plymouth. Legal routines and a special language established the form in which Americans declared their independence from Britain. The Civil War transformed the nature of property and consequently gave new meaning to citizenship for all Americans. In the early twentieth century, conservatives cloaked their interests as fundamental law. The response from New Deal liberals was to displace the old text with more flexible forms of authority. More recently, rights claimed by African Americans to equal protection became the mantle under which many disadvantaged groups organized their interests. In the Watergate and Iran-Contra scandals, overzealous officials were checked by invigorated constitutional limits. Agreements, proclamations, and talk of right and authority are the variegated sources of the terms of political discourse in the United States.

Yet we easily overstate the part that

legal phenomena[1] have played in American history. Legions of observers have commented on the prominence of laws as the subject of political controversy and drawn attention to the institutions of legal authority that democratic people employ. Alexis de Tocqueville described American legal doctrine and institutions in this light, and he depicted lawyers as the American aristocracy.[2] He spawned an industry of commentators who approached American politics as essentially legal politics, and he is known for the view that political issues in the United States ultimately turn into legal issues. James Willard Hurst was more cautious. He saw legal institutions as accessible to Americans, and legal forms as tools by which Americans do their business. He presented the authority of law as significant only in terms of other, often more important, factors such as the social and the economic.[3] In his view, social questions do not always become matters of law, but legal phenomena tend to matter in what become social questions. From Hurst, not de Tocqueville, we take our guidance in describing the role legal forms play in the constitution of political interests.

The "compact" is part of Pilgrim lore for us and presumably the process of making it reflected the notion of covenant so central to the theological debates of the time. The Federalists not only turned to a legal compact in order to rectify flaws in the first confederation, the Constitution and its creation have become the activity by which a generation is known.[4] Law is one basis for assuring freedom for labor after slavery. Old English legal ways figured prominently in the picture Oliver Wendell Holmes, Jr., drew in *The Common Law*. Woodrow Wilson understood trusts in terms of the laws that might regulate them, and also in terms of the laws that made them.[5] Due process rights incorporated into the Constitution from 1950 to 1970 make federal criminal procedure more national. Analogous forms are important in every kind of social endeavor in the United States. Because legal forms tend to be depicted as outside of social and political movements, I have tried to bring them inside, to demonstrate how they "inform" the language, purposes, and strategies of movement activity. When activists speak to one another, they use the language created for them by the legal system, even when they are voicing opposition to it.[6]

The Constitutive Dimension

We call practices operating on ways of thinking and acting—the law of the compact, of free or equal labor, or of due process rights—*constitutive*.

Legal practices in this sense are a part of the culture, part of our nature: our basic outlook on life is stamped by the compacts drawn up by the colonists; by the decision that all laborers, black or white, should be free; by the agreements concerning due process for the accused and the convicted and the proper roles of the police and the judiciary. The constitutive is a level in the analysis of legal practices; it comes from *constitute*, meaning to form or establish. When we say of a former slave after the Civil War that laws constitute his identity we do not mean to say that being free is his whole being, but rather that laws operate at the level where his being is determined, and that they operated, along with social position and physical characteristics (such as being black), to make him what was called at the time a "freedman." A constitutive approach has been suggested for the last fifteen years as a way to see the reach of law into social and political life.[7]

This level for analyzing legal phenomena has an affinity with the fundamental legal document of the United States, the Constitution. We use a derivative of *constitute* in referring to the fundamental law of the land. When laws operate at the foundational level of an activity, as the laws of marriage do for husband and wife or, perhaps, as sodomy laws do for homosexuality, legal phenomena play a constitutive rather than simply an instrumental role. Law in this sense need not be exclusive or exhaustive. To be legally constituted a sodomite, one who engages in an illegal sexual practice, may matter surprisingly little in the conduct of life most of the time. But because the law is there as a basis for action, possibly stimulating a mob or shielding a police raid, the social relations of the homosexual are inevitably distinctive. Even a law that is merely "on the books," such as the law on sodomy in Georgia when Michael Hardwick was arrested,[8] has more than an instrumental place in the affairs of sexual choice. The Georgia law delineates some same-sex relationships as illegal and thus plays a part in determining what those relationships are. All laws, in this sense, do what the Constitution does.

Constitutive law is most often contrasted with positive law, but they are not opposites. We see legal phenomena from within a positive frame when we accept a distinction between facts (or the world) on the one hand and ideas (or law) on the other. Legal phenomena are seen, in this sense, as operating from the outside of something that exists already. The traditional problematic of positive law, the issue of whether laws can regulate morality or instead depend for their efficacy upon a modicum of morality that is already in place, stems from the idea that legal

3

phenomena act on society from the outside. These phenomena are instrumental in that we use them. This preserves our social identity outside the reach of law and paradoxically leaves us fumbling as we try to figure in what way law matters. Positivism in social science offers some support to positive law. The distinction between law and society animates very narrow inquiry into the ways of legal institutions. The positivist conception in jurisprudence and in social science reinforces the distinction in liberalism between state and society and directs our attention away from the presence of laws in everyday life. The current popularity of a constitutive approach is more directly connected to German social science than to the constitutional project of the Founding Fathers.[9]

Controversy surrounds the notion that laws form part of our political life. Sometimes the controversy arises from sensitivity about calling the prevailing view "instrumental," and sometimes it arises as an objection to making too much of legal phenomena. Yet, by saying that laws constitute, we do not claim that laws either determine or fully encompass politics, but rather that they become part of politics in more than an instrumental way. This approach calls attention to the way we talk about politics and how we conduct its business. In the case of the Declaration of Independence, for instance, a group of citizens announce their opposition to the sovereign in a refined and distinctive politics of separation affirming their legal practices while denying the presumed source of these practices in the king. The legal form used in the Declaration does not capture all the aspects of identity and discontent that adhered in the politics of the American Revolution. It does, however, distinguish the politics in this phase of the movement for independence from what came after, the formation of a new nation.

In the preface to this volume, I mentioned a confrontation in contemporary social science between a constitutive perspective and traditional positive science in terms of a shift in the way variables are addressed. My understanding in addressing the history of this shift is that the pluralist tradition, like systems theory and the study of attitudes, has seen laws and legal institutions as the phenomena to be influenced. In interest-group terms, law is to be influenced, usually through the state or governing apparatus.[10] Some have proposed that making law the dependent variable was new.[11] I do not think that this move is new; moreover, the more important move is beyond variables altogether, because of the rigid frame that they impose.

By focusing on the laws that constitute politics, we move away from positivist legal science and legal phenomena as existing in texts, codes, or the pronouncements of governing elites. The constitutive perspective aspires to a less normative and regime-dependent approach that would rigorously depict the role of legal phenomena in society. While texts, codes, and other traditional legal phenomena are important,[12] by drawing from social practices—the way things are done—we lay a foundation for a more complete understanding of the role of legal phenomena in politics. In an early expression of the constitutive position, Douglas Hay discussed the meaning of judicial leniency in the face of severe codes, the "Black Acts" of Renaissance England, as an effective way of reinforcing the authority of the gentry.[13] The grace of the royal judges gave the law a power in practice that was not represented by the codes. The absence of the Declaration of Independence from texts on the Constitution also indicates a practice of distinguishing that initial break from the body of contemporary law. The birth of the nation is associated with the Declaration, and it is there that we know ourselves as a people. But the law is grounded in the Constitution, and it is constitutional practices that delineate who we are legally.

As form, laws come before as well as after people organize. Although people obviously think and act politically on a legal landscape that already exists, the way contemporary social science depicts legal politics makes it challenging to recognize this fact. We see legal practices and legal forms preceding the first women's rights convention at Seneca Falls, New York, in 1848. Women who had been active abolitionists organized the meeting.[14] They brought a framework of rights with them from the struggle over slavery, and they articulated this framework in the first sessions. Laws, in this sense, are embedded within society and form the contours of American life. Legal forms are salient in most areas of American life, in business, families, education, and literature. These forms operate as law's constitutive mechanism and are evident if you know how to look for them.[15] Here, we will be observing these forms within movement politics.

The prospect of engaging in a discussion about "what law is" tends to fill all but the most romantic scholars with dismay. Scholars resist and are often uninterested, as if such basic questions are an unnecessary return to matters that have long been settled. Yet, this phenomenon— the dismay of scholars—seems to be social rather than intellectual. The question is uninteresting because it seems to be settled; but it seems to be settled precisely because it is not talked about much, not because

5

there is nothing to figure out. Political scholarship asks what law is and seeks to reclaim political possibilities by keeping the fundamental issues alive. And such issues certainly exist. Felix Frankfurter made the case not so long ago: "It ought to be a needless platitude to say that there are many kinds of 'law' as administered by the courts, but unfortunately, it is not. The fact that the single term 'law' should cover the rule against perpetuities as well as the unconstitutionality of ticket-scalping legislation is a prolific source of confusion."[16] Frankfurter begins with the same disclaimer that I too felt obliged to make. We speak of law with a "single term" in spite of the plurality of the phenomena: "the law," as a generalization, is a settled usage. But breaking it down is essential. The variety of stuff that we call by the same term "law" contributes to our confusion and requires that we keep the inquiry open. Here, research into the symbolic order of political struggle joins concern about different legal forms with epistemological attention to the nature of law in society.

Beyond Symbolism and Pluralism

Positive legal philosophy from Jeremy Bentham to H. L. A. Hart , as well as conventional thinking, sees law as rules or commands from the sovereign. This perspective—whether backed by jack-booted state troopers or issuing from friendlier, albeit less imposing, legislatures—is as common to ordinary people as it is to philosophers. People speak of police as law enforcement and senators as lawmakers. The laws in each sense mean rules for the public, who are generally depicted as "down" there somewhere. The orders come from institutional sources, characteristically "up" above. This is a positivist view. Here, legal science stipulates that in order for jurisprudence to be scientific its propositions have to be divorced from norms. The state becomes the neutral site of legality, claiming a place of objectivity, a vantage point "above" the fray. Positivism treats the constitutions, statutes, and official government holdings as law. Consequently, the offices and institutions of the state determine what is legal. For example, the Supreme Court decision on abortion in 1973, *Roe v. Wade*, becomes the law on abortion in the United States. Although the decision was anything but final, as laws and prosecutorial decisions at the state level attest, many who find this decision appalling direct their attention to the Court or to Congress to make a change.

According to this tradition about what law is, people outside the institutions and offices of the "legal system" receive rather than generate legal authority. They may or may not know the rules. They may advocate change and apply pressure on the lawmakers or the public in general, but their advocacy is not itself understood as law. The "pro-life" movement, for instance, advocates a change in the Supreme Court's decision on abortion either through a new decision or a constitutional amendment.[17] In this framework movement politics, even when it has great significance, like when it determines the tenure of a senator or threatens the life of a judge, remains something other than law. Politics is set apart; it factors into legal outcomes but does not determine what law is. Hence, when a bishop proposes that "abortion is murder," we understand him to be preaching, not articulating a valid legal claim.

Legal phenomena studied in isolation from society offer limited insight into the social reality of particular laws and the rule of law more generally. We expect a gap between courts and society, and even when an effect between the two is posited it only confirms the usual absence of such effects. In either case, the research is painfully narrow. Systems theory is another illustration of studies that offer limited insight. In his book on the federal courts, *Hard Judicial Choices*,[18] political scientist Phillip Cooper organized the material on a systems theoretical basis. This framework parallels a familiar chronological arrangement of case material. Beginning with the trigger phase, systems theory moves on to the "liability phase," the "remedy phase," and "post decree issues." In this type of analysis the jargon gets heavy. For instance, the "post decree phase of a remedial decree case involves a parallel interactive relationship between remedy implementation and evaluation and remedy refinement."[19] Here, legal authority resides in the "system" and the society provides the raw material and generates demands, the hallmark of liberal jurisprudence. The law and society perspectives from which modern scholars describe law appear as normative "ideas" and scientific "facts." Ideas are debatable, and facts are the weapons of policy debate. Yet, a systematic bias in this view draws attention away from the processes by which laws constitute political phenomena.

Impact studies reflect this bias. Developed in the early 1960s, the behavioral period in social science, impact studies attempt to see if laws in action reflect the legal opinions announced by the appellate courts.[20] Indeed, this research coincided with decisions that many academics applauded, like those that promoted integration and nationalized the Bill of Rights. The late 1960s and early 1970s produced a wealth of scholarship that also reached outside the courtrooms and looked for law

7

in society. This work took legal opinions announced from on high as a starting point; law came from where positivism said it did, from appellate courts. As impact studies flourished, they influenced how we understand courts. What courts say, we learned, does not immediately or necessarily have any effect. For laws to matter, "other courts or . . . nonjudicial actors" must act.[21] Thus, we saw reception of appellate court decisions as political just as scholars made the court's process of deciding cases political a generation before. Impact analysis flourished in phrases such as "the *Miranda* decision impacted the police" or "the *Bakke* decision will impact universities," and conceptions in this language remain influential today.

The narrowest impact studies focused on compliance, the part of impact associated with individual decisions. Broader studies included, as the impact of decisions, such diverse phenomena as improvements in police work, the election of segregationist governors following the *Brown v. Board of Education* decision in 1954, and the defendant warning cards that followed Ernesto Miranda's successful appeal.[22] Institutional changes, political outcomes, and material artifacts such as the Miranda cards were all part of the picture. Although the object of study, law, was not very precisely drawn, the attention to phenomena outside courts was influential. We are asking new questions because the impact scholars have gotten us used to talking about legal phenomena while doing research out in communities.

The influence of legal material has now been pursued into the furthest reaches of society. Law is represented on television, in the practices of cops, lawyers, and judges. Law is central to political culture in Congress, in executive appointments, and of course in the judiciary. We hear law in ordinary conversation and find it in both the disputes and the harmony sometimes characteristic of daily life.[23] Laws operating in everyday life are recognized in standard materials—the cases before courts, the strategies of lawyers, and confrontations with police. The anthropological treatment of legal phenomena in a community describes the cultural context in which "courts and systems of formal law operate."[24] This research gives us much more than laws that leap from the pages of texts and compel obedience. It shows us how the life of laws differs from the *ideal* of "government of law" determined by texts and judicial orders. But the distinction between law and society is still there. This distinction extends the positive perspective and it is hard to shake.

By defining laws as what the sovereign orders, positivism has limited capacity to explain the generative significance of orders and the internalization of public authority. Positive legal theory overlooks how social action depends upon a generalized meaning of law because it separates society from governing institutions. In order to account for laws as they exist in the practices of those who deal with them, the research perspective needs to be shifted from law *and* society to one that recognizes law *in* society.[25] Thus, rather than joining the study of law with the study of society—for example, by studying what happens before or after a court makes a decision—the appropriate perspective incorporates laws in social relations. (See chapter 5, where I discuss the women's movement as a "rights" movement in the sense that it is constituted by the pursuit of rights.)

In the development of a legal doctrine, such as the perspective on separation of powers announced in the case of *Immigration and Naturalization Service v. Chada*,[26] the constitutional bar becomes more evident as an aspect of politics. We learn the names and nature of lawyers whose careers propel them into struggle over the meaning of articles and clauses in the Constitution. In a similar vein, we are learning about the "unobtrusive mobilization" that presses from within institutions.[27] This is part of what defines social movements as "new." Not only are new social movements less rigidly class based than the older labor movement, but they operate to restructure the forms of politics. These movements are organized around different forms of law. They are not outside, imagining law; rather, they are encompassed by law. And with this we are back essentially to where we started from—that is, we are describing how a fairly stable system of authority is maintained.

In this book, I propose that commands and rules structure the claims of political movements, and that movement political activity depends on available law. This formulation goes beyond the idea that laws in society are merely the result of social forces. Legal phenomena are a function of social knowledge. They are dependent on what groups know and how they act upon that knowledge. Freedom of expression is such a phenomenon that rules made by government quite commonly infuse and inform movement politics by influencing the thought of participants, the nature of their positions, and identification with the movement. We will consider how that happened in the antipornography movement.

The current conception of law as symbolic is rooted in the legal realism of the 1930s. From Thurman Arnold's *The Symbols of Government*[28] to Karl Llewellyn's *The Bramble Bush*,[29] the interplay of cultural and legal phenomena became the new framework for legal studies. Much later, scholars reacting to behaviorism in the social sciences turned to hermeneutics, semiotics, and ordinary language philosophy as bases for inquiry into the symbols of law.[30] This perspective on the rule of law appears in Joseph Gusfield's "symbolic politics" studies of the temperance movement and in Murray Edelman's symbolic uses of politics.[31] More recently, legal scholars are moving beyond recognition that symbols are important to understanding how our life is made up of symbolic considerations.

In the social sciences, scholars began to shift their approach in the mid-1970s. In political science, Stuart Scheingold, Isaac Balbus, and others renewed attention to the political role of laws by showing how rights "condition perceptions, establish role expectations, provide standards of legitimacy, and account for the institutional patterns of American politics."[32] By focusing on rights strategies in collective action, this work showed law as a political resource and elaborated how laws relate to material life.[33] As part of the larger "sociological movement in law,"[34] social scientists took law out of the hands of the professionals—the lawyers. They tried to stand outside the profession and observe its activities from close at hand. Much of the work was done in the United States, but access was often impeded by professional boundaries. As interdisciplinary scholars, sociologists of law often feel marginal in both sociology and law. Scholars in law schools lament their position relative to teachers of contracts or property, while sociologists and anthropologists who focus on law seldom dominate their disciplines. Often, however, the impact of the work belies this claim. The current realist core of legal scholarship and the importance of legal phenomena to scholarship in fields such as history, sociology, and political science have made the sociological movement in law more influential than it claims to be. And from Roscoe Pound to Frank Sander and Laura Nader—to name a few contemporaries—sociological scholarship has influenced the practice of law.

By pushing beyond the positive view of law, we bring into question the distinction between "the judicial process," including "the style and logic of appellate court decisions," and the acts of police, attorneys, and courts.[35] The authority of legal process, especially as it presents itself ritualistically, is an aspect of "state law." The "stuff" of legislation and appellate court decisions is an illusionary referent for law because it portrays an order that is "certain, consistent, and powerful."[36] Rather, the ritual and drama of the legal process lead us to the social reality of law. The conceptual life of the community is related to the conceptual parameters of case law, statutes, and the treatise literature (the "stuff" of the law school curriculum). To some, these "mandarin materials" represent "an exceptionally refined and concentrated version of legal consciousness."[37] In this view, the structures familiar to lawyers stand behind many of the ways ordinary people think about the world. Elite legal thinking may influence the vernacular, and elements of formal legal rules may be internalized by laypeople to be applied in contexts remote from officials and courts.[38] In an influential statement of this position, Robert Gordon argues that "field-level studies would reveal a lot of trickle-down effects—a lot of mandarin ideology reproduced in somewhat vulgarized forms."[39] Owen Fiss discusses law in society in terms of the "rich and generous body of decisions on free speech" produced by the Supreme Court, which he describes as a "Free Speech Tradition."[40] In this characterization, free speech has become "part of our general culture," and Fiss is not the only one given to "believe the decisions of the Court implanted that principle in our culture, nurtured it, and gave it much of its present shape."[41]

Ethnographic work on such traditions "in society" by anthropologists such as Sally Engle Merry focuses on legal ideology among "disputants" who use the courts. Merry finds that "[e]xperienced plaintiffs come to see rights as an opportunity, a basis for action, rather than a guarantee of protection."[42] In political science, a newer impact analysis challenges the assumptions on which the field was originally constructed. We get an enhanced picture of messages from the courts by calling attention to their reception by different audiences.[43] We know that groups react to court decisions differently, especially in controversial cases. In *Miller v. California*,[44] dealing with mail order pornography, the American Civil Liberties Union (ACLU) tended to withdraw, while publishing associations entered with greater enthusiasm. Newer impact analyses examine action that goes beyond the judicial orders traditionally associated with compliance. For example, the U.S. Senate in 1976 easily passed the Hyde Amendment barring the use of federal monies for abortion. The senators appear to have anticipated that the Supreme Court would strike down the provision. When the Court approved the congressional action, the situation changed. Initially inactive pro-choice senators mounted a more extended confrontation that became the first real battle of the modern abortion wars. The result was a three-month stalemate in the Senate. Similarly, the ACLU's involvement in *Skokie v. National Socialist Party* in the late 1970s led to a costly court victory. Although they won the litigation guaranteeing the Nazis' right to march through a predominately Jewish suburb of Chicago, the organization lost sixty thousand members. This broke the organization's growth trend and caused the ACLU to restrict its activities and reevaluate its priorities.[45]

We have learned to look beyond the behavioral questions to the ideological impact of judicial decisions. We now understand the importance of a decision's influence on the substantive discourse of politics. These developments require a more complex view of law, one that is sensitive to the channels of political action of which it is a part.[46] Taking account of the nature and significance of this research means allying ourselves with those who have jettisoned the positive baggage of law defined simply *as orders*.

Some contemporary scholars look at law that is not in or on "the books." This perspective is called *legal pluralism*. Even more obviously than the movement ideologies examined here, legal pluralism contains a view of law. And no less explicitly than these movements, legal pluralism sought to break down the domination of state law by positing other forms of law in society. As exemplified by the *Journal of Legal Pluralism (and Unofficial Law)* under the editorship of John Griffiths, and as evident in Mark Galanter's "Justice in Many Rooms" in the journal's 1981 issue, this perspective on law, like the law and society movement of which it is a part, sees law in places other than courts, as well as in the courts but outside the official gaze of the judge. Pluralism, in this formulation, is opposed to centralism, or the view that state law is at the center of the universe of norms. According to Griffiths, "[T]he state has no more empirical claim to being the center of the universe of legal phenomena than any other element of that whole system does."[47] Galanter points out that "courts resolve only a small fraction of all disputes that are brought to their attention."[48] The pluralist message is essentially the same as the more familiar, if less conceptually coherent, law and society framework. One might find evidence of contracting among businessman or an accounting of liabilities among the elders in a tribe or the homemakers in a neighborhood. One might also find many things that resemble law occurring in places such as the corridors of the courthouses.

The best of this scholarship includes "The Law of the Oppressed" by Boaventura de Sousa Santos,[49] "Marxism and Legal Pluralism" by Peter Fitzpatrick,[50] and Laura Nader's ongoing work.[51] Santos found in the *favellas*, or slums, of Rio de Janeiro an indigenous legal construction that he describes as law. Fitzpatrick took on Marxism in the interest of plural legal forms, which he found in post-colonial environments. Nader, in order to understand disputing, drew heavily on anthropology and developed an entire field that was sensitive to the cultural aspects of conflict. Summary articles on the contributions of the movement, such as the analysis by Merry, emphasize the discovery of law in formerly unrecognized or unrecognizable places[52]—or, as a recent critique pointed out with some concern, the paradox of finding law in nonlegal places.[53]

The problem with legal pluralism is evident in academic projects like a conference in 1989 that brought together legal pluralists with advocates for popular justice movements.[54] The conference was a call to utopian reification common in the liberal academy under positivism, where attention is drawn from the state apparatus in a move that seems to deny the legal authority underlying modern status relations. Certainly there are forms of law outside the state and thought generated independently of law and the state. But pluralism turns away from the effect of the state on aspects of social life: the family, bargaining, health and wealth. Conversely, it is important to recognize the penetration of state power into movement practice. To show how government law becomes part of the talk, aspirations, and social life of politics—that is, to take a constitutive perspective—is to challenge the positivist elements within legal pluralism.

Social scientists have been fascinated by other manifestations of law's "plurality."[55] Where scholars explore themes of hegemony and resistance, the work acknowledges the influence of a sovereign legal order.[56] One such contemporary perspective comes from Antonio Gramsci, who distinguished between the "dominant" and the "subaltern."[57] The subaltern, also known as "the other," is said to tell us who we are.[58] In order to describe the other as a part of the whole, we must place law in society. In an article focusing on native claims in the cultural appropriation controversy in Canada, Rosemary J. Coombe sees the characteristic feature of the other as representation "that projects upon non-Western peoples qualities and characteristics that are mirror opposites of the qualities the West claims for itself."[59] A parallel is evident in the language of colonialism. We have become self-conscious about the formation of national identities.

Social scientists are now looking at laws that enter into and determine social relations. Thus, in America the movement of white Europeans across the continent becomes the point of departure. Law must be held accountable for wiping out a native culture and creating an African slave class.[60] The earliest national legislation laid the groundwork for expansion by providing for the sale of fee simple titles at public auction after surveys that provided a more uniform marketable commodity (a parcel of land). Thus, a movement analysis starts with law because law draws attention to the place of rights, institutions, ideologies, and consciousness in political action.

In the late 1970s, Sally Falk Moore, an anthropologist at Harvard University, inquired into the nature of law and its relation to social change. Hers was a transitional conception of law as a "semi-autonomous social field," and she proposed this field as an appropriate subject of study. To Moore "'the law' is a short term for a very complex aggregation of principles, norms, ideas, rules, practices, and the agencies of legislation, administration, adjudication and enforcement, backed by political power and legitimacy. . . . The complex 'law,' thus condensed into one term, is abstracted from the social context in which it exists, and is spoken of as if it were an entity capable of controlling that context."[61] This presents problems that must be grasped in order to get beyond law as symbol.

As a research focus in the sociology of law, Moore's idea is "that the small field observable to an anthropologist be chosen and studied in terms of its semi-autonomy." This would amount to the fact that law "can generate rules and customs and symbols internally, but that it is also vulnerable to rules and decisions and other forces emanating from the larger world by which it is surrounded." Moore notes that "an emphasis on the capacity of the modern state to threaten to use physical force should not distract us from the other agencies and modes of inducing compliance." She goes on, in a very helpful vein, to say "that an inspection of semi-autonomous social fields strongly suggests that the various processes that make internally generated rules effective are often also the immediate forces that dictate the mode of compliance or non-compliance to state-made legal rules."[62] In sum, the point here is that "the semi-autonomous social field is defined and its boundaries identified not by its organization . . . but by a processual characteristic, the fact that it can generate rules and coerce or induce compliance to them."[63] There is no doubt that some norms develop in this way. But norms are also legislated by governments, dictated by administrative and judicial decisions, or imposed in other intentional ways by private agencies. These impinge on semi-autonomous social fields that already have rules and customs.

The call for semi-autonomy in law draws attention to aspects of law in society that anticipate the qualities to be taken up here. For instance,

Moore describes how law leverages political outcomes: "were it not for the vast amount of pertinent labor law, the union representative would never have come to have the powerful position he occupies"; and "were it not the legal right of the contractor to collect promptly the bills owed him by the jobber, his restraint in not pressing for collection would not be a favor." Thus, Moore notes that "the contrary can also be persuasively argued: that 'it is society that controls law and not the reverse.'"[64] Labor and contract law provide the foundation for exchange practices that barely look legal; however, law is always in the background as terrain, which may be its most significant quality. Thus right and law give birth to much more, as we shall see beginning in the next chapter.

Phillip Selznick and others have argued that sociology should have a "ready affinity for the philosophy of natural law" because both are "anti-formalist in spirit," looking beyond what is given to what is "latent and inchoate," and both are "committed to the study of 'nature.'"[65] Associating his position with the work of Eugen Ehrlich, who proposed in *The Fundamental Principles of the Sociology of Law*[66] that law is not to be found in formal institutions but in the "inner order" of society, Selznick calls on a "commitment to naturalism" that he associates with philosophical pragmatism rather than a narrow positivism.[67] Such analysis separates the legal status of laws from their content. Thus, the problem of the segregation laws in the early twentieth-century American South as immoral *and as law* would concern the sociologist of law interested in understanding more than simply the claims for law made from within the institutions of the state. For Selznick, natural law, like sociology, is a methodology, a way of looking for law, "a guide to inquiry."[68]

The concept of "form" has a tradition in the sociology of law that deserves special note. Out of the Marxist tradition I draw the concept of legal forms as correlated to social and economic forces in society. Had Isaac Balbus stayed in the sociology of law his significant contribution to the conception of legal form would no doubt have become more evident. Nonetheless, his article "Commodity Form and Legal Form: An Essay on the 'Relative Autonomy' of Law"[69] provides a foundation for this dimension of the theory of legal form. Balbus's work had corollaries of a distinctly British cast[70] and generated some interest among American scholars.[71]

In her article "Law and Capital," Doreen McBarnet discusses the role of legal form in maintaining economic enterprises.[72] McBarnet attempts

15

to invigorate the sociology of law, which in its sophistication had lost some of the vitality of earlier, more instrumental conceptions of the relation of law and capital. Where once the state was run by the ruling class and "capitalists were much in evidence," law came to be more narrowly defined, and the concentration on institutions was often to the exclusion of description of economic interests.[73] As McBarnet points out, bringing back the active human element requires "forging theoretical links between the structures of law and capital and the empirically observed human action which makes them work."[74] Her attention, and that of some of her colleagues at the Centre for Socio-Legal Studies, Oxford, is drawn to the armies of accountants, lawyers, and other professionals whose job it is to shape the laws to serve the immediate interests of very particular capitalists.[75]

Analysis of legal form grounded in social relations suggests affinities, corollaries, dichotomies, opposites, and continua as the social reality of law. Sometimes legal form is less articulated than we might expect and than those who count on the state for security might hope. This is generally true when we look at the property or political rights of the poor or movements of relatively marginal groups like gays and lesbians. At other times, penetration by the state may be far more significant than is generally realized, expected, or acknowledged. This is clearly the case with the realist movement in the law schools. The penetration of law in social relations becomes especially evident when we compare social movements.

In the analysis that follows, we will see that aspects of legal form, such as the belief that law is powerful, are shared by both gay rights activists and antipornography feminists, two movements generally at the margins and outside the institutions of legal authority. On the other hand, a belief in the powerlessness of law is shared by legal realists in law schools and the alternative dispute resolution movement, two movements that are heavily staffed by lawyers. One of the paradoxes is thus that the legal form associated with right suggests lawyers, while those with the most legal education—law teachers—declare the rhetoric of rights to be naive.[76]

Laws and Interests

The National Organization for Women's assault on the Supreme Court, following the pro-life movement's assault, has dominated the public life of the Court. These pressures to incorporate the political in law were preceded by pressures from liberal law writers of a decade before. Laws are obviously susceptible to group pressure. We make political pressure an element of the legal system by embedding law in a conception of democratic processes. Pressure has become an acceptable part of American law. Courts and legislatures are places where people bring wants and needs. While *Brown v. Board of Education* epitomized liberal politics in law, the civil rights movement demanded the reality of law and pressed for public demands from the government. Movement politics also brought institutional change, such as the sociological "Brandeis Brief," and with it Justice Louis Brandeis himself, who as a Jew exemplified a more diverse and inclusive Supreme Court.[77] Group resistance to civil rights, in the form of southern citizens councils with their control over government and law enforcement, also placed law at the center of political controversy. This resistance was aimed at preserving a way of life in which law oppressed a people. In this resistance, even when wrapped in legal form (the southern sheriff, the voting lists), politics took away the legal status of the resistance.

For the last fifty years, politics has been in the forefront of studies of law. The work of Clement Vose[78] broke new and important ground. Although initially Vose chose to focus on the restrictive covenant cases rather than *Brown*, thereby revealing the kind of intellectual curiosity that was driving his research, he provided elegant testimony to the subtlety and power of a framework. In his work the National Association for the Advancement of Colored People (NAACP), the National Consumer's League, and the ACLU became the central actors in the group struggle about law. With the NAACP the lore of movement struggle is rich and the contests among institutions and personalities are played out as a spectacle that defines the civil rights struggle: disagreements between Charles Hamilton Houston and W. E. B. Du Bois about the role of litigation, or the elevation of Thurgood Marshall to the Supreme Court. Women's movement groups were modeled on these progenitors, and they had great success with cases like *Roe v. Wade*. The success, in fact, was so great that these groups were slow in organizing at the grass roots.

One of the more vivid examples of the centrality of interests in a static or positive conception of law is in the research on "political trials," much of which was stimulated by the movements of the 1960s.[79] This research was done by "liberals" who were fascinated by the treatment of radicals in the courts. Theodore L. Becker, Kenneth M. Dolbeare, and Harry P. Stumpf, among the most engaged and important public law

17

scholars of their generation, contributed to disciplinary scholarship and to the politics of the 1960s. They were drawn by the aspirations of radicals, but they were concerned about the means employed, particularly the violence that often became the subject of trials. In the trials, means often became the focus of attention, shifting the scholarly gaze from politics to law. Generally, the trial showed the state as relatively autonomous with its own rules and standards for getting at the truth. In some cases this was more successful than others. An obvious failure was the trial of the Chicago Seven, where one of the defendants was bound and gagged. While the trial of Angela Davis put the radicalism of the black community under the microscope of liberal legalism, the institutional autonomy of the law was reaffirmed. In many respects these treatments of political trials are good case studies in the difficulty of seeing the constitutive power of law. A closer look at one of these cases reveals the pervasiveness of liberal law and the conceptions of interest that accompany it.

Stumpf and journalist Carrol W. Cagle chronicled "The Trial of Reies Lopez Tijerina" for the volume *Political Trials*, edited by Theodore Becker in 1971. The editor's disclaimer at the beginning of the book is important: "In a sense, *all* trials are political."[80] The statement reads as if Becker takes this observation for granted, as though he is saying, "Law is political, right? Okay, let's get on with what matters. Let's talk some politics." This shift from the inquiry into the obvious to the obviousness of the inquiry is a characteristic problem for the liberal framework as it addresses, or fails to address, the politics of law. There is a cuteness in the book's divisions that plays with scholarly distance from the material.[81] All the trials in the "pure" political sense are foreign. They include the Spiegel case, Indian trials, and one linking Great Britain and Nigeria. Here "the nature of the crime is clearly political and the impartiality of the judge . . . is not called into serious question."[82]

The chapter by Stumpf and Cagle covers the legal response to an event in early June 1967, when armed Hispanic land reformers entered the courthouse in Tierra Amarilla, New Mexico, and pushed around the occupants, including a number of government officials. The result was a shootout in the Old West style. Their account of the trial provides an opportunity to describe the construction of law at a level that is addressed infrequently, at least in American political science. The image of the shootout and the academy's response to it show us the role of social science scholarship on law in cooling the passions of the period and discrediting the movement claims.

In their account, politics is presented with a rich array of quotation marks. They are all over the place, even when no one is speaking. These quotes are used to indicate ambiguity and puzzlement. From the beginning we learn about "insurrectionists" and hear the details of the "courthouse raid" that included an "arrest." The subject of the trial, Tijerina, is first described as follows: "There, the mercurial Tijerina—eloquent, but with little formal education, and unversed in the law—confronted the man he had sought to 'arrest.'"[83] Later in the story, Stumpf and Cagle provide a detailed account of the legal issue underlying the event at the center of the trial—title to land. Their account, in part because of its detail, is informative, sensitive, and characteristic of the liberal ideology in law. Their sensitivity, however, is humanistic rather than legal. The separation of law from politics preserves the innocence of law, and ultimately the dominance of convention.

Thus, a conjunction of activisms—the activism in self-consciously political movements and the activism of the intellectuals, shows the construction of law in political science. At this level of cultural creativity we can see how the constructions of law contain political possibilities. In the face of concern about objectivity in research, political pluralists taught us acceptable forms. Though not as foreign, these followed the legalisms of *amicus* and *cert* very closely. One example of an institutional construction with political implications is Anthony Lewis's book *Gideon's Trumpet*.[84] In the guise of simply offering a more complete picture of the workings of the U.S. Supreme Court, the *New York Times* reporter brought a year of training at Harvard Law School to bear in a picture of the institution that subtly identifies it with biblical symbols of freedom and vehicles to challenge oppression. The power of the image has been so great that more recent books, such as Barbara Craig's *Chada: The Story of an Epic Constitutional Struggle*,[85] play off of the image of a trip "all the way to the Supreme Court" when this image is certainly not necessary and barely appropriate to the context.

Research in the politics of law has now become more sophisticated. It no longer simply takes on liberal interests. Conservatives before the courts as well as on them have become part of a continually illuminating story calling attention to the organized efforts by conservatives to transform the courts and their decisions through the Mountain States Legal Foundation, the Capital Legal Foundation, and other Washington institutions given prominence by the national media. These institutions affirm what the New Deal first taught, that political movements can

19

change the institutions of law themselves. They show that political activity can transform the processes of thought and the doctrinal relations on which cases are argued.

When activists talk about strategy and when they address each other in their movements, legal forms are more integral to their political activity than interest group pluralism suggests. Some movement discourse, like the feminist antipornography campaign, is a broadside against the oppression in laws. The alternative dispute resolution movement in the 1980s was built on a general critique of the legal process as encumbered and unsatisfactory. And, while gay activists sought fulfillment of legal promises they found in the Declaration of Independence, the critical legal studies movement in law schools was denying the authority of law's texts. The ideas about law held by these activists are not bound in standard law books, and they are not always petitions for a redress of grievances. They include conventions, articles of faith, and views about the world that activists take to be true. Ideas about law give meaning to social relations, and as law "in action" they must be understood as significant parts of the legal order. To attend to this aspect of law is to illuminate a part of law's social reality. Law that forms social life is real in the most elemental sense; its reality is evident in life's choices. More specifically, to look at law in this form is to see law informing social action in a new way. Such ideas and the relations they create are law *in* society.

Discursive Practices

Laws sometimes infuse American social life with elements that seem not quite natural. The due process guarantee that "the criminal goes free if the constable blunders" is one. A sense that judges are supposed to be different, wiser and more deliberate than other people, is another. Laws appear in political language as claims of right, like a right to privacy (or its derivative, the right to control one's body, in the pro-choice movement), and as the object of scorn, like the laws publisher Bob Guccione uses to protect *Penthouse*. In the chapters that follow, I will concentrate on four forms of law in society. Characterized as right, institutional realism, the ideology of remedy, and the radical consciousness, these forms capture a broad range of political action and legal signification. Of course, the categories are not exhaustive. Instead, they reveal some of the ways law works in politics that have not been developed very fully. Movement discourse—a stump speech, a keynote address, or a letter to the editor—may draw on ideas about law so settled and so distinctive that they define a movement's conventions.

The categories of legal form explored here provide some ideological breadth since they are linked to different kinds of movements, involve different kinds of political claims, and privilege various statements about what laws can do. Both gay rights and the form of legal consciousness evident in the movement against pornography, for instance, play off the view that law matters. In this view, laws offer protection from a society threatened by AIDS and create an environment for pornographers. Positivism is a legal form that depends on law schools and the judiciary for its impact. It operates from the premise of a formalism that is to be avoided by getting to the "real." Informalism is also a professional ideology, but one that speaks of court incapacity and a litigious society. Surprisingly, this legal form is the domain of lawyers and the movement is heavily influenced by lawyers. The link between rights and pornographers as insurgent movement forms and positivism and informalism as counterinsurgent forms is not altogether obvious, although some aspects of the relations are evident in the chronicles of legal politics. This is one of the most intriguing things about the framework. The existence of ideological forms in distinctive practices and the constitutive dimension of those practices for movement discourse will be elaborated in the following chapters in terms of debates in the gay media and in symposia, exchanges in law reviews (the forum for the legal academy), convention speeches, within paraprofessional organizations, and in the street language and alternative press favored by the antipornography movement.

21

In the following analysis, ideas, language, and conventions tied to a legal form will be called "practices." Practices are constituted by and in turn constitute different interpretive communities. Political language links legal form to the conventions of these interpretive communities. Consequently, the conventions can be seen in talk about purposes, in the style of discussion, and in political strategies. The discourse appearing in movement forums such as conference proceedings is distinct from academic or journalistic commentary on it. These forums establish the sociological dimension: people, by participating in them, constitute a community. Academic commentary is often comfortable with ideas outside of any time or place. The texts of journals or even academic conference papers in fields such as sociology or political science are seldom grounded in the communities that produce them. Grounding the conferences and presentations referred to here is an important part of this book. To comment on a conference, especially when not participating, is to observe as one might observe a subculture.[86]

The tradition of European social research has raised some of the problems inherent in observing subcultures: "How, in the final analysis, are we to make sense of subcultural style? One of the more obvious ways is to 'appreciate' it in orthodox aesthetic terms."[87] Whether one is observing the Hell's Angels, the Junior League, or professors at a conference, the cultural rather than instrumental approach has its advantages. There is more interest in the bonds that unite than in the forces that prevail. Each of the groups has qualities that are attractive, like the creativity of the gay community and the humanism of the mediators who drive informalism. Sometimes those are the qualities that associate the movement with law, sometimes they are not. This book seeks to establish the authority of law by focusing on political discourse with attention to the words and logic it employs.

From a vantage point less integrated into professional legal scholarship than some we have considered, Louis Althusser describes how different parts of the "social formation" perpetuate submission to the ruling ideology. Law appears as "domination of the ruling class 'in words.'" This formulation and related literature in the Marxist tradition develop the constitutive perspective discussed here. In "Ideology and the Ideological State Apparatuses," Althusser emphasizes that authority resides in the acceptance of words as a matter of practice in a social setting. Thus, the authority of law is material.[88] Law's authority calls people together in time and place and provides the focus of a social movement, is another way to describe the constitutive form of law and demonstrate its consequences.

The resulting perspective, as elaborated in this analysis, is that of constitutive law. Although this perspective has various sources and currents, an important statement of it is found in a 1979 article by Karl Klare. According to Klare, "The initial theoretical operation is to free the Marxist theory of law from . . . the notion that law is a mere instrument of class power."[89] Klare sees the project as one that tries "to conceive the legal process as, at least in part, a manner in which class relationships are created and articulated, that is, to view law-making as a form of praxis."[90] Although proposed some time ago, this project is only now getting off the ground. Klare has also examined the deradicalization and incorporation of the American working class as revealed in early Supreme Court Wagner Act decisions.[91]

A few classics from the rich tradition of British social research on law and class, such as Douglas Hay's "Property, Authority and the Criminal Law,"[92] show the interplay between property, forms of personal dependence, and criminal law. Hay shows how law displaced religion as the dominant legitimizing ideology in eighteenth-century England. According to Hay, the criminal statutes were infused with elements of terror, majesty, justice, and mercy. The rhetoric of the death sentence, the ever-present sanction of the gallows, and the localized and personal system by which the rural poor and occasionally the gentry were convicted, often released on technicalities, or pardoned, all produced a chaotic system by which respect for property and property owners was effected through the rule of law.

The law constructs through images in which people are placed. The Elizabethan Poor Law, sometimes taken by modern lawyers to represent the antithesis of welfare entitlement, was in fact widely understood at the time as establishing welfare as a right.[93] Yet, law's existence in general depictions of society raises the justifiable caution about seeing law everywhere. If we make this move too cavalierly and without caution, certainly nothing will be law—hence the attention here to state law and the ways in which it expands systems of authority. But in looking at law in movement practice some of the distinctive features of law seem to fall by the wayside. This may be the price we have to pay for seeing an important truth about law. Much of its authority is ideological.

Beyond legal pluralism and legal positivism we find a complex realm of social life organized around concepts that can be traced to an original articulation from some wing or corridor of the authoritative public platform we call the government or the state. Finding law in this realm requires transcending the distinction between public and private so central to traditional liberalism. As David Nelken puts it, "law enters into the production and reproduction of society."[94] In modern systems, and characteristically in the liberal state, the relation between social movements and law needs to be reexamined. Political movements, such as feminism, alternative dispute resolution, and others discussed below, are subject to this "production and reproduction." One of the most important modern feminist critiques of the law points out that the equality standard, whether the standard of "difference" or of "sameness," characterizes men as the standard.[95] In stopping to call attention to law beyond disputes over such things as comparable worth or occupational qualification, this analysis has suggested how law at the constitutive level operates.[96]

23

Movements are constituted in legal terms where participants see the world through concepts derived from state institutions and organize themselves according to these concepts. The concept of free expression in contemporary American politics is often derived from talk about the First Amendment. Thus, organizations as diverse as Women Against Pornography, when its adherents address a conventional notion of free inquiry, and the American Legion, when it advocated legislation in 1989 to protect the American flag, are constituted, at least in part, by the First Amendment. Legal forms are evident in the language, purposes, and strategies of movement activity as "practices."[97] When activists speak to one another in meetings, on picket lines, or over the phone, their language contains consistent ways of understanding or acting, that is, practices of, about, or in opposition to the legal system.

American feminists who met at Seneca Falls in the middle of the nineteenth century to start the women's rights struggle spoke of a "sense of right" familiar from the Declaration of Independence and abolitionist struggles. They rallied to the cry "Equality of Rights."[98] Similarly, when activists articulate political purposes their discourse is situated relative to law. Gay rights activists of the 1970s addressed claims to city councils for new ordinances to protect them from discrimination, and in the 1980s they extended protection for AIDS victims by establishing that the disease cannot be transmitted by "casual contact."[99] When activists develop strategies, they reveal a politically significant view of the legal system. The strategies followed by the civil rights movement, such as marches and sit-ins, were not always legal, and many were explicitly illegal; just as they were orchestrated to change laws in the long run, they were affected by laws that were in practice. Equally compelling, but harder to see, are the "post-consequentialist"[100] strategies of law and economics or the radical consequentialism of critical legal studies. From Klare's "Judicial Deradicalization of the Wagner Act" to William Forbath's *Law and the Shaping of the American Labor Movement*, critical legal studies has done considerable work on the labor movement in the tradition of constitutive law.[101] In general, scholarship on race relations has availed itself of a constitutive perspective more fully than most chronicles of our political life. Eugene Genovese's *Roll, Jordan, Roll* is an outstanding example in this regard, as is Mark Tushnet's movement analysis work on the NAACP.[102]

David Silverman and Brian Torode's discussion of the constitutive character of language and symbols, appropriately titled *The Material*

Word,[103] proposes to reverse the assumption that speech refers to an external reality in exchange for "attention to speech as a reality in its own right."[104] These British authors develop Althusser's materialist theory of ideology, to which I will refer throughout this study. Silverman and Torode describe practices as existing within ideologies that relate individuals to one another and to the conditions of their existence. For example, they look at the ideology of the Christian religion as evident when we address "a human individual called, say, 'Peter.'" They point out that the name is produced from within an ideology since it is a biblical name and that it is granted by an ideological practice, baptism, and they argue that these practices tell you that "God exists and that you are answerable to Him."

While much of society's law is evident in the opinions of judges and bills passed by legislatures, the scholar who looks to these sources is looking for law in all the wrong places today because we have been looking there for too long. It is now time to recognize that the social reality of particular laws and the stature of law generally are evident in the shared practices that we find throughout American life, including movement activities. In movements, forms of law help define basic social relations, such as who is in, who is out, and how we know there is a movement. What I hope to do here is highlight the operations of this constitutive dimension of law by pointing to its manifestations in the formative language of various political movements.

The chapters that follow cover four contemporary social movements and depict law as it constitutes movement practice. In chapter 2 I discuss rights by focusing on the gay reaction to public hysteria about AIDS, a situation in which this form of law characterized at least one aspect of a political controversy. Events such as the closing of bathhouses in San Francisco in the 1980s manifest the belief in rights as an important form of law. I begin here because rights have become a very familiar conception of law, particularly as the reach of federal law has been extended into states and localities and as the Western conception of law has been exported around the world. In chapter 3 I turn to the denial of the reach of rights in legal realism. Critical legal studies and law and economics, movements on the opposite reaches of the political spectrum, have both allied themselves to realism, resulting in the predominance of realism in law schools. In chapter 4 I discuss the influence of established legal institutions in the informalist or alternative dispute resolution movement, a form that is remedial in that it is both based in

25

reformist claims and seeks remedy over right. In chapter 5 I examine a form that in some sense is the opposite of rights—that is, the tendency in political movements on the right and the left to attribute great power to law but to find the impact of law to be highly negative. Today we see this kind of rage in the militia movement. A decade ago rage at legal protection of pornography was prominent in radical feminism and the antipornography movement, especially at its inception (1978–1982), when movement activists sought to raise consciousness of legal complicity in women's oppression.

When compared to one another, these movements reveal some curious aspects of law's consequence for politics. Gay activists, among the least powerful and certainly the most threatened of the groups, work to advance a right to equal treatment in the interest of empowerment and pride. Dispute resolution or informalism would not exist as an organized interest without a conception of law against which it could posit its alternative form. Realism in law schools is self-consciously attentive to a reformulation of law as politics rather than promise. Thus, from professors at institutions like Harvard and Yale we hear that it is naive to make claims about legal obligation while antipornography feminists hold law responsible for the construction of sexuality in America.

Each chapter unfolds in roughly the same fashion. First, I provide a theoretical background for the legal form at issue, which helps to systematize the comparison between forms. In each case, the form is associated with a body of scholarship and tied to issues in jurisprudence. This discussion is followed by a description of the historical and political background necessary for understanding the specific cases used to illustrate the form. At the heart of each chapter is discursive material revealing the way activists talk about law. This is the basis for the interpretation of form as a political practice in each movement. Finally, I compare the general characteristics of legal form across movements whenever possible. This comparison is amplified and deepened in chapter 6.

The study of legal form in movement discourse builds a conception of law from the way people talk and therefore think about law in politics. What people think of as inequality or discrimination is really a framework through which we view events such as how people are treated. Very often the perception of right and wrong is derived at least in part from legal decisions and operates not as an order but as a way of thinking. From this perspective we realize that rules and commands permeate the social consciousness and structure social action. Rather than simply existing as orders, as if law were like the instructions promulgated by an imperious drill sergeant, law is presented as a part of society, a part of the way we think and act. The result is a number of counterintuitive findings about which forms attach to which sort of movements.

27

Rights to Profligacy?
Sex and AIDS, the Early Years

Chapter 2

Tradition is the
custody of that which
is already there and its
essence is expressed in
the separation of spirit
from substance. . . .
[O]nly in death, in
articulo mortis, can the
subject perceive the
secret of law.

—Peter Goodrich,
Languages of Law

Rights demand a response from people in authority. As an artifact of the law, they claim an obligation from government generally and usually litigation processes in particular. Yet rights also signal a vulnerable community turning to law, often simply in the hope of surviving. Americans, at least those of the recent past, have heralded rights. From Clarence Earl Gideon, a small-time crook in Florida who claimed to have a right to an attorney, to contemporary AIDS activists, rights have demanded that people respond.[1] When George Whitmore, an author who died of AIDS in 1989, was refused service at a Greenwich Village dental clinic, he sued for a violation of his civil rights. The clinic was fined $47,000 by the New York City Human Rights Commission, forcing it to close (it was later opened as a nursing home for AIDS patients).

The ideology of right, long part of the American experience, provides a warrant for movements to organize around taking or refusing to take an action. The claim of right is rooted in the past and its form reflects the adversarial structure of Anglo-American law. The result for politics is that movements that organize around rights engage in distinctive forms of political action. From African Americans before the Civil War to gays since Stonewall, those who attempt to mobilize as activists to express interest to the state are themselves affected by these forms.[2] Indeed, even the conceptualization of a movement in terms of rights gives politics its form and situates it in public life in a distinctive manner.

Struggles in the early years of the AIDS epidemic exemplify the relationship between rights and the identity of a movement. In the late 1980s, as the struggle against AIDS moved beyond the closing of bathhouses, the strategy shifted and the more liberal conception of law as rights ceased to be in the vanguard. The position developed in this chapter is that the impact of AIDS on group identity was mediated by legal forms. Initially, rights appeared as a bulwark against a society pressing on gays already at risk for the disease. Later, as queer activists took the place of lawyers, the bourgeois form of right went the way of the presumption that coming out was a matter of individual choice.[3]

Rights as Practice

Rights are a way of doing things. The orientation toward rights, with its litany of institutional channels and deference to professional discourses, contributes to political stability in the United States. Thus, the same rights that seem to propel us forward also hold us back. This is becoming evident with reference to the civil rights legacy in the late twentieth century, when the nondiscrimination rights that helped Supreme Court Justice Clarence Thomas, NBC anchor Bryant Gumbel, Ford Foundation President Franklin Thomas, and General Colin Powell get to the top of the social heap also keep most people of color at the bottom.[4] In invoking the state, rights require that a certain homage be paid. Rights excite us, drawing our attention to the few who get ahead, rather than the many kept behind.[5]

Rights may rely on rules backed by threats or appeals to some higher authority, as in the Declaration of Independence, where the claim that "All men are created equal" challenged the law on the books. Rights again make such sweeping claims in the Seneca Falls declaration of women's rights. Similar claims defining equality in terms of universal tolerance fuel the struggle for racial equality today as they have since slavery was accommodated in the U.S. Constitution. In the early 1980s, barely ten years after the Stonewall riot that launched modern gay liberation, rights played a key roll in the response of the gay community to AIDS. Only a few years into the AIDS epidemic, some gay activists made rights central to their political strategy while others tried to introduce the competing concerns of public health. The claim of rights in the controversy over the baths is analogous to the critical discourse on sexual repression more generally. Like the polarities of mourning and rage so prominent since the onslaught of AIDS, the practice of rights contains within itself both protection and repression. Contemporary scholarship in the social sciences calls attention to the constitutive qualities of such debate-framing dichotomies. According to Michel Foucault, the focus on repression and liberation in the history of sexuality limits insight.[6] Eve Kosofsky Sedgwick characterizes identity debates in the gay community, which pit social construction against biological essentialism, in much the same way.[7] We ought to be able to see beyond repression in the relationships among public health concerns, the gay community, and the law. Here, the terrain of the rights claim, rather than its validity, is of primary interest.

Rights fit into the instrumental picture of politics in the modern state. Groups, generally those considered "outside," present claims to a government that may or may not respond. This framework makes it difficult to see law constituting movements. We find it hard to fathom the extent to which Martin Luther King, Jr., and the civil rights movement operated "inside" the state (or Attorney General Robert Kennedy practiced "outside" it). Gay rights activists in the early years of the AIDS epidemic were also seen as outsiders appealing to the constitutive norms that legitimize authority, against the practices of particular government officials. Though conventional, this framework fails to capture important aspects of politics and law in America. San Francisco, with a powerful gay community, closed its baths while other cities like New York, Los Angeles, and San Diego waited or did not close them at all. The proposition developed here is that San Francisco's gay community was more fully constituted in realms beyond rights. That is, in San Francisco the gay community was influential and played a role in formulating health policy, which made the rights claim less monolithic, less constitutive of the entire community.

Rights claims move to "trump" mere policy consideration by claiming to be operating at a higher level.[8] Rights claims assert that the state will eventually support one's position. In the case of AIDS, some gay activists appealed to legal rights in order to resist what they saw as sexual repres-

31

sion. Others challenged the rights claim in the interests of the health of the community. Where governments denied the rights claim, as in San Francisco, the failure of this form of activism may be a sign of community strength, of gay penetration into the structure of power, rather than a sign of weakness.[9] Although all political struggles manifest some relation to law, those who claimed rights in the early days of the epidemic differed from more political activists. The rights claims seemed at the time to be more characteristic of gay activism. In retrospect, these claims may actually have been an expression of a more legally constituted segment, perhaps even a more politically immature part of the community. Nevertheless, in the early struggles over AIDS policy at least part of the gay community was clearly constituted in relation to rights.

Modern political and legal practice distinguishes individual rights from the rights of a community.[10] Contemporary scholars assert that the Greeks appear not to have employed what we call individual rights.[11] Before the bourgeois revolutions of the late eighteenth century, people turned to ideas of justice and right conduct, what we now call "natural" law. Before "nature" became a modifier of law,[12] nature or God *was* the law and law made things happen. Law in this sense was not an official statement of how people should act, but rather a description of action. Earlier people treated "the legal precepts that governed kings, counsellors, and courts"[13] similarly, as descriptions.

Before there were "rights" in the Western tradition there was custom. The Romans administered their empire through rules formulated to govern strangers, and they handled political problems that had been obscured by the homogeneity of the Greek polis through universal values drawn from cultural norms.[14] These universals amounted to a sort of "common law" for the Roman Empire, which helped to promote a workable citizenship.[15] When collected in codes, they became a source of "higher law" in the Middle Ages. There they could be appealed to against the "sinfulness" of mankind and could serve as a limitation on rulers. While the Greek concept of justice "enter[ed] into the more deliberate acts of human authority," the more modern higher law checked and limited authority "from without."[16] But medieval jurists lacked a basis for secular authority to recolonize individual consciousness.

Law is said to have shifted in the Middle Ages to a notion of right action, which was characterized as the "right reason" of learned men. The Inns of Court in medieval England provided an expertise independent of popular custom. Although they claimed public authority, the

Inns depended on separation and professional mystery—the "science of bench and bar"—which expanded with the rise of a marketplace ideology of individualism in the nineteenth century.[17] The expansion of this form of power transformed the professional mysteries of lawyers and judges into a generic unit of political exchange comparable to money in the economic sphere. In the United States, rights appear to precede society because of the "autonomous individual" depicted in liberalism. But society remains the source for rights, and individuals are expected to satisfy their interests and desires within stipulated limits. Developing from this basis, American government depends on practices that dissolved natural law into the natural rights of "life, liberty, and estate"—liberalism, in the "classic Lockeian sense."[18] Rights ground social relations in the formal autonomy of individuals while basing the claim in the community. Rights, understood as practices,[19] reflect the ways we know the world. Rights depend on knowledge and coexist along with other social practices, such as honor and exchange. The practice of rights comes from specific rights to have or do something, such as receiving a social security benefit. Because rights are more than matters of opinion,[20] a group relies on them when it feels threatened. When right simply asserts an individual opinion, and fails to draw from the authority of practice it is likely to fail.[21]

Rights may appear selfish and may seem not to blend very well with values such as gratitude or loyalty. As rights assert entitlement and appeal to the government for protection, they function very differently from social attributes such as generosity or friendship. In the AIDS epidemic, all sorts of social relationships are tested relative to rights established in law. In the handbook "Legal Answers about AIDS" put out by Gay Men's Health Crisis in 1989, the issues come from family life: the desire to continue to live in an apartment after one partner dies; the desire to visit in the hospital or have children taken care of. The responses, often in terms of right and its analogues—contracts, probate, and property—seem strained, minimally reassuring, and often cold. Although we cannot isolate rights from more communitarian and familial concepts, rights in their most familiar manifestations are incongruous with relationships like sisterhood or feelings like love.[22] Relationships of this sort affect us more deeply than rights—and we don't look to governments to enforce them.

Wesley Hohfeld, an American law professor writing in the early twentieth century, produced a catalogue of rights, and his description of

33

the practice of rights has become a grammar for how to use them.[23] Somewhat modified by Richard Flathman,[24] Hohfeld's analysis introduces the varieties of right: powers, claims, immunities, and liberties. *Powers* are available to people by virtue of specific authority or provisions in law. Hohfeld's formulation requires no specific grants of consent, although powers in a constitutional democracy depend on popular acquiescence. The government has the power to prosecute people it believes to have committed crimes. Rights in the strict sense, or claims, are the expectations between individuals, or between individuals and the government. *Claims* exist where a person or institution has a definite duty to a right holder. In the case of government officials, for instance, claims of public responsibility exist. Similarly, welfare recipients and the holders of entitlement provided for by statutes have claims to certain benefits if they meet the eligibility criteria. The rights conventionally associated with civil liberties Hohfeld calls immunities and liberties. An *immunity* is an exception to a power such as the Fourth Amendment protection against unreasonable searches and seizures. *Liberties* are rights held against authorities that limit interference with a variety of activities deemed worthy of special protection. The government's duty not to interfere with the exercise of free speech comes, not from the freedom to speak, but from the right or liberty not to be interfered with in the exercise of certain expression.

In each of these forms, rights exist as practices characteristic of the American political experience. Clarence Gideon's appeal is featured in books and movies; Martin Luther King, Jr.'s contribution to civil rights gets a national holiday; and claims that reach the Supreme Court receive much attention. Like elections, where we struggle over votes, our contests over rights display our politics, and a politics of rights is a key to the American experience that can be brought to bear in politically significant ways. Both flag burning and criminal due process became central to the 1988 presidential election campaign between George Bush and Michael Dukakis.[25] At about the same time, minority scholars began defending rights from the contemporary position in law school, which tended to focus on their lack of meaning.[26] Because they are social practices, rights in general, and particularly the claims, immunities, and liberties described here, are recognizable forms by which interests are asserted and thus law enters into politics.

Modern liberal jurists such as John Rawls, Ronald Dworkin, and Michael Walzer cannot be separated from communitarian concerns as readily as the stereotypical liberalism we legitimately associate with the prevailing conceptions about right in law. They are not, as scholars such as Roberto Alejandro, Susan Moller Okin, and Linda C. McClain have pointed out, trapped in an "atomistic man" framework.[27] In my efforts here to see the social relations in rights that constitute movement practices, I do not wish to caricature rights as without roots and without community. Rather, I want to say that a relationship built on rights is usually bonded in a different way from one built on family relations or love. But the battles raging in political theory point out the need to develop the character of liberalism beyond the relative autonomy of the individual to include assumptions about the rightness and reach of law that is essential to the hegemony of liberalism.[28]

In his response to the minority critiques of the critical legal studies movement,[29] Alan Freeman concedes a lesson learned from minority scholars, in this case Patricia Williams, that "the experience of rights-assertion has been of both solidarity and freedom, of empowerment of an internal and very personal sort; it has been a process of finding the self," an experience of particular importance to the "historically disempowered."[30] At their height in the late 1980s, these debates were over the nature of the practice of rights. Although politics drove the debates, the social practice of rights—different for white male intellectuals than for women, Asian-American, Chicano, and African-American intellectuals—determined the place of the intellectual in the politics.

Rights Movements

Today, it is hard to understand the power of legal rights even while they seem omnipresent. Since at least the first years of the New Deal, "legal realism" in law schools and "judicial behaviorism" in social science departments asserted a political view of law[31] and people in the academy, surrounded as they were by the artifacts of law, tended to lose track of distinctly legal processes. The action was in politics and in society, and hence the law did not seem as significant. Conceptualizing power in America as distinctly political, however, is stilted. By appealing to rights or calling attention to possible transgressions, rights have empowered and often changed those who invoke them.

Although America was born out of declarations of natural right, it took a century to satisfy the most basic claims of human equality and launch the modern period of rights. Frederick Douglass refused to vote and participate in the polity delineated by the Constitution because it accommodated slavery.[32] William Lloyd Garrison and other northern middle class reformers challenged the complicity of the state with the evil of slavery.[33] The abolitionists may have been the first group to make a constitutional claim in the modern sense.[34] Later in the nineteenth century, rights served industrial capital with a vengeance and women's equality less energetically.

The Seneca Falls Convention, held in 1848, produced a Declaration of Principles that demanded the extension of political rights to women in terms nearly identical to those in the Declaration of Independence.[35] To most women outside the convention the control of property, guardianship, divorce, and education may well have been more pressing than the vote, but it was political rights of this sort that exemplified the equity claim and its particular political form.[36] As a result, this movement has been identified closely with subsequent political demands made by women. Among the descendants of the Seneca Falls movement, first the Bloomers and much later feminists in the academy became identified with equal rights as articulated in the original declaration.

Struggles for equality by other groups turned into legal victories for women only sporadically. The Fourteenth Amendment, a major victory for free labor, placed "male" in the Constitution for the first time, thereby demonstrating the falsehood that the generic pronouns of the Constitution could easily be read to include women. The Fifteenth Amendment could have included sex since it listed "race, color, or previous condition of servitude," but it did not. Suffrage for women did not develop as a right until the perception of sexual equality was more advanced. A problematic relationship between the struggle for equal rights and women in the workforce who identify more completely with workers' struggles exemplifies the distinctive quality of rights as a legal form.

By mobilizing masses of people around legal rights, civil liberties shifted public consciousness toward greater appreciation of law as a resource. Those who fought for free labor, most notably in the Thirteenth, Fourteenth, and Fifteenth Amendments, initiated later expansion of constitutional rights and liberties. The craftsmanship of various legal scholars and Supreme Court justices in the late nineteenth century exemplified creative development focused on the protection of property.[37] After Franklin Roosevelt remade the Supreme Court by appointing three new justices, the Court shifted its attention to political rights. Groups such as the American Civil Liberties Union and the National

Association for the Advancement of Colored People's Legal Defense Fund facilitated this shift in such important cases as *Near v. Minnesota* and *Brown v. Board of Education*.[38] The results transformed the Bill of Rights from a document whose application was limited to the federal government to one that applied to all Americans.

The public interest law movement reconceived the relationship between movements and law. Lawyers made legal change a basis for mobilization. Stuart Scheingold's response to this movement in the 1970s considered rights strategies as part of "the myth of rights" and described rights as beliefs to which one could appeal.[39] He located the significance of rights in political practice and identified legal power that extended beyond the courtroom by political mobilization based on appeals to rights. Other natural rights claims surround us. Activists from Eastern Europe to China proclaim fealty to rights and other artifacts of Western "liberty" as a substitute for socialism. Rights also characterize less celebrated domestic struggles such as the contemporary squatter movements. Here, the claim of right to particular buildings stands starkly against the more popular efforts to house the homeless. Squatters from the Lower East Side of New York City to Amsterdam and London confront property by the act of squatting, and their claim of entitlement draws from natural law rather than charity.[40]

37

Rights movements have become a type of political action. In many cases movements that may be about identity are cast as rights movements because it is so much more comprehensible politically. This seems to be true of the struggle over abortion rights, which may really be a dispute over lifestyle and conceptions of the family.[41] One suspects that rights movements fit so nicely with a pluralist vision of appeal to the state that even occasional excess is not enough to deter public enthusiasm for demands of rights. In some cases the assertion of rights, such as those of the elderly and people with disabilities, have transformed the landscape in the form of new entrances to buildings and have redefined traditionally age-specific occupations such as airline steward or professor. In the case of people with disabilities, realizing rights was possible by extending the civil rights tradition. In the case of the elderly, political influence seems to have played a greater role.

The conventional assumptions about rights movements have provoked questions and given meaning to "new social movements" that appear unconventional. These are movements that do not easily situate themselves on the spectrum from left to right, a spectrum provided by movement orientation to politically constituted authority. The new movements for environmental sensitivity, for peace and disarmament, against nuclear power and weapons, as well as the many lifestyle movements concerned with health, mysticism, and consciousness, mobilize but either do not challenge the state or, in some less classically political sense, present a challenge to all states. These movements challenge boundaries set by traditional movement practice that is strongly associated with rights struggles.[42] Conversely, or perhaps dialectically, these movements and the scholarship that takes account of them have expanded our conception of the larger impact of rights movements themselves on their participants.

A Latina teacher in San Jose, California, is quoted by Blanca Silvestrini as noting that "you have to confess first, and then you can claim a right."[43] Rights claims, particularly those associated with social movements, require the acceptance of certain identities or relations to the state. Sometimes these are "required" upon entrance to the embrace of the movement; at other times they enter into individual consciousness through the shaping that is characteristic of the movement. Rights do not always constrain the participants in this way; often rights are used in an instrumental sense to mobilize. This is the picture we have of the early organizing of the civil rights movement,[44] and it is reflected in the observations of activists about the meaning political struggle has had for them.[45] This sense of rights is also revealed in the work of Michael McCann on comparable worth.[46] But our understanding of the extent to which movement politics creates identity—the way in which it enters the consciousness and becomes indicative of the social place of movement practitioners—is still relatively underdeveloped. The picture that needs to be filled in is outlined by Kristin Bumiller in *The Civil Rights Society*, that is, the picture of people within law; people who have taken on aspects of legality not fully acknowledged by the aspirational addresses of movement practice.[47] In Bumiller's frame, the status of victim reflects in practice what Alan Freeman describes as the doctrinal stance of civil rights law, a stance that limits the aspirations of participants.[48]

Gay Rights and AIDS

AIDS brings to everything it touches a sense of urgency. Rights have been touched in this way. This urgency was particularly evident in the initial hysteria as the disease emerged in California in 1983. Public reaction made it difficult for city buses to move through San Francisco's Castro District or, in other parts of the country, for infected children like Ryan White to go to school. Such urgency was due in part to the blistering pace with which the disease has spread since it was first identified.[49]

After the period covered in this study, urgency led activists to adopt bold strategies in order to demonstrate the failures of a government operating under ordinary practices.[50] Thus ACT-UP and Queer Nation shut down institutions such as the Food and Drug Administration in Rockville, Maryland, and *Cosmopolitan* magazine.[51] This was a boldness grounded in the vulnerability of most affected groups and the failure of rights strategies to promise protection. In the early years, rights claims were seen as protecting gays against society.

A movement's assertion of a right is based upon the existence of a group. For gays, sexual preference is central to but not determinative of identity. As an ancient predisposition, homosexuality is a movement rooted in basic social relations. In the West in the twentieth century, gay men have created a social structure and group identity. By the 1960s, this group identity was evident in all aspects of society, language, culture, and social relations. The existence of a gay language, for instance, is described by Bruce Boone in the context of a poetry review.[52] In the work of beat poet Frank O'Hara, Boone finds evidence of group praxis characterized by repressed violence, cynicism, and guilt, as well as links to the world of the arts and the avant-garde.[53] The image Boone identifies is one of opposition incorporating and coopting dominant practices. In this language of group identity we also find the basis of the rights content of gay liberation struggles, as well as the rights orientation of the gay community's initial response to AIDS.

Since the 1960s, homosexuals have raised claims for protection against discrimination on the basis of sexual preference. Gay liberation, with an affinity for the guarantees of the civil rights movement, erupted with a new militancy following the Stonewall riots of June 1968.[54] The conventional picture of gay life in America until the 1950s was one in which gay men and lesbians had little security. After the national expansion of rights to expression, equality, and due process associated with legal liberalism in the 1950s and early 1960s, security for gays and lesbians became a realistic aspiration. New demands were brought by gay politicians such as San Francisco's Harvey Milk, and public interest

39

law groups such as the Lambda Legal Defense Fund.[55] Gay rights statutes were passed in many American cities in the 1970s and 1980s. But in Miami, and then a little later in California, there was a backlash.[56] Although ordinances against discrimination were being passed as late as 1989,[57] they were also being repealed with much fanfare.

Beyond the dominant equal protection claim at the root of the gay rights movement, there has also been a rights link with privacy. For years the right to privacy, which had emerged from the due process changes in the 1960s and had given women the right to abortion, promised to offer security to gay men and women. Until the Supreme Court decision in *Bowers v. Hardwick* in 1986, however, there was more political action than significant judicial decision in this area.[58] To gay activists in groups like the Lambda Legal Defense Fund, the *Bowers* decision was disappointing because the movement had supported Michael Hardwick's attempt to apply the right of constitutional privacy to homosexual relations. Having gone all the way to the Supreme Court and lost magnified the impact of the decision.[59] This was the legal environment in which closing bathhouses surfaced as a political issue.

AIDS was first identified in 1981. By 1983, just enough had been learned about the disease to create a panic. In San Francisco, people began calling the AIDS Foundation with questions about shared toothbrushes and gay waiters, while city bus drivers whose routes brought them through gay neighborhoods were reported in the *San Francisco Chronicle* to be wearing surgical masks.[60] While the federal government resisted addressing the issue, ostensibly because gay sex was illegal in half the states, a group called Bay Area Physicians for Human Rights began producing materials "to eroticize safe sex." This new concept of sexuality would eventually have profound consequences for social practices.

As the initial terror subsided and the magnitude of the crisis began to present itself, rights issues began to surface. They appeared as the response to an asserted link between morality and disease. Characteristically, some would juxtapose rights claims in the context of AIDS against the interests of the community—rights versus public health.[61] By early 1984, public health officials in San Francisco were describing gay bathhouses as "sex establishments" where men engaged in "high-volume, high-frequency sex." This was the context for a struggle over strategic responses in the gay community, first in San Francisco and later in New York, Los Angeles, and San Diego.[62]

The Baths

Evolving from historic establishments where men had gone for generations to get a steam, a massage, and the fellowship of other men, gay baths became the focus of the early struggle over AIDS. Baths such as those on the Lower East Side of New York were public facilities that promoted physical hygiene—often in response to the urging of the "better" classes. The "better" classes also had their own facilities, such as the all-male Olympic Club in San Francisco. In an unflattering portrayal that predates the epidemic by fifteen years, Martin Hoffman describes the baths in detail as institutions developed by a population restricted from the traditional places for sex.[63] The baths of that period were divided into private rooms, initially changing and rest areas, and the public areas around a pool or steam bath. In the next decade, the gay liberation movement of the 1970s is reported to have made the hundreds of "bathhouses and sex clubs" a $100-million industry across the United States and Canada.[64]

Concern about sexual practices was a feature of reports on the epidemic by Randy Shilts, the *San Francisco Chronicle*'s AIDS correspondent. In his book *And the Band Played On*, Shilts quotes a 1980 interview in the New York City gay magazine *Christopher Street*, where Dan William addresses the rise in erotic practices:

> sex has been institutionalized and franchised. Twenty years ago, there may have been a thousand men on any one night having sex in New York baths or parks. Now there are ten or twenty thousand—at the baths, the back-room bars, bookstores, porno theaters, the Rambles, and a wide range of other places as well. The plethora of opportunities poses a public health problem.[65]

Drawing from ads for the baths from the 1980s, Shilts notes that the Handball Express's motto was "find your limits," while "the Glory Holes pledged to be 'the most unusual sex place in the world'; the Jaguar sex club in the Castro hyped 'your fantasy, your pleasure'; while the coeducational Sutro Baths had a 'Bisexual Boogie' every weekend."[66]

The YMCA's indoor pools, steam baths, and massage facilities provided a model for the gay baths.[67] This particular institutional lineage seems to go back to the period before World War II, when the Navy conducted a major investigation of the Newport YMCA branch.[68]

In the late 1970s, Dr. David Ostrow, an expert on gay diseases, described the baths as "a horrible breeding ground." Later, in his book on the control of AIDS, he ranked them the fourth most dangerous out of

seven locations where gay and bisexual men met for sexual encoun-
ters.[69] Other studies confirmed this observation:

> A Seattle study of gay men suffering from shigellosis, for example, dis-
> covered that 69 percent culled their sexual partners from bathhouses. A
> Denver study found that an average bathhouse patron having his typical
> 2.7 sexual contacts a night risked a 33 percent chance of walking out of
> the tubs with syphilis or gonorrhea, because about one in eight of those
> wandering the hallways had asymptomatic cases of these diseases.[70]

As epidemiologists from the Centers for Disease Control (CDC) entered
the effort, the baths came to head the list of locations and behaviors
identified with the spread of AIDS. Shilts summarizes the position of
Mary Guinan from CDC in his typically vivid fashion: "This disease was
being spread through sex by people depositing their infected semen in
sundry orifices of their partners. . . . Gays were just getting it more fre-
quently because they were more active sexually and they had institutions like bathhouses that were virtual Federal Reserve Banks for
massive semen deposition."[71]

By the mid-1980s, these bastions of nonconformity were becoming
lightning rods for a community concerned about repression. The baths
became symbols of tolerance and a barometer of the gay community's
vulnerability, and they were also linked to political leadership in the gay
community. Shilts describes bathhouse owners as influential in major
American cities, "by virtue of their substantial largess to the always-
starved gay political community."[72] The link between the economic via-
bility of the baths and public health issues around AIDS was the subtext
of conversations between bathhouse owners and public health officials.
Cleve Jones of the Kaposi Sarcoma Education and Research Foundation
is said to have tentatively suggested, "I think it's a sexually transmitted
disease that's caused by a virus," and he mentioned the baths tangen-
tially, "Nobody has advocated closing the baths, but I think there need
to be changes."[73]

The "Crunch"

A powerful connection exists between law and the material conditions
that affect business or corporate bodies as well as bodies infected with
AIDS. The Alice B. Toklas Gay and Lesbian Democratic Club in San Francisco opposed closure of the baths, but some gay activists described
bathhouse owners as capitalists cynically trying to make themselves out
as civil libertarians.[74] Civil liberties lawyers defended the baths in the

42

abstract without defending the actual institutions or the practices they facilitated.[75] On the other side, activists ranged from advocates of voluntary closure, the position held by the Harvey Milk Lesbian and Gay Democratic Club in San Francisco in 1983, to those who believed that mandatory closure was inevitable.

Shilts's book and the television movie made from it describe growing recognition, first in San Francisco and then in other communities, that the baths had to be closed. This development began with Selma Dritz,[76] the infectious disease specialist for San Francisco's Department of Public Health. Shilts's treatment of the issue, beginning with work he did for the *Chronicle*, pits public health against the claim of rights. About Dritz, he writes, "She had never been overly fond of the institutions. It wasn't that she had any moral qualms. . . . But bathhouses were biological cesspools for infection. . . . 'Of course, from an old-fashioned textbook public health standpoint, you might go in and close the places down." Dritz adds, "Of course, some might argue that there were civil liberties issues involved," and Shilts describes "her voice trailing off in a way that suggested she did not think for one minute that civil liberties were the central issues involved here."[77] Shilts describes the split over tactics in the context of activist concern that "talking about the gay community's prodigious promiscuity was part of a 'blame-the-victim mentality.'" The Gay Men's Health Crisis in New York, which advocated safe sex education, was on record at the time as seeing important civil rights issues in bathhouse closure.[78]

In San Francisco during the spring of 1983, activists sought to move beyond the "safe sex" campaign. A manifesto by Bill Kraus, an aid to Congressman Philip Burton, proposed, "We believe it is time to speak the simple truth. . . . Unsafe sex is—quite literally—killing us. . . . [U]nsafe sex at bathhouses and sex clubs is particularly dangerous."[79] With this, the campaign against the baths was launched publicly.[80] The baths issue was central to the struggle between a sense of right within at least part of the gay community and the regulation of community health. The civil libertarians were led by businessmen such as the owner of the Sutro Baths, who shouted to a public health official in San Francisco, "If you try to shut them down, I'll have you in court a day later with a temporary restraining order."[81]

In early 1983 the public health community still had doubts about the legality of closing the baths. Dritz "asked for an opinion on the legality of closure from the city attorney's office," knowing "that a closure order might be difficult to get because doctors had not yet isolated an AIDS virus." Mervyn Silverman, Dritz's boss as director of public health for San Francisco, said it would be "illegal for me to close down all bathhouses and other such places that are used for anonymous and multiple sex contacts." Dritz, however, "thought the posting of signs [about the dangers of AIDS in bathhouses] was a cop-out," and she held that while "[t]he U.S. Constitution might be construed to allow the right to commit suicide . . . [t]he Constitution did not grant the right to take other people with you."[82] Even after San Francisco mayor Dianne Feinstein quietly began to advocate closing the baths in 1982, public health officials hesitated for two years.

By February 1984, however, doctors at the San Francisco General Hospital announced their support for closing the bathhouses.[83] In March, the public health department concurred, but the city did not implement the decision until that fall, leading conservative supervisors like Wendy Nelder to lament the slow pace at which the city was moving.[84] On October 9, Silverman announced that the city would close fourteen baths that "promote and profit from the spread of AIDS." He went on to add at a news conference, "These 14 establishments are not fostering gay liberation. They are fostering disease and death.'"[85]

The reaction from the bathhouse owners and the civil libertarian community linked economics with rights claims.[86] One gay business association called closure "an intrusion on private enterprise," and the Bay Area Lawyers for Individual Freedom expressed concern that gays throughout the country were in danger of losing their rights.[87] Six of the bathhouse owners defied Silverman's order and sought court injunctions allowing them to remain open until the civil rights suits could be heard.[88] Although reports at the time held that the baths were becoming less popular,[89] they were a locus of struggle in law. The bathhouse owners formed the Committee to Preserve Our Sexual and Civil Liberties and fought the closing in San Francisco's courts, while it was reported that other cities were unlikely to close their baths.[90] On October 11, 1984, the city sought a temporary restraining order listing the fourteen baths and fifty-six defendants. Feinstein, in supporting the order, said that the defiant owners were "putting the profit motive ahead of the health and life of those who patronize their establishments."[91] On October 16, the baths were ordered to close temporarily by Judge William Mullins of the San Francisco Superior Court, who found a "real public health menace."[92] The ban was upheld on October 24 by the State Court of Appeals on a 2–1 vote with J. Anthony Kline dissenting.

When San Francisco ordered the baths closed, there were 714 AIDS cases reported in the city. This was one third of the total for New York, where the struggle over closing the baths did not fully emerge until a year later. In October 1985, Governor Mario Cuomo declined to recommend closing the baths in the state, offering new regulations instead.[93] Two weeks later, the *New York Times* reported favorably on San Francisco's effort, which had led to court mandated restrictions on behaviors in the baths and "a dramatic decline" in sexually transmitted diseases among homosexuals.[94] The mayoral election in New York that fall pitted conservatives advocating closing against liberals Carol Bellamy and Edward Koch who opposed closing. As the state health commissioner moved closer to closing the baths, the debate in New York saw little advocacy from the gay community in favor of closing the baths.

Other Cities

In San Diego, J. Douglas Scott, president of the Democratic Club, addressing the possibility of closing the baths in that city, argued for voluntary measures. He figured it would be good public relations for the gay community and might stem the threat of more extreme action by public authority. In Scott's words, "If we aren't seen as cooperating and are seen as little children saying 'no, don't take this away,' they'll feel perfectly justified in whatever actions they take. They'll go further than the baths."[95] Although the public health community was beginning to feel a need to respond to the epidemic, the preemptive call for closure was seen by many as capitulation.

Reacting to the call put forth by Scott as the controversy in San Diego raged through the winter of 1985–86, gay activists developed the civil libertarian position that was evident in a number of publications. The letters to the editor of the *Gayzette* contained calls for an aggressive assertion of the rights in the Constitution, including the right to property, free association, and liberty. This call was emblematic of past struggles. It claimed a new legal definition through the clarification of already recognized values in the midst of a crisis. The assertion of right came as a response to the threat not only of closure for the baths, but of genocide fueled by the fear in the straight community. In this case, many in the gay community felt threatened by public reaction to the spread of AIDS and the resulting pressure to close the bathhouses.[96] But the AIDS crisis also arrived during a political shift to the right in the United States that put leverage on the culture to disavow a more liberal past. In this context, activists in the gay community saw voluntary closure as a "co-conspiracy . . . with the forces of reaction." In one comment in the *Gayzette*, the issue surrounding bathhouse closure was whether gays and lesbians would work in an illicit alliance with those who would wipe them out in order to respond to the immediate situation. Such an alliance, the writer says, would "rob us of our fifth amendment constitutional right to due process in the protection of our life, liberty and property."[97] Here the claim of right rejected the public health strategy. In this sense, the writer was operating according to the same polarity recognized by conservatives, one that pitted rights claims against public health interests.

The letter writer's assertion is of a vested right, and it brings to bear a tradition of honoring that right. Although the earlier gay rights movements relied on equal protection rather than due process, property, privacy, and assembly rights, the demand from law is for protection. However, the writer also argues that the baths perform a public health service: "The baths in the 1960s brought together under one roof these myriad forms of sexuality in a safe gay haven. . . . Close down the baths and our brothers are back on the streets as outlaws." This threat, as an aside, represents the potential for a sort of germ warfare. As part of the public health debate, however, it escalated the threat beyond the claim of right.

The language in the response is fearful. It lacks the confidence in a better future seen in some rights struggles—the speeches of Martin Luther King, Jr., for example—although it shares an apocalyptic threat with such struggles: "Most of the heterosexual majority hates us. . . . We are fatally deluded if we think that by punishing our 'perverts' and 'tainted merchants' we will be miraculously spared." At this stage in the struggle, neither the radical disobedience of ACT-UP nor the culturally evocative NAMES project had provided a voice for the community. It was a period of growing terror and very real prospects for the kind of mass violations of rights that California had tolerated in interring Japanese Americans during the World War II. The threat to the baths came only a year after the voters of California rejected a Lyndon LaRouche–sponsored initiative that would have required all persons with Human Immunodeficiency Virus (HIV) to report their condition to the State Department of Health.[98]

Back in New York, in December 1985 the city obtained a court order to close the New St. Marks Baths on the basis of findings of unsafe sex by city health inspectors. Two weeks earlier, the city had closed a club frequented by heterosexuals on the grounds that prostitution was tak-ing place. The sequence was reported as an effort to demonstrate that the city was not acting against homosexuals in closing the New St. Marks Baths.[99] Some reports described this bath as one of the more responsible in providing safe sex material, but a vivid portrayal of life in the baths by Philip Weiss for the *New Republic* described plenty of unsafe activity.[100] In the New York Supreme Court opinion handed down in January 1986, Judge Richard W. Wallach emphasized the rapid spread of the epidemic and its link to sexual practices such as anal inter-course and fellatio.[101] He found the closing authorized by regulations created by the State Public Health Council two months earlier.

The claims against closure in the first years of the epidemic denied public health concerns and invoked traditional cultural symbols of right. Although lawyers were involved, the discourse of the struggle is not deferential to them. It is not mediated by professionals to any great extent. The discourse, the practice, in this struggle is about right. In the end, the rights claim is a stance, a political position. In this sense, it is directed within a movement context, not to the outside and the uncon-verted. The special significance of right in this movement context explains the choice of this strategy over others. The assertion of a legal right indicates the social relations the legal form constitutes. Many gays in San Francisco, New York, and San Diego resisted the public health moves of the government in an expression of their solidarity and con-cern about the repression they felt sure would follow any assertion of authority from the state.

The struggle against AIDS has not only been fought within the lan-guage of social structure, it has produced new social structures in the steps taken by cities such as San Francisco to provide education and treatment in response to the disease. Paradoxically, however, the asser-tion of what on the surface sounds formal and legalistic is more accu-rately seen as an assertion of community identity. In this case, the rights claim reflects the post-Stonewall tradition among gays in the United States of making identity a central feature of cultural politics. In the case of the baths, the identification appears both natural and des-perate, which is in the nature of the identity politics so prevalent fol-lowing the civil rights era in the United States. Here, however, resistance may have been romanticized.[102] Though not as evident a form of hegemonic power as silence, resistance is nevertheless an expression of state power.

47

Law and Social Relations

Academic study of rights teaches that rights are a political resource because they contain beliefs about how things should be done. Stuart Scheingold calls this belief the "myth of rights."[103] The significance of rights in this framework lies less in the political power behind them than in their congruence with beliefs about social justice or right conduct. In the late 1960s and early 1970s, the public interest law movement, with its mobilization of people around legal rights, sought appreciation of law as a resource. In the conservative 1980s the critical legal studies movement's critique of law turned away from rights.[104] But life with AIDS teaches that rights do matter, at least to people subject to the disease.

Historically and epistemologically, society is the source for the meaning and significance of rights. Rights appear to come first because of a picture of the "autonomous individual" associated with liberal legal practice in the United States. Despite this emphasis, rights involve interactions and cannot have any meaning simply in terms of individuals. In fact they have produced a situation cleverly described by Thomas Haskell as the "curious persistence of rights talk in the 'Age of Interpretation.'"[105] In a society (or intersubjective moral order) the rights "lay claim to a kind of knowledge that is not merely personal and subjective, but impersonal and objective."[106] For many, the reality is conventional, a form of "moderate historicism"; for some, the historicism is more troubling.[107] In the academy, the historicism of Friedrich Nietzsche and Martin Heidegger thrives while in the polity, particularly around law and social movements, the language of right seduces.[108] The answer to why rights persist lies in their social reality.

Practice and talk about practice matter.[109] This, of course, results in recognition of willful conduct rather than a paradox in the persistence of rights. Haskell and others predict "the intensification of rights talk as more and more people shed their illusions about objectivity and come to see in the old superstitions about natural rights a useful device for manipulating the gullible."[110] Beyond the challenge of historicism, the natural rights challenge to conventionalism attacks an absence of standards. On the other hand, "admitting that rights talk has a fictive element loses its dismissive implications, and . . . even gains some potentially constructive ones."[111]

The gay community in the mid-1980s, like the women's community 150 years earlier, drew on a rights/law base in mobilizing a community response to a crisis. Right in the gay community was something to mobilize around, something to "come out" to. Now that the political struggle against AIDS has matured with ACT-UP, the politics of "outing," and Queer Nation, these earlier moves in a mobilization around rights seem immature, as naive as the sentiment that dismissed the first manifestations of the disease. Groups continue to reconstitute themselves with reference to their environment. The initial response to AIDS owed much to the period of rights consciousness following the Stonewall riot and the emergence of the San Francisco gay community in the 1970s. Subsequent developments took some of their meaning from the transformation of social relations brought on by the epidemic itself, including the aftermath of the struggle to keep the baths open.

As the struggle matured, right seemed to be subsumed in larger cultural constructions. As Lucinda Furlong pointed out in "AIDS Media," her introduction to the show at the Whitney Museum in the winter of 1989, "It is precisely because cultural biases are inscribed in language that AIDS activists have contested the terminology used to describe the disease and have substituted the phrase 'people with AIDS' for 'AIDS victims.'"[112] In his book *Policing Desire: Pornography, AIDS, and the Media*,[113] Simon Watney calls attention to the "crisis of representation" associated with the epidemic. Work such as that of Furlong and Watney deconstructs, in what seems to be an opposition to rights. And, with regard to political activity generally, rights claims have not necessarily predominated. At the level of culture, the appeal to rights reinforced the very victim status in the gay community that later activism would work to break down.[114] Like the polarities of mourning and rage that come together and fly apart, the practice of right contains within itself both protection and repression.[115] To paraphrase Foucault, we ought to say that the relationship between public health concerns and the gay community is not characterized by repression, which would "risk falling into a sterile paradox." The question is not, "Was closing the baths repressive?" but rather, "Why do we say, with so much passion and so much resentment, that we are repressed?"[116]

AIDS activism has appeared to draw on bonds between gay men and lesbians. This is a strange alliance given the misogyny in some gay literature. In the important movement groups, such as the Lambda Legal Defense Fund, gay and lesbian lawyers present a united front. In ACT-UP, the alliance of homosexual men and women looks quite striking. Yet the alliance may not be as formidable as public discussion makes it out

49

to be. There may be a synthesis of group interests, but there is little doubt that this alliance affirms law's authority as a terrain for struggling over the construction of gay identity. Of course, in many instances, the two cultures are profoundly divergent. The lesbian community, particularly much of the radical lesbian community, is generally anti-men, and the gay community, particularly the more libertine elements, is anti-women in much the same respect. This is not always evident on the surface, where rights as ordinary discourse forge superficial links, but in the literature and life of the communities one sees evidence that the alliances and the common enemy, which are synthesized in rights terms, mask deep divisions.

Rights provide us with a paradigm from which to consider the presence of legal form in political discourse. Here, law is not legal in the positive sense—that is, it is not a command of the sovereign. Drawing as it did from the civil rights and the women's rights movements, which were themselves grounded in the Declaration of Independence, the resistance to closing the baths was a movement about rights. Here, the practice of rights made sense for a group under siege, particularly when that group had flourished under a more tolerant legal climate and aspired to liberation under a banner of tolerance and equality. As both the climate and the material environment degenerated, a rights strategy expressed a longing for community.

Some gay men living through the start of a mysterious epidemic that was singling them out and killing them relentlessly reached for a tradition in law that had empowered homosexuals since the Stonewall riots. These years roughly coincided with a grand expansion of civil rights and liberties. In claims of rights, protectors of the baths took a stand as "incumbents" of a tradition hoping to evoke some of the features of that tradition, and perhaps even "those dark letters that are law for us," as Peter Goodrich has described it.[117]

This inquiry has examined the claim of right in a besieged community with a history of reliance on rights. The prominence of this form of law in the early years of the AIDS epidemic is part of the problem of the persistence of this claim in an age of interpretation. Thus we return to Goodrich's description of tradition in English Law as "the custody of that which is already there . . . expressed in the separation of spirit from substance."[118] Asserted in the face of AIDS, law is indeed an authority that carries the specter of death.

Professions of Realism
An Institutional Form

Chapter 3

When we came, they
were like a priesthood
that had lost their faith
and kept their jobs.
They stood in tedious
embarrassment before
cold altars. But we
turned away from those
altars and found the
mind's opportunity in
the heart's revenge.

—Roberto M. Unger,
*The Critical Legal
Studies Movement*

In the late spring of 1990, Derrick Bell—a professor at Harvard Law School, the distinguished author of "The Civil Rights Chronicles," *And We Are Not Saved*, and *Faces at the Bottom of the Well*, and former dean of the University of Oregon Law School—announced that he would turn down his salary in protest over Harvard's failure to hire a black woman in a tenured position at the law school. Bell's salary, considerable in comparison to most Americans, and the prestige of his position made his sacrifice significant. But the publicity occasioned by this event was also a consequence of the tactical pig in the law school poke. Direct action is not the traditional stuff of the legal academy. Duncan Kennedy, a leader of the critical legal studies (CLS) movement, responding to Bell's protest, said such tactics were "not his style."[1] Although three years earlier Bell had a "sit-in" in his own office to protest personnel actions taken by Harvard's president Derek Bok against faculty associated with the CLS movement, such public display is clearly not law school style.[2]

Bell's earlier protest took place the same year that Robert Bork, an appellate judge identified with the economic model of law, was nominated to the Supreme Court.[3] The nomination was questioned by a Bar Association committee on which Harvard was well represented. At the hearings, Laurence Tribe and other Harvard professors played a major role. The publicity around Bork's nomination struggle was widely seen by the bar to be unfortunate. It was, however, nothing compared to the unfortunate developments surrounding the subsequent nomination of Judge Clarence Thomas to the Supreme Court. During the Thomas hearings the usually unseen relations in the legal academy came prominently to the fore. Unlike successfully managed nominations, like those of judges Ruth Bader Ginsburg and Steven Breyer to the Court, law schools were evident in the prosecution and defense of Clarence Thomas. We saw Yale against Yale being judged by Yale, Harvard, Syracuse, and others.

Events on the legal left and right that make it to the public stage merely suggest the nature of politics in and around the legal academy. In the last quarter of the twentieth century, the professionally constituted halls of academe have occasionally been rent by political struggle. These struggles, however, have generally been behind the scenes. This is true in large part because the most dynamic political movements in law—CLS on the left and law and economics on the right—are rooted in a jurisprudential ideology first proposed in the 1930s. As intellectual movements they bury their politics in the cloistered life of the legal academy. Legal realism sets the epistemological parameters and determines the rhetorical constructions for waging these legal struggles. It also diverts attention. Both political movements adopt the realist framework as they set themselves against traditional dogma.

This chapter is about how realism, as a theory of law, operates in conjunction with law schools to maintain the law. Realism in law schools has become a perpetual insurgency that keeps alive the foil of formalism in constituting contemporary struggles. Through realism, which was once offered to expose the interests behind law, the ideologies of law mask the politics at law schools and resist academic inquiry. By restating the obvious—that law is about interests—and going no further, the role of the legal profession and the legal academy in law is ignored. Politics formed in realist terms draw attention away from professional communities while maintaining the power of those communities by means of a professional shyness. Politics in the legal academy invokes old formalisms that shield the conflicts and draw attention away from the hierarchies that constitute legal power. The authority behind modern law is found only partly in the public institutions of the judiciary; the legal academy also plays a major role in constructing the authority of law by determining what the public thinks law is.

Politics in the legal academy, specifically the struggles between law professors, though sometimes disruptive, tend to affirm the authority of the institutions in which they take place. Thus, struggles at Harvard Law School over tenure are important because the law school is important. Disagreements at Yale Law School over Clarence Thomas's nomination tended to affirm the centrality of Yale in the national legal arena. In the first section of this chapter, I focus on elements of constituted practice in a professional community.[4] In the following sections I consider the tradition of realism in law schools with attention to the way jurisprudential ideologies have been used to maintain professional power, including the place of oppositional politics in maintaining the contemporary legal establishment.[5] I conclude by examining the social functions of positivism, in its epistemological and legal sense. Positivism is the law in law school, but the hegemony of this ideology has been challenged in the debate over the racial and ethnic makeup of law faculties and the racial and gender challenges to the nature of legal scholarship.

Ideologies in a Profession

An enduring fact of professional life described in the academic language of our time by Yves Dezalay, a French sociologist of law, is that scholarship on law maintains a "silence on the role of the legal profession."[6] While true silences are rare these days, given all the attention to different voices, the institutional and professional relations themselves have been heard relatively little. The extraordinary consequence of this silence is the absence of "the subject" in the discourses of law. The idea that judges, lawyers, and legal academics are silent or self-effacing is not intuitively obvious. Yet, at least in matters relating to where their power comes from—the institutions, language, and conventions of the profession—the bar is shy. This is evident in its sensitivity to advertising, in its caution about opening up its processes, and in the desire of law professors to be seen as academics and not as lawyers. In this chapter I try to overcome that shyness by linking the professional community—the bar and the professors—to the authority and meaning of law.

The authority examined here is in the academy. Of course people think that the legal academy has something to do with the authority of law, but attention is deflected from the role played by the professional life of the law in the academy in delineating contemporary legal authority. In one respect, the law schools, like the bar associations, are seen as mere servants to the bench. While we focus on the Rehnquists and the Borks, the Warrens and the Burgers, the men and women who decide who will practice before the courts in California and Massachusetts and the professors who determine the curriculum future practitioners will study disclaim jurisprudential responsibility with a democratic demur and a cavalier shrug.

Identifying lawyers as the subject calls attention to a powerful fraternity and to the bonds of professionals in terms of particular institutions and specific communities. By charting the common ways lawyers understand things we can present an aspect of professional power as a form of law that is taught to the community more widely. This law exists behind the law of courts and legislatures in common ways of thinking and speaking. The nature of linguistic practice as social phenomenon has seldom been described with greater flair than in Peter Goodrich's *The Languages of Law*. "In institutional terms," he says, "the profession also stands between justice, 'lady and queen of all moral virtues,' and barbarism." Without the lawyers, he continues, "justice would have no tongue."[7] The practices evident in legal language are institutional practices upon which the social life of law is built. Justice without its distinct language, without the practices carried by it, is not legal.

The practices that delineate the legal community—the imposing edifices, the archaic language, the fat books—are like the rules for polite dining, such as the arrangement of the forks at a dinner party. Like the rules for dining (a popular way of portraying the characteristics of class),[8] the practice of acknowledging law's forms, whether the hierarchy of law schools or the discourses on the Constitution, affirms a "community." Law's practices, like other social practices, are mediating devices in that the participants "are not simply speaking as individuals to one another" but are engaging as members of a group.[9] In the legal profession, as with medicine or political science, such practices establish authority. Knowing when to use a free-speech argument or where to file a petition is as crucial to wielding the authority of law as the conventions of dining are to maintaining class relations.[10] Along with relations such as old school ties or the arrangements for partnership in a firm, fundamental jurisprudential practices are practices of the profession.

Realism as jurisprudential practice determines the way torts or contracts is taught or whether a particular doctrine of equal protection is authoritative. It is the basis for excluding some forms of scholarship, such as when that scholarship is said to be insufficiently "developed" or lacking in "a respectable basis," as feminism was described to the late Mary Joe Frug by the head of the Contracts Section of the Association of American Law Schools in 1988.[11] These principles of jurisprudence form the domain of legal philosophy and its institutional life. All have implications for control of the classroom, with its access to bench and bar, and thus they are the subject of heated discussion in the clubs and cloakrooms of legal power. The jurisprudential ideologies control the basic assumptions beneath the surface controversies of any given moment.[12] They say who is part of the group.

The story of the legal profession in law is like the story Roland Barthes tells of the Eiffel Tower and the ways some Parisians have dealt with its domination of the landscape.[13] Guy de Maupassant, a great foe of the Eiffel Tower, dined contentedly in the tower restaurant although he is said not to have cared for the food. The restaurant was, however, according to Barthes the only place Maupassant did not have to look at the tower. In many respects the tower is like the legal profession, and legal scholars have been much like Maupassant. Although the tower dominates the landscape, it can be avoided by those on the inside. In the legal academy, the power of the profession and even of law more generally is often denied. Realism is at the heart of the denial. Much as lunch in the Eiffel Tower allowed its critics in the early part of this century to turn away from the monstrous presence looming over the city, being realistic in the academy, quite paradoxically, allows the legal professional to draw insight from the mythology of the ideal. As law professors and lawyers point to the formal and mechanical, the stuffy and the archaic in law, they draw attention to behaviors and away from institutional power.

Legal history is, of course, full of stories about the professional projects of lawyers.[14] The late-nineteenth-century lawyer has been the focus of attention for Robert Gordon, who has established the role of the elite bar in New York City as "architects of ideas and institutions,"[15] creators of law schools, the American Law Institute "restatements," and the uniform codes. This work is of great interest to the legal community, as evidenced by the reception Gordon's work has received. In his Holmes Lectures on the subject at Harvard Law School in the mid-1980s, Gordon

55

drew attention to the efforts of lawyers a century ago to establish a high ground for their practice.[16] According to this version of a "Civic-Republican" ideal, these lawyers used their new position to help the corporations extract themselves from the strictures of "classical legal science."[17] The result was that corporate lawyers emerged at the vanguard of the progressive legal reform movements of the early twentieth century.

The Realist Tradition

Legal scholars still contest the nature and significance of realism as they continue to discover it. Thus, long after the influence of similar movements toward "realism" in the United States, such as those in art and philosophy,[18] has declined, contemporary academic lawyers call up the bad old formalism that is the hallmark of the realist insight. Thus, the scene for a contemporary academic battle is set by Phillip E. Areeda, a professor at Harvard Law School, when he observes, "Twenty years ago our mission was to teach law in the grand manner."[19] In a *New York Times Magazine* article on the struggles between left and right in the legal academy, Areeda is posed behind a stack of ancient law books, and his comments about method and the "grand manner" are brought to bear through allusions to Socrates, the settled nature of law, and wellworn cultural artifacts of formal legal authority popularized in *The Paper Chase*.[20] The discussion in this chapter draws on contemporary disputes over legal form that maintain its institutional authority.

Although legal histories written by lawyers are not above suspicion that they might tend—like corporate histories—to avoid offense, they do show the importance of realism to legal formations grounded in the academy. From such tales we learn the names and dates, the geography and the ethnography of the professional movements in law. One influential history of law schooling in the United States actually begins with "Once Upon a Time."[21] In this treatment, legal education emerges in something like the modern "law school" form by 1850. This recent "Once Upon a Time" is in the nature of modern academic ideology about the profession. Early American legal education, still grounded largely in the practice of apprenticeships, had by the nation's founding, produced some schools around distinguished practitioners such as Tapping Reeve of the Litchfield School in Connecticut. Chairs in law at the universities had been established as early as that for George Wythe at William and Mary in 1779. But it was not until the 1820s that the universities began to integrate anything even remotely like professional legal education into their curricula. For the next thirty years this emerging aristocracy had to defend itself from the populism of the Jacksonian period. Yet, by the 1850s an institutional foundation existed for law in universities.

The growth of law as a profession in the universities followed. Robert Stevens traces this to a point when "the market explodes," as he described the rapid expansion of the profession around the turn of the century.[22] Legal education in the universities would have much the same qualities as liberal education. Its mission would be to train gentleman, although law would place a bit more emphasis on the practical dimensions of what it meant to be a gentleman. Stevens described the scene at New York University in the 1860s: "There are thousands of young men in the United States who are in possession, or will come into possession, of large estates. . . . [N]early all are anxious to avail themselves of the advantages conferred by admission to some one of the learned professions."[23] It is necessary to rethink the university in order to understand its nature in the nineteenth century compared to present institutions. The creation of professional schools changed the nature of the university. Isolation and specialization led to separate communities that drew from the authority of the university and linked it to practice.

By the early twentieth century, the legal profession had firmly planted itself in the universities.[24] As a learned profession in the modern sense, academic practice supplanted class and other institutional relations as the foundation for legal authority. One of the more interesting developments pointed out by Stevens is that the law school took on an extraordinary homogeneity "in the cause of institutionalization and interchangeability."[25] Rather than representing the many facets of legal practice in different institutions, all institutions aspired to look as much alike as possible, given huge differences in stature, influence, and wealth. As law schools became affiliated with universities, the length of the program, the curriculum, the teaching style, and ultimately the intellectual climate became standardized. Today the standardization of form and rhetoric presents considerable unity in the face of diverse regional identifications.

Legal realism had its foundation in the elite law schools, and the nature of the movement expresses itself in the abstract thinking and materialist methodology characteristic of those places by the early twentieth century. The institutional changes that brought law under the umbrella of the academy, the bane of law students and liberal faculty who want more practical teaching, enhanced protection of the legal monopoly. These changes also led inevitably to a realist foundation for law that was more consistent with the dominant scientific orientation of the academy than were the class or theological underpinnings of earlier legal formations. The push of scientific method, evident throughout the academy in the post–Civil War years, further transformed the ideology of law. The work of Christopher Columbus Langdell, the use of his case method at Harvard, and the creation of the modern university by Harvard's president Charles Eliot provide the generally acknowledged foundation for the modern legal academy. Harvard stood nearly alone until at least the beginning of World War I, providing law in the form of graduate education.[26]

Out of this academic culture, realism is a manifestation of the social research concerns that dominated the academy after World War I. Dean Roscoe Pound of the Harvard Law School is a major figure here, and although he has recently been linked more closely to progressivism, Pound's method (like Justice Holmes's aphorisms) is part of the tradition. Realism in the 1930s portrays itself against a backdrop, not of the Langdellian avant-garde, but of formalism.[27] Its terrain is a romantic if not altogether accurate picture of English legal education.[28] This propensity to place the informed present against the darkest past is an ongoing proposition. Jerome Frank and Karl Llewellyn, two early proponents, capture these and other currents of the realist tradition. Llewellyn's The Bramble Bush[29] and Frank's Law and the Modern Mind[30] elaborate the realist project. These volumes tell us little of the influence of the movement, but they present ideas that are still current, as if they had just been minted.

This movement also stemmed from fascination with the social sciences on the part of Dean Pound at Harvard and Llewellyn at Columbia. Social scientists have embraced realism and have generally supported the picture provided by movement's participants, one that depicts realism as critique and realists as dissidents who "broke from the sociological school and mounted a fresh assault on the still highly orthodox declaratory theory."[31] Realism is conventionally compared to theories drawn from materials like Blackstone's Commentaries and associated with "Holmes's dictum" that the law is made up of "prophecies of what the courts will do in fact." Just as with realism in law schools, however, the political science variant has become an ideology by which we know the institutions of the law. In discussing the existence of neutral principles, many have noted the obvious currency of the view that law is a characteristically political process rather than one determined by neutral principles. But realism is no longer critical. Indeed, "the perspective seems to have demonstrated its authority."[32] In a nice characterization of the puzzling persistence of realism, Harry Stumpf notes that we are inclined to "read most of critical legal thought with a big yawn, concluding that law professors, or at least a vocal minority of them, have finally joined the club."[33]

It seems that perhaps the realism of the early figures was more interested in revealing the sources of law than the retro-realism we see in law schools today. The early realists carved out a place by establishing links with philosophical movements, on the one hand, and reform movements in politics, on the other. Realism was an aspect of the social scientific advance in the academy, reflecting in one community the much larger characteristic of the Western and particularly American experience of a world that must be known through science if it is to be "really" known.[34] Although speaking to epistemology, realism also had a reform aspect that linked ideology and social relations more explicitly. Realism in the 1930s was part of the progressive effort to control governing institutions with professional elites. With its analogues in the urban struggles by the middle class to take control of the city from political machines, realism in law school operated within the institutions to wrest control from established elites and link the academy to emerging administrative structures, particularly at the federal level.[35]

Thus, a striking characteristic of this movement, and a central element of its legal formation, is that it links institutional and epistemological considerations. "Holmes's dictum" is institutional. When he calls attention to the judge, the realist suggests that he is undercutting the role of the law. The epistemological consequence of the exhortation is clear. Holmes tells us how we are to know the law, and it will not be in books (except as guides to what the judges will do). The realistic perspective associated with Frank, especially in *Courts on Trial*,[36] approaches law from the perspective of what "really" occurs. Frank makes an epistemological claim about what determines the outcomes in cases before the bench. These poles are blended together in the jurisprudential practice of the law schools as well as in judicial practice and popular commentary. The consequence in practice is that the schools are supported by a cynicism that leaves institutional arrangement unexamined and intact.[37]

59

Scholars have woven realism into jurisprudence and even spoken of it as a project for the legal profession,[38] but only rarely do they note the impact of realism on the maintenance of legal power, including the way social science research on law is channeled. Laura Kalman has argued that "[a]t least since the 1930s, the view that the establishment is naive and trapped in a formal orientation to rules has grown progressively more influential until it became the framework of the legal establishment."[39] And Gary Peller is among a number of scholars who have noted that the most interesting thing about realism is how this perspective is continually advanced as a vanguard project.[40] Christine Harrington and I said nearly the same thing in an article some time ago: "With its widespread acceptance for nearly 30 years, there has been remarkably little change in legal thinking beyond the initial insights of Realism." We conclude that "[s]ocio-legal scholars, particularly in America, have understood law through a version of realism for some time." To us, a central paradox about realism is its propensity to be reinvented. We saw realism operating from "an essentially anti-law rhetoric . . . while serving as a rationale for law reform movements and as the basis of a modern legal orthodoxy."[41] The capacity for realism to maintain itself seems to derive from the ideological role the orthodoxy plays in the curriculum at institutions such as Harvard and Yale law schools.

Harrington and I point out that "Realism as legal authority promotes the view that law is indeterminate but leaves intact social arrangements and institutions determined by law."[42] We note that "[t]he new emphasis on the plurality of law is preoccupied with diversity and difference," and that a political orientation linked to realism "asserts a desire to be free from the authority of the privileged voices it attributes to official law."[43] Yet the impact of realism has been just the opposite. Contemporary American jurisprudence places the judge at the center of the law and emphasizes the importance of the context in which law is practiced.[44] This gives the appellate courts immense power. We now assume, as a truth about the legal process, that the judge, not the law, is the authority.[45] The result of realism is that judges have become the definitive source of the fundamental law in the United States. The sociological consequence is a jurisprudence in the law schools that is closely linked to appellate courts.[46]

In the case of law schools, realism is not just a jurisprudence, it is an episteme, a way of knowing. The fact that law is now located in law schools at research universities, where science is supreme, reinforces this way of knowing.[47] Thus, a lawyer knows the law as ideal and the nuances of the moment as reality. He still may expect the citizen to respect the authority of courts, but his sense of the real leads him to be far less reverent to the forms of law as applied to himself. These ideas about law are part of the institutional practice. They are law that constitutes. Legal power in America with its institutional hierarchies is reinforced by the fact of a shared way of proceeding, the most important part of which is agreement on the importance of what is real.

The centrality of realism to the intellectual life of the legal academy is evident in the work done by ideologists of the profession, such as Bruce Ackerman, whose *Reconstructing American Law* draws on realist principles. His call on the profession to take control of its intellectual environment makes the lessons of realism the necessary antidote for the ills of the present. This is done with considerable skill, in a way that is indicative of professional attention to the strains of intellectual life that the lawyer must respect. Ackerman compares the methodology of modern social scientists to the old method of the "common lawyer." The comparison is weighted in favor of social science due to the imperative to respond to new ways of proceeding. In the end, Ackerman takes on the role of practical philosopher and becomes the profession's therapist. In this role, he warns the profession by elaboration from the realist tradition. This look at realism through the aspirations of a second-generation legal economist and Yale Law School faculty member is an appropriate transition to the current manifestations of realism in the CLS and law and economics movements.

Contemporary Manifestations

In American law schools in the last quarter of the twentieth century, the major academic traditions draw from a foundation heavily influenced by legal realism. Critics, who meet under the banner of critical legal studies and call themselves "crits" and their movement CLS, claim that the true legacy of legal realism is progressive, that is, on the political left (as opposed to allied with the progressive movement). Conservatives in the law and economics movement also rely on realist insights about the law balancing interests through the opinions of judges, although they say less about their realist heritage. Both movements have some links to the social sciences in general, and in the case of CLS and legal economists such as Robert Ellickson and Lewis Kornhauser, there are specific links to the law and society movement, the inheritors of the sociological tradition originally linked to realism under the title "sociology of law."[48]

Critical Legal Studies

CLS is a post-1960s law school movement that began at Yale and is now situated at schools such as Harvard and Stanford, with outposts at the University of Miami, Northeastern, and Cardozo. At Harvard its proponents number a half dozen and at Stanford a few less. Around the country it may have a couple of hundred adherents. Its influence on law students and in the intellectual community fostered by the legal academy is far greater than it is in the profession generally or in the courts. It has also received a great deal of attention in the print media: The *New Republic* called it "radicalism for yuppies"; *Boston Globe Magazine* reported on the "Feud at H.L.S."; the *Journal of Higher Education* spoke of "Crits" versus the Legal Academy; and the *New Yorker* called it "the new left played out in law." Its distinctive presence has been felt in disputes over tenure at law schools and in the decorum associated with these august institutions. The movement's key theoretical position is old-fashioned legal realism with a sixties twist that emphasizes the role of law in maintaining the dominant relations of power.

The manifesto of the movement, perhaps its high point, was a dramatic presentation by Roberto Unger at the CLS meeting held in Cambridge, Massachusetts, in November 1981.[49] Unger is an enigmatic figure who has injected a level of mystery (and mysticism) into a profession marked, by its own admission, with a cynical godlessness. Unger, from Brazil, was trained as a Jesuit and has a priestly persona that adds considerably to his intensity. (The priestly element in law school movements has often been commented upon. We heard it early in the realist era from Oliver Wendell Holmes, Jr., in describing Dean Langdell[50] and more recently in postmodern work by Peter Goodrich about how law speaks of itself.[51]) Unger gave this particular speech to a packed hall, with students and faculty nearly hanging from the rafters. Dressed in black and standing alone on the floor, without a lectern and without notes, he spoke for nearly two hours. The unusual length of this after-dinner speech to an audience of five hundred produced a certain amount of discomfort, yet few departed. The core of the speech was built on the realist tradition, from which Unger drew familiar links to a legacy of critique and concern with activism within the legal profession. The nature of his critique was twofold: "the critique of formalism and objectivity."[52] But in addition to critique, Unger held out the promise of action; CLS was on the move and the territory to be invaded was the law school. Action has been the most dramatic aspect of the CLS movement. From sit-ins to law review articles that are as engaged as one might imagine given the forum, the movement has been characterized by a rather purified activism. The activism extends to the critique so that the characteristic form of intellectual engagement for a time was "trashing," a scholarly bashing of the existing niceties of legal thought. The juxtaposition of thought and action is a classic aspect of the positivism at the root of legal realism in the United States.

Unger's speech concluded with the declaration that provides the epigraph to this chapter. Few of us got the idea when we first heard it, but more than a few were intrigued. Years later its realist roots surfaced, breaking through the mysticism. The key element of realism, whether modern or of the older fashion, is that some other must be standing, thinking, or speaking in a way that is patently naive. The priesthood of law professors Unger spoke of has the same place in the modern variation of realism as those Holmes and Frank characterized as naive enough to believe the truth was in the words of the law. Unger, however, builds on the loss of faith and sees in these moderns a vacuous institutional attachment. The "cold altar" of Kingsfield's lectern provides CLS with the opportunity for revenge.

Unger's purpose, in his speech and through his influence on American law, was to create a stir. He offered faith in a mystical, relativized world. The CLS movement at the time was reeling from its first brushes with the academic old guard. It had been expelled from Yale but had set down roots at Harvard. In this environment during the late 1970s, faith in the CLS project coexisted with a critique of positivism in the academy. In the years that followed, the next generation seemed to replace Unger's Latin American mysticism with Anglo-American summer camps, rock concerts, and lampoonesque versions of legal scholarship. These maintained a community of left-liberal scholars in the face of reaction from the outside and of feminism and diversity within. Given the nature of the academy, this was also a period of tremendous scholarly production.

CLS drew from critical theory, an intellectual movement grounded in German scholarship of the 1930s, and the "fancy French philosophers" of post-structuralism. CLS has from its inception led the inquiry into "the domination of the ruling class in words."[53] The words studied have been law words, often the words and language of elite legal thinking or mandarin legal consciousness, a particularly important form of ideology. The link between critical theory and realism is elusive. Kennedy has described Marx as a "formalist" and called attention to the insights of "realism." Following Marx, Kennedy draws out a relationship between the commodity mode of production and "its constitutive legal consciousness." Early CLS scholarship saw law as more than epiphenomenon and speculated that its constitutive dimensions would become apparent.[54] This was the context in which the movement absorbed realism. The foundations in the 1960s meant the discussions prior to the embrace of realism concerned ideology and the law that constitutes. With the realist tone, ideology took on a distinctive indeterminate quality and the interest in constitutive law dropped out.

Three texts provide a wealth of material for examination: *The Politics of Law*, edited by David Kairys (1982); the "Critical Legal Studies Symposium" in the *Stanford Law Review* (1984); and Mark Kelman's *A Guide to Critical Legal Studies* (1987).[55] Although they only begin to reflect the range of legal scholarship that has been associated with the movement, these works represent CLS at the stage being considered here. Kelman is a critical scholar who directed a great deal of his attention to the law and economics movement, and his book reflects that interest.[56] The book also reflects some of the demographic biases of the movement, especially its maleness and its situation in the law schools.[57] The *Stanford Law Review* symposium is an expression of maturity and institutional position: the CLS movement is able to command an entire volume, over six hundred pages, in the law review of one of the nation's richest law schools. The volume incorporates a somewhat greater range of contributors, from adherents to law and economics such as Lewis Kornhauser from New York University Law School to colleagues from the old left such as the late Ed Sparer of the University of Pennsylvania Law School. The stunning fact—given that it was published in the mid 1980s—is that all eighteen contributors are male, and all are drawn from the academy of professional law.[58] The Kairys volume was more diverse, and some of its female contributors became influential feminist legal scholars a few years later.

Not long after Unger's speech and in response to an increasingly dramatic CLS presence, some of the more retrograde members of the legal profession rose in defense of the old order, giving life to the requisite realist foil. The result was a heated exchange in 1984–85 between Robert Gordon, a professor at Stanford Law School, and Paul Carrington, dean of the law school at Duke University. This exchange is important because unlike some left movements, CLS depends on its place in elite institutions. It speaks from academic positions in the imperial city and the legal consciousness it studies is the mandarin consciousness of the legal academy and the elite bench and bar. The "trash" as CLS methodology depended on its unsettling effect in a professional environment held together by manipulation of the tradition of legal discourse. The paradox is the centrality of realism to that tradition.

The Carrington-inspired exchange plays a central role in Sanford Levinson's study of belief surrounding the Constitution. Levinson's analysis of this exchange provides a fine basis for evaluating the functions of realism and its role in maintaining the authority of lawyers. Levinson's book *Constitutional Faith*[59] begins with a quote from David Mamet, whose collection *Writing in Restaurants* includes a discussion of those deeper commitments that occasionally make ordinary practices transcendental. Mamet writes, "If you take the belief out of Law, all you have is litigation."[60] Levinson examines Felix Frankfurter's support for swearing allegiance to the United States. Where Frankfurter's analysis veers in the direction of flag waving, Levinson suggests that patriotism has been sullied by "its joinder with American involvement in Vietnam." Levinson says he is not interested in patriotism, at least not "ordinary patriotism" or love of country, but rather in ideals that he calls "constitutional faith"—that is, wholehearted attachment to the Constitution as the center of one's (and ultimately the nation's) political life. This includes "what it means to be an American," that is, "what bonds us (or could bond us) into a coherent political community, especially after the triumph of a distinctly (post)modernist sense of the contingencies of our own culture and the fragility of any community memberships."[61] Levinson's title is meant to call to mind Barbara Jordan's "faith in the Constitution," as expressed during the Watergate investigation, and Richard Nixon's "breach of faith," in a chronicle of the same period by Theodore White.

Of course, in the constitutional setting the conception of the founding document is central, and differences between Thomas Jefferson and James Madison loom large. Jefferson's idea was that "[w]e might as well require a man to wear still the coat which fitted him when a boy, as civilized society to remain as under the regimen of their barbarous ancestors."[62] Madison felt that "frequent appeals would in great measure deprive the government of that veneration, which time bestows on everything, and without which perhaps the wisest and freest govern-ments would not possess the requisite stability."[63] In the context of the law schools, belief in law more generally serves as a measure of what Levinson calls a "faith community."[64] He compares CLS professors in the law schools to atheists teaching in divinity schools, reflecting the dis-may expressed by Carrington. These "Legal Nihilists" are the ones of "little faith." According to Levinson, Carrington's position is that to be a professor of law one also must have "some minimal belief in the idea of law and the institutions that enforce it."[65]

The debate over CLS is instructive with regard to the role of realism in the legal academy. It is not that everyone believes in an autonomous law, though at some level the possibility of a government under law is impor-tant, as when Levinson writes, "Carrington cannot be dismissed as a naive cheerleader for law. He confesses to his own dark nights of the soul, in which the 'dread in disbelief' makes its appearance."[66] It is rather that the engine of realism, like the devil within, is the source of refinement, the disciplining mechanism, and the temptation, so that those who can stand the heat advance to the head of the profession, while the choirboys are left behind. The debate takes place on matters of truth, as would be expected in a faith community, and the ability to live with partial truth has long been a hallmark of the avant-garde, the new, the modern.

The nature of the CLS movement must be seen in terms of style and pragmatics. Earlier radical left law movements have been based in the practices of radical professionals, such as those in the Lawyers Guild, who worked in the centers of poverty and other sites of resistance. CLS is different—and more like the law and economics movement than the Lawyers Guild—because its base has been in the law schools. Instru-mentally, the significance of the law school base is that Harvard pro-duces about one-third of the law teachers in the country and Yale another one-fifth, so that a movement institutionally situated in these institutions and able to influence how they think will be influential in law. This is why tenure and appointment struggles have helped define the movement, and it is the way in which the insights of realism have been central to the movement. Thus, although CLS claims to be a radical movement,[67] I consider its primary legal form, realism, to be well within the dominant channels of legal power. The CLS position is that the legal arena has always been a context through which the dominant classes have sought to justify their place in the social order. CLS has criticized the view of law as an unmediated instrument of class power. Rather than articulating and foreshadowing the legal forms of the future, CLS has developed the method of "trashing." This method, along with the movement's identification with political activity such as the organization of rent strikes and its support for racial and gender diversity in the law schools, forms the basis for its claim to be a radical movement.

Law and Economics

Realism is also at the heart of the most significant conservative movement in the legal academy, the law and economics movement. Law professors across the country have been shifting to this movement, which has increasingly defined the conventional language of the academy. In little over two decades, it has become de rigueur to maximize utilities, look for efficiencies, and discount externalities. There are lawyers and lower court judges ready to be appointed to the Supreme Court with this perspective. Law and economics was part of the ideology prominently displayed by Robert Bork at his confirmation hearings (though it was not his only distinctive feature). The former dean of Yale Law School, Guido Calabresi, is one of its originators, but movement's center is in Chicago, where it draws on the relentless advocacy of Richard Epstein,[68] and the continuing influence of Judge Richard Posner.[69] While the CLS movement immersed itself in its "fancy French philosophers" and warded off the pragmatic orientation of clinical practice, the law and economics movement became a source of rigorous policy analysis for conservatives.

67

As its name indicates, the movement approaches law from the perspective of economics. Two of the things it takes from this approach are individualistic actors and a marketplace. The actors in this model are not the same as people we run into on any given day. They are *profit maximizers* in the hypothetical extreme. They seek to maximize their interests every moment and in everything they do. The economists call this behavior rational and give it an inevitable quality by holding that its context is a market. These profit maximizers meet to *freely exchange goods and services* in markets where the buyer and seller do not know or care to know one another and no one can be made better off without someone else being made worse off. *Efficiency* is the name given to the situation in which the interests of all are taken into account, and this defines the optimum situation for society's well-being.

Because this approach more closely resembles economics when it first began as a science of society than it does the economics of the recent past, it is called *neoclassical*. Its practitioners began by applying economic theory to the areas of regulation with Calabresi's study of air pollution[70] and the work on antitrust by Posner and others.[71] With ever-expanding claims, the method was applied to contracts, torts, and property rights by Richard Epstein and Bernard Siegan and to crime by Kate Stith.[72] The economist eschews the romance of traditional discourse and talks of the "supply and demand" for crime and the penalty as a "price" to engage in crime.

The movement began with R. H. Coase's article, "The Problem of Social Cost,"[73] which contained a bold application and a theorem that stated: "in the absence of transaction costs, the efficiency of resource allocation is independent of the placement of liability" (or, conversely, the initial assignment of rights). Coase applied the theorem to a situation in which running a train beside a farmer's field will destroy some of the farmer's crops (impose a "negative externality"). The economist as lawyer is interested in the socially efficient outcome, that combination of train trips and damaged crops that is best for society. He proposes that the most efficient outcome will result regardless of which party has the initial right if the right is traded at the most efficient price.

Kornhauser characterized law and economics as a perspective in legal academic writing where every article displays one or more of four distinct claims:

1. Economic theory provides a good theory for predicting how people will behave under rules of law.
2. The law ought to be efficient.
3. The (common) law is in fact efficient.
4. The common law tends to select efficient rules, although not every rule will, at any given time, be efficient.[74]

These claims provide that rules of law be treated like prices and legal actors like rational individuals, that the best law is efficient, and that the common law is generally efficient.

The realist presence is evident throughout the law and economics movement. Like other manifestations of realism, the language of economics is offered as a means of cutting through cultural categories. These categories are often dismissed as externalities in the language of the economist. Realism in the law and economics movement differs in political orientation from CLS as the left in politics differs from the right. These positions become points on a realism spectrum. Just as left and right in ordinary politics often share institutions (like Congress), left and right in law share in maintaining the institutional status quo. Law and economics emphasizes the impediment of traditional rights analysis to rational decision making. At the same time it offers the promise that economic analysis will reveal solutions consistent with the traditional equities worked out through the common law.

CLS and law and economics talk to each other in scholarly journals. From 1975 to 1980, a series of CLS articles critical of the law and economics position appeared in leading law journals and anthologies. The primary contributors were Mark Kelman, Tom Heller, and Duncan Kennedy.[75] As Kornhauser describes the nature of the CLS critique, it proposes a different understanding of how law functions in society that is difficult to discern because CLS does not share a common methodology to the extent that proponents of law and economics do.[76] But generally the CLS position is that law and economics passes itself off as value-neutral scientific analysis and that it is internally inconsistent because it demands a form of motivation—rational action—that is rarely practiced.

Where CLS promoted a sort of "retro" realism using the traditional language of politics,[77] law and economics introduced economic terminology and theoretical frameworks. The authority of the legal academy for what judges do and how law is analyzed is established as these movements travel on a parallel track. The key element in the politics is wealth maximization for law and economics and equalization of wealth for CLS. Realism as a form of law in these academic movements is evident in the relationship between what is traditionally viewed as law and the view of law offered by the movement. The claim of a fresh, but often a very familiar, point of view is characteristic of legal realism and evident in law school movements on the right and the left.[78] The currency of this claim to be offering something new against a backdrop of traditional formalism indicates a reliance in both instances on a realist perspective. With realism a sense of discovery links the present to a familiar and generally acceptable tradition.

One thing CLS seems to lack and the conservative movement to have developed to a high degree is a rigorous method. The significance of the law and economics movement has been not just in the substantive implications of its findings, but also in the seduction of its neoclassical doctrines to lawyers and judges. The attractiveness of this dogma reaches beyond the legal academy and is but another way in which activities within the law show the influences of the outside. For some, the meth-

69

ods of law and economics, sometimes called "public choice," have resulted in the substitution of efficiency for justice as the basis for law.

Many cheap shots are taken at CLS. Most are on matters of style. However, the incapacity of CLS to provide tools and vision for socialist strategies to match the challenge of law and economics has affected growth of the movement. While law and economics is transforming the way American law is taught, practiced, and decided, the left has failed to respond. Movements on the left in law have relied on compassion, utopianism, and networking to effect change. Where the right has supplanted, the left has critiqued. Not only is its growth far less dramatic, but CLS appears to be stagnating without dogmatics, without a program.

Some of the roots of a program are there. Crits are attentive to the transformative potential of the vast array of understandings about justice, democracy, equality, and liberty that legitimize the state. Social science is appealed to, with some trepidation, as a potential methodology, and important critical scholars such as Richard Abel of UCLA and David Trubek of the University of Wisconsin are active in the law and society movement.[79] There is more to the limited growth of CLS, however, than its failure to develop a coherent method. For one thing, the American legal academy is a conservative place. It is certainly not the most conservative place in America, relative to most corporations or military installations. But the legal academy is conservative enough in style and nature to favor conservative movements and subsume progressive, critical movements whether or not they have highly developed methodologies.

These two movements express the political significance of realism. To the extent that the traditions depend on distinctive characterizations built around this orientation, the social relations (explicit with CLS and implicit with law and economics) determine the politics in the legal academy. The movements have a great deal in common. As Ken Emerson pointed out in his *New York Times Magazine* article, both sides enlist similar imagery, with the conservatives seeking to "help the wheels of commerce turn" and the crits pointing out that "greasing the wheels of the system" is mostly what lawyers do.[80] A crucial difference, especially as a basis for organization, is the extent to which these two movements have produced coherent social theories and practical political guidelines to go beyond the realist insight. In this regard, law and economics has been much more successful.

CLS failed to maintain its stature in the academy for a number of reasons, not the least of which were conservative administrations in Washington and an increasingly conservative federal judiciary. The ability of law and economics scholars to further distract attention from the social relations constituted by law, as well as their ability to create a super-structure consisting of forms that guide thought while denying the position from which they direct, represent perhaps the fullest expression of the contemporary realist legal project. It is with this dimension of realism that I conclude this analysis.

Positivism as the Academy

This inquiry into the academic manifestations of legal realism raises a number of questions. One is the perennial issue of the positivism at the heart of the realist enterprise. The realist ideology bears comparison with a framework on which it depends heavily—common sense. Realism has become the common sense of the legal academy and an increasing number of other places in the culture. It is fully embedded in political science and through that discipline influences the conceptions of citizenship and public affairs. Realism is increasingly a prominent aspect of the politics of trial and appellate courts. As common sense, neither realist scholarship nor the critique of formalism is its biggest contribution. Realism is responsible for displacing the play of power away from the bar and law schools.

One of the features of legal realism is the parallel between institutional and the epistemological claims. Realists say that the law is what the judges say it is *and* that behavior or what the judge wants to do reflects the reality of the legal processes, that it is law. This double-barreled quality of realism is a key to its significance in the academy. As a relatively new institution, the legal academy has established an intimate relationship with the discourse of judges by making their words and actions central. Among the losers, to some extent, are texts, which no longer have a central place in the system of authority behind law. In a realist framework it is naive to place texts above people. Instead, in American law today, the professional triumvirate of practicing attorneys, law professors, and judges becomes the relevant community.[81]

This jurisprudence radiates from the law schools into other parts of the legal academy, such as academic law programs outside the professional schools and at the research institute established by the American Bar Association, the Bar Foundation. A study by Austin Sarat and William Felstiner, discussing the practical significance of law in the lawyer's office, shows the reach of the realist framework to mask the power of the profession.[82] The authors taped interviews of 115 lawyer–client conferences in California and Massachusetts in the early 1980s. They were interested in the power relations between the lawyer and the client as an aspect of legal power and outlined what they called "modes of discourse about law," namely, formalism, equity, and realism. Finding that the lawyers were critical of the law, the authors posit a realist mode as dominant and suggest that because this mode is critical, it may be responsible for some of the popular dissatisfaction with the law. One wonders, however, how the cynicism of the lawyer gets translated into legal power.

In an earlier article using the same data, the authors explicitly address the question of power.[83] They conclude that lawyers construct more flexible clients than the ones that walk into their offices. The power wielded in these constructions and evident in the transcripts they report on is realist power. Much of it is cynical. The client is brought into a world that is unfamiliar and pays for the lawyer's insight about the judge or about legal strategy. The client is disabused of naive belief that the law is an idealized tool for correcting injustice. "A major professional function therefore is to attempt to limit clients' expectations to realistic levels."[84] However useful this insight about what lawyers do to clients, it does not stray far from the traditional insights of realism, and like realism in the law schools, it leaves the structures of professional power intact. The cynicism of realism does not, as Felstiner and Sarat would have us believe, "chip away at the legal facade," it *is* the legal facade.[85] Though we might become a little cynical in learning how we are treated by legal practitioners, we learn nothing to rattle the structures of legal power, especially if we simply adopt the realist frame suggesting that justice is not really relevant to legal practice.

Both of the movements in the law schools, as well as this additional example from another part of the legal academy, draw attention away from the mundane practices whereby lawyers wield power that citizens do not have: the power to know when and where the judge will be sitting; the nature of the calendar; who controls the docket; and the papers that need to be filed. The realism here is a professional and institutional one. It is hard to see with a traditional conception of the legal system. To fully understand its dynamic we need to go beyond the critique of legal form and show how realist jurisprudence perpetuates hierarchies. Ultimately, the power in law and the legal profession is wielded in opposition to the expectations we have received from the past. Where legal mystery and reverence once held the scepter aloft, now candor and irreverence do the job. Texts would also make law accessible to many more people, especially where the text is relatively simple, as with the American Constitution.

According to Gary Peller and others identified with CLS, the law/politics dichotomy of contemporary realism has impoverished the conception of politics because "[i]t reduces the conception of politics from the wide notion of struggle over the exercises of contingent social power to the narrow conception of how to adapt to the limited possibilities presented by the functional necessities of social life."[86] This concern is focused on the shift from formalism in general and the liberty of contract formulations in particular, to realism as it developed from its initial more radical assertion in the 1930s to its "domesticated" incorporation into mainstream legal discourse. The shift, which domesticated realism presents as radical, Peller sees as perpetuating the "organization of conceptual space which took individual subjects as the ultimate source of social relations."[87] Where "the central representational dichotomy in the liberty of contract discourse was the public/private distinction," according to Peller, "Realism relied on similar spatial metaphors."[88] These included distinctions between words and things, rights and remedies, the is and the ought, and facts and values. In the opposition between formalism and instrumentalism, realism in jurisprudence perpetuates the metaphysics of liberalism and constitutes legal power around those relationships. Like divisions between thought and experience, form and substance, or reason and will, the distinction between law and politics perpetuates legal authority over the rules of the game and limits politics to the margins and the surfaces.[89] These divisions are most prominent in the law and economics movement, which in fact moves, in some sense, partway back to the liberty of contract formulation. The positivist divisions are also evident in judicial behaviorism in political science and in the social research on alternative dispute resolution.[90] Not surprisingly, they are also evident in the critical school. We can conclude by exploring the critiques leveled at that school by minority faculty.

Minority politics in the legal academy has focused attention on struggles to diversify law school faculties and at the same time has introduced a new form of legal discourse that is neither formal nor realist. The most prominent example of both efforts is Derrick Bell, whose protests began this discussion. He begins his book *And We Are Not Saved* with a quote from the Bible: "The harvest is past, the summer is ended, and we are not saved" (Jeremiah 8:20).[91] The book was a reaction to what the U.S. Supreme Court had done and the perceptions of equality that both support the Court's decisions and affirm an intention to change little in the practice of race relations. "Today, while all manner of civil rights laws and precedents are in place, the protection they provide is diluted by lax enforcement, by the establishment of difficult-to-meet standards of proof, and worst of all, by the increasing irrelevance of antidiscrimination laws to race-related disadvantages, now as likely to be a result as much of social class as of color."[92] For Kimberlé Crenshaw, an influential critical race theorist, at least part of the effort must be to show a new way to present law: "Through the allegory, we can discuss legal doctrine in a way that does not replicate the abstractions of legal discourse."[93] Very early in Bell's book, he turns to faculty meetings and conferences as part of the world of law. In this context, Howard Law School and Charles Houston are recognized for their contribution to the civil rights movement, the predecessor to critical race theory. This is followed by a series of allegorical "Chronicles." The first, "The Chronicle of the Constitutional Contradiction (The Real Status of Blacks Today)," focuses on the way law has been bound up with oppression, from "the sanction of slavery in the Constitution" to the idea that "'republican' equality in Virginia rested on slavery."[94]

All through the Chronicles, Bell the lawyer is speaking to Bell the African American. In "The Chronicle of the Celestial Curia (The Benefits to Whites of Civil Rights Litigation)," the issue is the capacity of law and litigation to achieve meaningful reform for the victims of racial and economic inequality. Bell parodies presumed progressive developments in the law as emanating from conservatives who would stir the disinherited to revolt. Within the community of civil rights lawyers, a hegemonic liberal position is shown in the case of Lewis M. Steel from late 1960s. Steel was an NAACP staff attorney who criticized the Supreme Court's decisions while Earl Warren was Chief Justice. He argued that the decisions benefited the white rather than the black community.[95] Steel was fired by the national board the day after the article appeared.

Bell also argues that anything short of quotas draws energy away from fundamental social change. Thus, school desegregation through racial balance is described in "The Chronicle of the Sacrificed Black Schoolchildren (Neither Separate Schools nor Mixed Schools)" as a distraction. In Bell's work, the power of law to mystify through its abstractions is addressed by the allegorical form. Minority scholars present an alternative jurisprudential form featuring a focus on the institutional seats of power and a challenge to the way law has been written in those places.

The qualities evident in the practices of realism and minority politics in the legal academy are the key to the contemporary picture of the powerlessness of law. Peter Fitzpatrick has linked positivism to what he calls the "liberal cosmology," which provides "a particular protection of law's innocence."[96] He shows how the separation of law from material life distracts us from the responsibility of law for the constitution of social relations and ultimately for much of material life. Realism, with its denial of law's power, is a paradoxical picture of law for those who have so much power—the judges, the legal academics, and at least to some extent the practicing attorneys. It is certainly at odds with the picture of law I have described in the gay community, a threatened and relatively powerless community that sought protection from majority hysteria surrounding AIDS. The powerlessness of law leaves the legal community without responsibility. This position makes it naive to ask much of the law, and analogously it becomes unthinkable to ask who the lawyers, legal academics, and judges are.

An approach sometimes called "relational" embeds legal thought in human relations and social institutions. Alan Hunt's interest is much the same as I have been pursuing here.[97] He makes an effort to transcend the limitations of a liberal framework in order to liberate scholarship on law from the inability to look critically at its social foundations. This attention to social relations is emphasized here as a basis for moving from the realist perspective to a constitutive picture of law. The separation of law from its literature and its culture through immersion in its institutions makes it impossible to see the institutions themselves. The common sense political view by which we have come to accept this cultural separation is an outgrowth of realism. This function of what we take to be an ordinary common sense perspective so permeates scholarship that the critique of positivism in the academy leads to the call for a constitutive theory of law. Such a theory is necessary to understand the part realism plays in maintaining the institutions of law.

Remedial Law
The Ideology of Informalism

Chapter 4

It is time to explore
new ways to deal with
such family problems
as marriage, child
custody and adoptions
outside the formality
and potentially
traumatic atmosphere
of courts.

—Chief Justice
Warren E. Burger,
"Agenda for 2000 A.D."

A desire for peace, for conciliation—a remedial urge—this is
the social consequence of informalism, the "alternative" to law that has
been such a preoccupation around
the legal profession since it surfaced
in the 1970s. For the last twenty-five
years, the remedial orientation, as
informalism, spawned a new profession with associations, conferences,
and careers. Groups such as the Society for Professionals in Dispute Resolution (SPIDR) and the National
Conference on Peacemaking and Conflict Resolution offered the opportunity
for growth in a professional direction
following the activism of the 1960s.
Informalists built centers, like the
National Institute for Dispute Resolution (NIDR) in Washington, D.C.,
where they drew millions of dollars
from foundations such as Ford,
Aetna, and Hewlett. From these institutions they went forth to prosely-
tize. Unlike activists in the previous
decades, informalists in the 1980s
were closely linked to institutions—
churches, courts, foundations, and
the legal profession—and in this
sense informalism has been a movement in law.

As a legal practice, informalism

has made disputes its business. Just as the practice of medicine claims illness, informalists work to heal conflict. From within the movement, the remedial urge is not a political demand or a vision of social processes, but rather the discovery of something latent, a fact of life. The "process of disputing"—the natural and seemingly inevitable eruptions in the social fabric—preoccupies these mediators. This perception of disputes as an elemental form of social life presents them as inevitable.[1] Conflict and the urge to resolve it are conceptualized by informalists as prehistoric. According to practitioners of the remedial arts, men and women have disputed from the biblical Cain and Abel to contemporary Israel and Palestine. Nature becomes an ally against the inevitable counterarguments that link disputes to professional interests and a particular configuration in social history. Working under the shadow of a biblical tradition, as well as a legal one, the peacemakers, according to this movement, will inherit the earth.

Informalism, or alternative dispute resolution (ADR), is a movement constructed by men and women following their sense of what needs to be done. The construction of disputes, or the disputes paradigm, serves the remedial urge and is neither particularly natural nor inevitable, but the participants prefer to hide their roles in nature. The shyness about agency seen in the legal academy and attributed to realism is also characteristic of informalists operating from remedial premises in law. Law offers a cover for politics, and informalism makes use of this cover in various ways. Unlike some political movements, where getting credit and publicity are expected aspects of the political process, informalism would prefer not to be seen as a movement at all. As the inevitable response to natural phenomena rather than a political process, informalists mask the representation of interests. But informalism is more accurately associated with politics than nature. From the outside, informalism as a movement may indeed appear to be an industry.

Informalists operating under the remedial impulse needed disputes to work on—that is, there had to be disputes before there could be remedies. Informalists not only found people in conflict, they also developed a framework in social science that makes disputing central. According to scholars in the sociology of law, this framework came from anthropology and conflict theory. The anthropologists built on the work of Max Gluckman, P. H. Gulliver, and Karl Llewellyn and Edward Hoebel.[2] These scholars applied the principles of American jurisprudence to other societies, which they called primitive. They also developed a case approach like the one American law schools had instituted fifty years before. Rather than reflecting the body of precedent associated with English law, cases were viewed as the conventional response of ordinary people dealing with inevitable social problems. In conflict theory beginning in the 1960s, scholars incorporated the practices of arbitration into a more intellectually sophisticated picture of social processes. For instance, in the work of Wilhelm Aubert, an important early sociologist of law, conflict became a building block for a new theory of social control incorporating the perception that disputes are natural.[3] With these academic tools providing the basis for an energetic scholarship, the informalist movement could build its empire.

Informalism was not without its critics, who emerged at the height of the movement's activity. Some of this critical work helped to highlight informalism as politics. British scholar Maureen Cain and Hungarian constitutional lawyer Kalman Kulcsar published an influential article during the academic frenzy over disputes in the early 1980s. The article, titled "Thinking Disputes: An Essay on the Origins of the Dispute Industry," was a response to sudden growth of informalism and the prominence of the remedial urge.[4] Cain and Kulcsar argued that the assumptions of academics, when instituted in a movement practice, constitute an ideology.[5] They elaborated the ideology of the informalist movement as a way of calling attention to its politics and to associate its ideas with its practitioners. The ideology of informalism, in their view, includes a belief in *universality*, whereby disputes are everywhere in human society; *functionalism*, whereby disputes and their remedies serve as vital parts of society;[6] and *settlement practices*, where the critique of courts leads informalists to new institutions.[7] Universality, functionalism, and settlement practices are some shared characteristics of the orientation to disputes that allow us to identify the movement.[8] The practitioners might acknowledge these characteristics of informalism at the same time that they would deny the movement nature of their activity.[9]

Remedy, as the social manifestation of informalism, supplants social practices traditionally associated with disputes, such as law. Informalists present remedy as a righteous crusade and a trump to other forms derived from law, like the autonomous expectations associated with the claim of right. In the world of labor negotiation, where informalism flourishes as arbitration, dispute resolution processes are available as alternatives to strikes and labor violence. Informalists offer remedy as a higher social practice than the fights and rights of the litigation process.

Viewed within the movement's ideological form, this seems attractive enough. But in the context of politics, problems have arisen. For example, in the past decade African Americans have challenged feminists on the "myth of the Black rapist," which places African American men at the forefront of the problem of violence against women.[10] The informalist response to issues of race and rape tends to be remedial, that is, that such issues are subject to settlement rather than the basis for calls for justice. In fact, the clash between informalist ideology and contemporary concern for domestic violence has led to changes in the articulated practice in places where the ideology of mediation does not seem appropriate. For instance, battered women are discouraged from using mediation.

When informalism sits in the place traditionally left for law in theories of public authority we say of this social practice that it constitutes a community in law. The form differs from the right asserted by gays in the controversy over the baths in San Francisco, and from the rage against pornography to be discussed in the next chapter. Because informalism is so close to law in a professional and institutional sense, it is more akin to realism in the law schools. Some of the features of law's magisterium, like the robe and the gavel, are clearly jettisoned in favor of the urge to resolve rather than judge. But the lawyer and his or her professional forms are very much in evidence. Along with the professional orientation of the participants, many of whom are lawyers, there is also the way the movement depicts itself as standing against the pagan masses.[11] This key feature of modern legal ideology, described by Peter Goodrich as "institutional," means that "the profession also stands between justice, 'lady and queen of all moral virtues', and barbarism."[12] The architecture of many of our law buildings testifies to the centrality of those images—Greek temples house our most important courts. In the case of family disputes, informalism becomes institutionalized as alternative dispute resolution and mediation. Programs from court diversion to institutional grievance procedures are advanced by members of the legal profession, court administrators, and attorneys in private practice.

As a form of conflict management, informalism occupies in history the soil tilled by the progressive revolt against formal processes in the courts. In the early twentieth century, legal activists and reformers articulated a range of alternatives to the inherited legal process, often called formalism. Roscoe Pound, in his 1906 speech "Popular Dissatisfaction with the Administration of Justice,"[13] expressed a desire for greater efficiency and access from which informalism grew as a movement advocating new methods. The informalists depicted legal actors and their processes in a highly critical fashion. The old form, the ground that launches informalism, is epitomized by embattled courts and battling lawyers with their own institutional interests in the forefront. Thus, the legal shark and the court bureaucracy become a foil for remedial interests, and the opposition against which informalists propose to make their contribution. Like realism, informalism is associated with law schools and, like realism, it operates from denial of a traditional legal form. In the process, conflict resolution has become a central aspect of law and has come to represent remedial practices. Thus, remedy and informalism, mediation, conflict resolution, disputes processing, and ADR, along with delegalization, have enough in common to constitute a movement when looked at from the perspective of law and law reform.[14]

My aim here is to highlight the extent to which the movement depends on a distinctive form. Informalism puts forth settlement as the overriding concern. It is far better, in this framework, for mother and daughter, Egypt and Israel, even the tobacco industry and the American Cancer Society, to "settle" than to fight for a right. The movement ideology is remedial because of this commitment to reaching a resolution; "getting to yes" is elevated to a matter of principle.[15] The Holy Grail of agreement becomes an article of faith in the movement.

Law Reform as Form of Law

The remedial orientation manifested as informalism constitutes a form of law in a number of senses. Practitioners place the importance of a remedy in opposition to the legal process. They first characterize the law in formal terms, much as the realists have done. They depict their own activity in opposition as informalism. In the guise of institutional practices like "mediation," informalism claims to be different from the traditional legal process. Mediators disavow procedural rules and sometimes even theories of practice.[16] On the surface they affect a militant casualness in dress (shorts, golf shirts, even Birkenstocks in certain contexts) and style of speech. In the case of Howard Bellman, a regulatory negotiator charged with bringing industry and environmentalists together on the matter of a federal nuclear waste dump, the form of presentation is illustrative. During negotiations in 1990 he offered the following summation: "I think the formal process is going to expire either in a few hours or after this next meeting. The informal process was going on a hell of a long time before we started and is going to continue, I presume, for decades, as a matter of fact."[17] This casual style asserts the opposition of informal and formal and suggests an alternative to traditional professional practice.

Informalism is grounded in an assessment of law by lawyers. Lawyers may not have been the first to think of elevating the importance of remedies, although there are a number of instances, such as plea bargaining and settlement conferences, where remedy is the operative feature of law. Lawyers have appropriated informalism to become its primary benefactors and some of its foremost advocates. But lawyers like former Chief Justice Warren Burger brought it to the courts. Lawyers like Joel Handler sold it to the foundations. And lawyers like Janet Rifkin make it more acceptable to the public. Burger was an early proponent of ADR, as will be noted below. Handler, who teaches at the UCLA Law School and was president of the Law and Society Association 1991–93, consulted with the Ford Foundation in the early 1970s when it helped to set up NIDR. Rifkin, professor of legal studies at the University of Massachusetts, Amherst, has held a number of advocacy positions in the American Bar Association and participated actively in the dispute resolution community. In addition, the prominence of legal authority in some disciplines, such as academic social science relating to law, leads many who have only a passing association with the profession to embrace informalism as one of its current techniques.

This, of course, appears paradoxical because the ideology of informalism is based on a critique of traditional legal forms. Lawyers inevitably bring the movement close to the state apparatus even while informal procedures and remedial interests eschew the state's traditional forms. Remedial practice, informalism, and the alternatives movement seek to build a community around the absence of both rage and right. Yet, as a movement practice, remedy is closely associated with institutions of law. As a legal form, informalism is linked to realism and movements like critical legal studies (CLS). Thus, informal alternatives to law are intricately connected to courts, the bar, and the law schools. The form appears in a variety of settings, from plea-bargaining to family mediation, and participants take pride in their orientation to procedural rather than substantive issues.

Christine B. Harrington's work on mediation and informal justice shows the movement character of informalism and how it is rooted in law reform.[18] She draws parallels with the progressive reforms advocated in the first few decades of the twentieth century. Those movements were associated, through Dean Pound, with sociological jurisprudence, an approach to law grounded in positivism and linked to legal realism.[19] Sociological jurisprudence, which along with legal realism is the intellectual precursor to law and society, drew on the new German social science becoming popular in the academy during the first quarter of the twentieth century. In public administration, the progressive reformers reclaimed government for the middle classes with science and research. In addressing the courts, the progressives advocated "'business-like' management,"[20] which they claimed would defuse public criticism of the law. This links informalism with reform in the tradition of the liberal state.

The progressive period in legal reform was driven by a framework for public authority aptly characterized as the "Corporate Ideal." In a book carrying this title, James Weinstein offers two theses that run counter to prevailing opinion about the role the state plays in the interests of business.[21] The first is that the liberal state had been established by the end of World War I. The second is that the liberal corporate social order was developed by those with political hegemony, the corporate financial establishment. The pressure for change may have come from the bottom, but the reforms were put in place by liberal leaders. They were elite efforts to stem the tide of socialism and expand the political economy. The social theory of this framework holds that the liberal state requires federal intervention and that it cannot survive in a truly laissez-faire order. According to Weinstein, the ideology of federal intervention does not capture the nature of American liberalism. Rather, liberalism promotes the idea that the state is in opposition to capital.

This opposition, like that between the formal and the informal, is one way that beliefs can be organized to maintain the dominance of the given social order. Liberalism, then, has been the ideology of the dominant economic groups since the nineteenth century. In the days of Jacksonian democracy, the thrust against monopoly included such achievements as free public education and popular suffrage. In this period "business leaders sponsored institutional adjustments to their needs, and supported political ideologies that appealed to large numbers of people of different social classes in order to gain, and retain, popular support for their entrepreneurial activity."[22] But by the end of World War I, leaders of the large corporations and banks emerged secure in a "loose hegemony" over the political structure. Control operated in the name of corporate liberalism in the progressive era (1900–1920). In large part because class struggle raged throughout the period, many business leaders came to believe that cut throat capitalism threatened social stability. Thus, the National Civic Federation opposed socialists, radicals, and middle-class reformers on the one hand, while the libertarians in their own ranks, the business establishment, organized as the National Association of Manufacturers. Marcus Hanna was the first president of the National Civic Federation, and Samuel Gompers was the vice president from its founding until his death in 1924. Andrew Carnegie was its biggest contributor. According to Weinstein, "in large corporations, such as United States Steel, the 'anarchists' tended to be those men who came from the manufacturing end of the business while the progressives were those who represented the bank or were second-generation managers."[23] But when they were "unable to establish hegemony over the business community on the basis of its trade union policies, Federal leaders turned to welfare as an area of work that would appeal particularly to anti-union employers."[24]

One of the specific reforms brought by corporate liberalism was workmen's compensation. The reaction to entrepreneurial greed served those who would stabilize the economy. In terms of injuries to workers, the industrial system took a severe toll. In U.S. Steel's South Chicago plant, 46 men were killed and 598 injured in 1906. In the early nineteenth century, recourse to damages was through the courts and was based on laws (e.g., the fellow servant rule, the assumption of risk, and contributory negligence) that kept recovery low and made it difficult to establish responsibility for working conditions. Labor attacked these defenses and did not generally support workmen's compensation. The amounts specified in compensation laws were suspect, and most unions opposed government regulation on the theory that government was controlled by business. Workmen's compensation, they thought, might also reduce loyalty to the unions.

At the same time, a mounting attack on courts was being thwarted by industrialists. One aspect of labor's new look at politics from 1905 to 1908 was a fear that increasing use of court injunctions against labor would move the American Federation of Labor (AFL) to political action to limit the judiciary. So when Carnegie contributed to labor's legal fund in an important case as part of his work with the NCF, he warned that he would not give "the slightest countenance to attacks on the Supreme Court."[25] But for labor reformers the courts were the enemy. For instance, in 1911 the New York Court of Appeals held in *Ives* v. *South*

Buffalo Railroad Co.[26] that the "conservative" compensation act of New York (relying on private insurance) was unconstitutional. In New York, an amendment backed by Theodore Roosevelt was passed to reverse the *Ives* decision. As President Roosevelt often told big business, social reform was truly conservative. By 1920 every state but six in the South had workmen's compensation and the federal government had a program for civil employees.

Another area of early reform was in the city commission and city manager movements, where the bywords were "efficiency" and "reduced costs." Locally, to rationalize government and make a city more attractive meant more business. Under the banner of business management and social science, small businesspeople created the commission and council manager form of government. Business was connected to the need for paving, harbors, the elections system, and water, fire, and sewer services. The result was often businesspeople at the helm. The city manager form was opposed by the northern political machines, socialists, and trade unionists. The plans eliminated ward representation, and hence minorities; concentrated power, making it hard to mobilize opposition; and eliminated the partisan ballot concentrating on a politics of personality. "Efficiency" and "reduced costs" ushered in new forms of government.[27]

Reform struggled along in other arenas of the industrial front from 1913 to 1915. These included the United States Commission on Industrial Relations. The commission was formed under President William Howard Taft following violence at the *Los Angeles Times*, an open-shop paper. The idea of an industrial relations commission was supported by prominent reformers such as Lincoln Steffens. President Woodrow Wilson continued to link the academy to reform with the appointment of such important members as Frank Walsh as chair and John R. Commons, author of *The Legal Foundations of Capitalism*, as researcher. Walsh, a radical social justice advocate, believed in publicity about the conditions under which labor worked. He looked into the activities of Colorado Fuel and Iron and the role of John D. Rockefeller in controlling Standard Oil as well as producing the Ludlow massacre. These movements during the most contentious years in the struggle between labor and capital reveal a relationship between economic and political power. This is the relationship that produces reform in the spirit of democracy.

In the end, the more radical alternatives presented the greatest threat to the legacy of the National Civic Federation reformers. Their "politics of social responsibility" was a basis for the emerging corporate system. Their reforms clouded class identification during a period when socialists such as Victor Berger were elected to Congress and seventy-three cities elected socialist mayors. Supported by liberal business leaders and reformers like Jane Addams, the federation's Industrial Economic Department investigated the menace of socialism. The reaction linked the "informal" with the harsh and final, as economist Scott Nearing was fired from the University of Pennsylvania in 1915. Though it failed to destroy the socialist movement, National Civic Federation activity set limits. By moving to the left it absorbed some of the social issues on which socialist strategy was based.

By analyzing the constraints of legal form in the informalist movement, we draw out the tension in critical realism—that is, we see the underside and implications for a movement in law even in the words it uses. Grant McConnell saw a number of paradoxes in progressivism. Although linked to rural populism, progressivism was an urban movement. Although speaking for the masses, it was hostile to organized labor. For McConnell this same tension was characterized in the progressive movement's paradoxical support for private power through its critique of itself.[28] This analysis of progressive interests and ideologies rests on a view of law that is quite complementary to the one offered here. The law does not nor can it simply "contain" private interests; rather, it must be understood as constituting those interests. Only at this depth of analysis can we hope to understand the way law and legal institutions determine politics.

Progressives gave a great deal of attention to arbitration processes and "voluntary tribunals," such as the Chamber of Commerce Committee on Arbitration of the State of New York, which were developed by business leaders during the progressive period as mechanisms to cut down on the rate of litigation.[29] Through such vehicles as the New York State Bar Association's Committee on Prevention of Unnecessary Litigation (formed in 1916), a somewhat less mature bar played a major role in developing this alternative framework. Although these ideologies persist, and barely seem to have aged after half a century, groups such as the American Bar Association have changed a great deal with the growth of a national system of law.

Many of the reforms instituted in this period were attempts by the self-defined "better" classes to transform the values and limit the power of the immigrants who had come to dominate the urban landscape.[30] In her analysis of this phenomenon, Harrington cites comments to the Committee on Small Claims and Conciliation by Reginald Heber Smith, who "hailed small claims courts as socialization agents worth more to the cause of Americanization than any amount of talk."[31] Lower costs and expanded access would perform the socialization function all the more comprehensively and, most importantly—in the argot of the time—more efficiently. Although the movement expressed an affection for the "less formal," it was also highly "professional," the new code for gentry control.

In another "progressive" movement, the one to eliminate lay or non-professional judges, the consequences of bourgeois reform during this period are evident. Lay judges are remnants of an earlier and more democratic populism that has become inconsistent with professional interests as these interests have been articulated by the organized bar in the twentieth century.[32] There is a widespread presumption that non-lawyers, like laypeople, are incapable of adhering to legal rules and rendering judgment. While there have always been nonlawyer judges in America, the challenges to their suitability have been fairly recent. Early attempts to limit this popular and essentially less formal institution of the state relied on the requirement in some state constitutions that judges be "learned in the law." The common-law principle, however, was that no learning was needed. In the 1960s, the old "learned in the law" expectation for judicial competence began to be couched in terms of constitutional due process protection, but most courts turned down claims that nonlawyer judges could not constitutionally instruct juries, act in nuisance prosecutions, conduct preliminary exams in felony cases, or carry out other duties typical of misdemeanor judges. The Supreme Court accepted nonlawyer judges in *Colton* v. *Kentucky*, a case involving a conviction before a lay judges.

Contemporary academics have infused remedial practices with forms of law that reflect some of the reformist tendencies reviewed in the previous chapter in conjunction with realism in law schools. Like realism, remedial practices are nurtured by liberals and conservatives alike. We see this in Mark Kelman's book, *A Guide to Critical Legal Studies*, and in Richard Posner's economic analysis.[33] The interest in informalism, in a practical sense, comes out of the same epistemological critique that lies at the heart of legal realism. Thus it is linked to the neorealism of CLS and to law and economics. The latter, with a more coherent method, shares the critique of practice with the ADR movement. Some of this we can see in Posner's effort to look more closely at the interpretivist movement in law. But law and economics, rather than being immersed in the epistemological controversies, creates an alternative normative scheme, an economic formalism that ultimately has little connection to ADR.

The description of mainstream legal thought by CLS scholars contains the remedial notion of the state as intervenor, which is central to liberal ideology. According to Kelman, this body of thought is simultaneously beset by internal contradictions and "repression of the presence of these contradictions."[34] These contradictions appear again at the heart of the ADR movement. In generally unselfconscious ways, remedial practices attempt to resolve the contradictions identified by CLS scholars and others in the last twenty years. The three central contradictions are between (1) "a commitment to mechanically applicable rules as the appropriate form for resolving disputes . . . and a commitment to situation-sensitive, ad hoc standards"; (2) "a commitment to the traditional liberal notion that values or desires are arbitrary, subjective, individual, and individuating . . . *and* a commitment to the ideal that we can 'know' social and ethical truths objectively"; and (3) "a commitment to an intentionalistic discourse, in which human action is seen as the product of a self-determining individual will, and determinist discourse, in which the activity of nominal subjects . . . is simply deemed the expected outcome of existing structures."[35] The heart of contemporary realism and the foundation for the ADR movement is the indeterminacy position. This is a characteristic of CLS, where governance by rules is made to look impossible because cases require human intervention in the form of interpretation. The CLS position draws on modern conceptions of language and elevates practice and convention over the traditional formal exegesis. Similarly, on the need for purposive intervention, CLS, drawing from law and society, calls attention to the law in action and thereby focuses on the law's essentially political character.

The realist/CLS view of conflict also has affinities to ADR. Conflict is more natural than order, and the fact that failures of normative order may be embraced by left and right alike is a source of support for the realist position. For the Crits, "[T]he idea that state power is often exercised on behalf of those who capture influence in battle certainly seems to be the common wisdom."[36] While Crits profess to avoid a faith in pluralism because of its failure to recognize the influence of entrenched interests, they are also reluctant to accept the frameworks of the first realist period which focused on capture of governing institutions by elites. In this avoidance of the determinative, their epistemological skepticism makes them less radical than their predecessors and much more like the informalists who deny the role of institutional coercion.

The continued interest in grand theories and the inevitable pull toward more structural explanations ultimately separate the academic realism of CLS from the institutional realism of ADR. In the case of law and economics, the market orientation to bargaining is similar to the operative framework driving informalism, but the doctrinal payoff for law and economics goes in a different direction from the practical changes sought by the ADR movement. As part of their position in the academy, Crits project a theoretical cynicism that clashes with the optimism of informalists. While Crits do not put much stock in the benevolence that may or may not be part of the rule of law,[37] this is certainly a feature of informalism. The ADR movement is less self-conscious than the law and economics and CLS movements about the power that rests in even the least formal institutional arrangements. ADR's proponents seem to have trouble recognizing the more ordinary psychological convention that acknowledges transference—of the sort commonly practiced by mediators—to be a form of manipulation.

Perhaps the most telling feature of academic discussion of informalism is the propensity to maintain that this movement is organized around an "alternative" practice. Informalism, in positing itself in opposition to law, resists the incorporation of law into the "alternatives" framework.[38] With regard to law reform as a form of law, however, I have described a number of respects in which facets of law are central to the mediation "alternative."[39] In the mid-1980s, a more sophisticated presentation of informalism seems to have developed that more fully acknowledges the extent to which the movement is a part of the legal process. To observe this development in movement practice, I turn first to the earliest articulations of the informalist creed, and then to the critiques as they emerged from the application of informal processes in the area of family law.

The Pound Conferences

Three historic twentieth-century speeches reflect the concerns of the ADR movement and link them to the law: Roscoe Pound's 1906 address to the American Bar Association (ABA); Chief Justice Warren Burger's speech to a 1976 conference that sought to build on the concerns expressed by Pound; and a speech at the same conference by Frank E. A. Sander of Harvard Law School, an influential contributor to the ideology of informalism. These speeches, and two conferences at which they were given, form the basis for examining what my colleagues have aptly called "the production of ideology."[40] Like other phenomena that relate law's forms to its social life, speeches in conference settings, where people meet to develop strategies and generate support to institutionalize their position, are evidence of law *in* society.

Pound's speech, "The Causes of Popular Dissatisfaction with the Administrations of Justice,"[41] which is quite famous in law reform circles, was given at a conference of the fledgling ABA held in St. Paul, Minnesota, in 1906, and attended by two to three hundred members.[42] The ABA, formed in the late nineteenth century, had only just reached a place of prominence, but not yet national significance, and Pound himself was relatively unknown. Born in 1870 on the Nebraska frontier, by the time of the conference the 36-year-old Pound had acquired a Ph.D. in Botany from the University of Nebraska and studied law for a year at Harvard. He had taught botany, publishing fifteen professional papers on the subject, and also practiced law, where five of his papers had been published, including "The Decadence of Equity."[43] He began teaching Roman law at the University of Nebraska in 1895 and was dean of the law school from 1903. Historically, both the conference and its speaker placed alternatives to the inherited legal system on the national agenda.

Pound's "sociological jurisprudence," which was the driving force behind his speech, claimed a place for social science in the national legal establishment. It predated Justice Louis Brandeis's sociological brief in *Muller v. Oregon*[44] by two years but was basically part of the same movement. Just as Brandeis would link academic scholarship to the record in a case before the Supreme Court and be acknowledged in the opinion for the usefulness of this technique, Pound is known for having expanded the empirical foundations for understanding courts. In this he differs somewhat from later realists such as Jerome Frank and Thurman Arnold, whose analytic critique of process and theory has more affinity with some of the more vocal contemporary manifestations of realism.[45]

He begins the speech historically in an attempt to ground dissatisfaction in the fabric and history of Anglo-Saxon law. From its roots in the early contests over royal sovereignty in the Middle Ages to democratic resistance in nineteenth-century America, the various dissatisfactions to which Pound alludes do indeed depict the growth of the law. From the claim of equal justice for rich and poor to concern over corruption by judges in courts, which served as a newly institutionalized Renaissance expression of the technologies of governance, Pound depicts dissatisfaction as an engine for growth. In the United States, especially in the early twentieth century, some of the dissatisfaction was a democratic resistance to control of courts by conservative interests. Pound's work is in part a response to those forces, which, like the reform orientations discussed earlier in this chapter, met redistributive demands with institutional refinements.

Pound presents a picture of the courts as overburdened and inefficient, one that is still with us today. Initially, it was not simply the flood of cases that bothered Pound, but rather how they were handled. According to Pound, the court system in the United States needed attention in three different respects: multiple courts, concurrent jurisdictions, and a waste of judicial manpower. Commentators note that this system of classification reflected his botanist's training and was a style Pound would employ throughout his scholarship.[46] Pound denounces the "mechanical" operations of the law, foreshadowing the mechanical jurisprudence that was to become such an important foil for realism, which suggests links rather than strong divisions between Pound and the realists.

While the details of Pound's perspective get lost in history, the image of an overburdened court system persists. This image of the legal system seems to be as enduring as Alexis de Tocqueville's dictum that everything in America inevitably ends up in litigation. Pound spoke in a language that appears remarkably fresh:

91

> Judicial power may be wasted . . . by rigid districts or courts or jurisdictions, so that business may be congested in one court while judges in another are idle.
>
> Uncertainty, delay and expense, and above all, the injustice of deciding cases upon points of practice—have created a deep-seated desire to keep out of court, right or wrong, on the part of every sensible business man in the community.

Indeed, the freshness of Pound's words is as much a function of the success of the movement attached to this position as it is to the speaker's ability to anticipate developments in the law. In laying a foundation for the contemporary "litigation crisis" mentality, as well as for informalism, this picture is among the most compelling depicting American courts. Yet, except in the broad sense, it is not entirely clear how law reform and the critique of the administration of justice becomes a foundation for the ADR movement.

One of the particularly creative parts of Pound's speech condemns "the sporting theory of justice," in which lawyers tend to seek private advantage instead of searching for truth and justice: "With the passing of the doctrine that politics, too, is a mere game to be played for its own sake, we may look forward confidently to deliverance from the sporting theory of justice." This depiction was ultimately embedded in realism through the work of Jerome Frank in *Courts on Trial*. The depiction of the fight-for-its-own-sake or empty-contest aspect of the American system became the basis for informal alternatives such as mediation and arbitration.

The legacy of Pound's speech is important for understanding the contemporary ADR movement, including its relation to ideological movements in law like realism and contemporary critical perspectives, as well as its links to reform movements of the past. The speech is still available in pamphlet form from the American Judicature Society of Chicago, a group that traces its formation in 1913 to the speech. And, according to John Wigmore, it was "the spark that kindled the white flame of progress."[47] Although not initially as enthusiastically received—a resolution at the conference calling for mass printing of the speech was defeated—it is an icon of court reform. Wigmore, who observed the speech, was a dean at Northwestern University Law School, and he brought Pound to Evanston, a major step in Pound's journey from the frontier to the citadel of legal power.

In 1976, the National Conference on the Causes of Popular Dissatisfaction with the Administration of Justice was held at St. Paul, Minnesota, in the same hall where Pound had initially spoken seventy years before. The conference, whose title echoed Pound's speech, came during a time when the bicentennial of the Declaration of Independence had generated a rhetoric of renewal. The keynote address was given by then Chief Justice Burger, who applauded Pound's effort "to bring rationality and order to the economic and social chaos caused by the industrial revolution, by the subsequent growth of our cities and by the waves of immigration."[48] The conference sought to mobilize the leadership of the bar and the judiciary, and it is a key source of interest in the ideology of informalism. Sponsors included the American Bar Association, the Conference of Chief Justices, and the Judicial Conference of the United States. Proceedings were published in *Federal Rules Decisions*, the official federal agency publication.[49]

Burger's keynote, titled "Agenda for 2000 A.D.," included a call for reform in the direction of ADR. Amid an extraordinary number of references to Pound's speech, Burger emphasized the need for fundamental change. No minor tinkering, as Pound had initially pointed out, would do.[50] Change was important to the Chief Justice, though one had to admit that he was a quite solidly situated baron of the bar. Changes in legal practice would be the necessary response to other massive changes the country would be facing. Burger looked to institutional structures as a way to measure the success and health of the official normative order. The ABA helped found the National Center for State Courts. Lawyers and judges formed the American Judicature Society, in part, as a response to Pound's speech. They also created the Judicial Conference of the United States, the American Law Institute, and the Institute of Judicial Administration, each with an interest in professional reform through institutional change. Expansion of the federal judiciary is one of the keys to institutional reform suggested by Burger, but the structural element of Burger's presentation is also reflected in the ADR movement. In the guise of alternative institutions, which despite their name take the establishment of law-related programs as a measure of their success, ADR is a largely a lawyer's movement.

Another concern Burger borrowed from Pound and the progressives and made to work in the interest of the judicial establishment was efficiency. Although not "an end in itself," said Burger, efficiency "has as its objective the very purpose of the whole system—to do justice."[51] Small litigants, he said, "are often exploited by the litigant with the longest purse" who can use delay to his advantage. But the small guy, especially if he has been judged guilty or condemned to die, is less salient in the argument when the issue of efficiency is taken to bear on appeals and the jury system.

In anticipating the charge that the conference was stacked in favor of those who would reduce access to courts, Burger cited as the first of his fundamental changes the need to find ways to "resolve minor disputes more fairly and more swiftly than any present judicial mechanisms make possible."[52] Lawyers are not feasible for many minor or small claims like "shoddy merchandise . . . or a poor roofing job," and Burger suggests that nonlawyers might be brought in for neighborhood or community disputes. Similarly, Burger added, "It is time to explore new ways to deal with such family problems as marriage, child custody and adoptions" outside what he called "the formality and potentially traumatic atmosphere of courts."

There is no indication that participants at the conference were uncomfortable with the tenor of this critique of law, even though most were lawyers. The demand for change was a central part of the program, and there was little that criticized the way this change was supposed to develop. Only Simon Rifkind and Laura Nader decried the absence of talk of rights and charged that the conference sought to close access to the courts. But Burger had anticipated their concerns in his expressed desire for "the speediest and the least expensive means of meeting the legitimate needs of the people in resolving disputes." Burger thus presented informal mechanisms as an alternative to court congestion, a classic argument of remedial practice advocates. The orientation of the gathering was at least in part an expression of preference for a different style of politics with clear class implications.

During the 1976 conference, Frank Sander, who was to become a key activist in the ADR movement, drew images from an academic past in a talk titled "Varieties of Dispute Processing."[53] Although late in the movement, by comparison to Pound's progressive-period oration, this presentation came as organized interests were arrayed around new institutions championing alternative ways of resolving disputes. Informalism had risen to significance as an instrument of liberal reform.

Family Mediation Alternatives

Juvenile courts stem from the progressive period, as do domestic relations or family courts. The first domestic relations court was established in Buffalo upon the recommendation of the New York State Probation Commission in 1910. Built on the same model as the juvenile court, with its emphasis on social justice over due process and its paternalistic conception of the relationship between the state and the defendant, the New York court dealt with cases of wife abandonment, illegitimacy, failure to support, offenses against minors, and custody disputes.[54] At the height of the contemporary informalist movement, activists targeted family-related disputes, along with consumer, environmental, and business disputes, as objects of reform.[55]

Robert Mnookin and Lewis Kornhauser, law professors who were early supporters of the ADR movement in family situations, describe informalism in the area of domestic relations as "an alternative way of thinking about the role of law at the time of divorce."[56] Rather than viewing law as "imposing order from above," they see mediation "as providing a framework within which divorcing couples can themselves determine their post-dissolution rights and responsibilities." The academic foundation for moving from courts to informal appendages was the belief that mediation would lead to a form of "private ordering," or what Lon Fuller called the "law" that parties bring into existence by agreement.[57] While the media broadened support for ADR in the form of dramatic presentations of law's failure, such as the popular movie *Kramer vs. Kramer* with Dustin Hoffman and Meryl Streep, a community of attentive and interested professionals came increasingly to represent an institutionalized force for informalism within the law.

Sander's June 1982 keynote address at the First ABA Conference on Alternative Means of Family Dispute Resolution, titled "Family Mediation: Problems and Prospects,"[58] provides a basis for analyzing the discourse of informalism. Sander had chaired the ABA's Special Committee on Dispute Resolution and helped to organize the conference, which took place in Washington, D.C., and was funded by the bar association and various foundations. It also received support and programmatic assistance from newly established groups like NIDR, funded by the Ford and the William and Flora Hewlett foundation. Sander's address, with its specific concern for family mediation, is a good example of movement discourse. It epitomizes a focus on remedial action as it is structured by a view of the legal system.

The most obvious aspect of Sander's discussion of "alternatives" is its disputes focus. It is infused with a discursive practice familiar largely to lawyers and those who are around courts or who define themselves in terms of lawyers and courts. It is not that the law is the only place we find disputes or that disputes inevitably lead to legal issues, but rather that disputing is a term of art for a particular movement. Disputes are the social reality on which this form of law is based. As it is used by Sander, the disputes paradigm is a practice for the movement. The movement has built a structure of understandings that transform a social phenomenon, disputes, into a highly organized aspect of political culture.

Sander pays homage to Fuller as a legal theorist interested in alternatives, and he plays down the issues of court congestion that Burger introduced as the basis for his interest in alternatives to court. The "problem" addressed by the movement is grounded in anthropological research and community relations. Sander presents "reports from the field" in the form of commentary from "litigators." His search is for a better way, and he interposes the skill of the intermediary as a new path

away from the "donnybrook" toward "civilization." Sander links the
ADR movement to the family environment in terms of characteristics to
which informal processes are addressed, such as intensity of feeling and
the existence of continuing relations.

The inevitability of disputes demands an institutional response. Consequently, a characteristic of Sander's speech is its heavily procedural
and institutional orientation. Although it deals with conflict in the family, its real detail and its passion are linked to the various forms for chan-
neling the disputes rather than the substance of the conflict. The listing
of institutional forms is impressive. Just in terms of those linked to
courts, Sander lists "small claims mediation, court-annexed arbitration
for routine middle-sized claims, medical malpractice screening tribunals, and the mini-trial used in large and complex litigation."[59] This
attention to institutions and the separation of process from substance,
though not unique to the legal profession, is a skill more finely honed
among lawyers than among most of the citizenry.

At a more superficial level, the authority for the discussion clearly lies
in the legal profession. The author is a Harvard professor, the bibliogra-
phy is overwhelmingly from law reviews or about law, the authorities
from whom Sander draws his material are either in law or part of the
growing paraprofessional community in dispute resolution. This community relies heavily on the institutions of the law, particularly law
reviews, but it approaches the material from the concerns of often critical social research. This symbiosis has been essential to the emergence of
the ADR movement. The academic community came out in force in the
late 1980s to review the book *Dispute Resolution* by Stephen B. Goldberg, Eric D. Green, and Sander.[60]

Such closely linked networks pursuing shared goals are among the
most important considerations for ensuring that remedial practices such
as the disputes focus and the substantive/procedural split are carried by
a political movement. Shared practices associated with the legal profession identify law as a problem and offer the informal alternative as part
of a strategy with significant consequences for how power is wielded in
the United States. The Third National Conference on Peacemaking and
Conflict Resolution in 1986 carried an impressive list of supporting organizations, headed by the William and Flora Hewlett Foundation.[61] Even
greater evidence of links with the law can be found in the SPIDR conference held in New York City in 1987, where the opening plenary session
was addressed by Margaret Shaw, director of the Institute of Judicial

Administration, and Peter S. Adler, director of the Program on Alternative Dispute Resolution, Hawaii State Judiciary. Both of these conferences included sessions on family mediation and "issues" sessions devoted to the family. Only a few years after Sander's call for family mediation, however, the family as a center of mediation practice seemed to be in decline.

Critics of informalism in the family mediation area have been among the most vocal in opposition to the remedial orientation. In an essay in the *New York Times*,[62] Lenore J. Weitzman, Herbert Jacob, and Mary Ann Glendon argued that women fare worse under no-fault divorce. Their essay drew responses from practicing lawyers who argued that the process of divorce, like criminal prosecution, goes to trial less than 10 percent of the time. The Natioanl Organization for Women (NOW) Legal Defense and Education Fund's 1984 pamphlet "Divorce Mediation: A Guide for Women" has a more extensive treatment of the subject. Written by attorneys Judith Avner, from the Family Law Project, and Susan Herman, from the Institute for Mediation and Conflict Resolution, the work contends that feminists need to respond to the growth of informal alternatives.

The NOW pamphlet begins with a caution that divorce mediation should be carefully examined and scrutinized because the woman is often the more vulnerable partner in a divorce. The authors warn that "subtle prejudices" such as economic dependency and the desire to avoid conflict, which often relegate women to an inferior status, may hurt a woman in the mediation process. Stressing that divorce mediation is a voluntary process, the authors also distinguish it from going to court on the basis of its lack of formality. Some states, like California, mandate mediation in cases of divorce; others, like Massachusetts, encourage the parties to work with court officers to try and resolve differences prior to going before a judge. Using a question-and-answer format, the pamphlet leads women through the possibilities, concluding with the proposition that the appropriateness of mediation depends on each woman's situation.

At about the same time that the NOW pamphlet appeared, the Family Law Project of the University of Michigan Law School offered the following concerns to the participants at a Conference on Women and Mediation at New York University: (1) the parties should be of relatively equal bargaining power for mediation to be desirable; (2) because women "feel greater responsibility for the quality and success of a relationship and family life," they might be misinterpreted as blameworthy; and (3) women feeling the threat to custody of children may be willing to bargain away nearly everything else in the interest of maintaining a position as the primary caregiver. These caveats shift to dire warnings where there is violence in the family. They reflect the view, which became more common in the mid-1980s, that where there is violence in a relationship mediation is inappropriate. The authors hold that "[m]ediation provides no deterrent to the assailant and even gives him a protected right to speak his mind about his wife, who because of the peculiar characteristics of victimization, will often agree with him when he enumerates her many failings."[63]

In this critique, informalism collides with feminism. It is a clash that seems inevitable, considering the absence of attention to feminist issues in documents like Sander's speech.[64] By 1987 cautions were being raised about the extension of mediation into family disputes,[65] and by the end of the decade the warnings had become a chorus.[66] A relatively enthusiastic movement discourse gave way to the more guarded product of the political process and the rare academic critique became the norm. Posner's consideration of family law and the application of economic analysis to family relations links family mediation directly to academic thinking, and suggests law and economics as a rehabilitative framework.[67] I conclude the treatment of informalism with more material links between the movement and the academy.

Difference and the State

A façade of folksy informality and therapeutic conviction masks the institutional structures supporting informalism and makes it difficult to assess transformations in the nature of law. Here, the law that looks accessible, human, therapeutic, even friendly, is produced by people well situated within the state. Informalists also mix informality with the language of social science, which gives their presentations a complex passivity. To quote the negotiator Howard Bellman again: "Now it seems to me that we can end this with some sort of a bundle of input that all of you may or may not fully like . . . but hopefully is a consensus as initially defined."[68] The terms "bundle of input" and "consensus" emerge as nontechnical terms of art that help define a separate practice and situate it in opposition to traditional legal practice.

In discussing remedial practices in law I have drawn on elements of social relations in order to suggest some of the distinctive interests we need to take account of in order to understand informalism. These relations, as well as some analytic similarities, have linked informalism and remedial practices to realism. In this section, I expand my analysis to indicate some of the implications of this movement for various arms of state power. In particular, the expansion of a form of power in which efficiency is more salient than justice and remedies more highly prized than rights portends a legal form that constructs claimants out of citizens.

Remedial practices exist in communities, where they provide the legal forms that are the modern manifestation of state power. Three aspects of state control as social practice deserve note in this context. The first is direct corporate sponsorship and its correlate the various indirect attachments characteristic of the Harvard Program on Negotiation and its would-be competitors. The second is foundation support, which is sometimes an aspect of indirect attachments, but also exists on its own as part of the cultural environment in which remedial practices thrive (e.g., NIDR and its substantial Ford Foundation support). Third, in the only slightly removed arena of the academy, there is the life of institutions, careers, and professional relationships that facilitate this aspect of informalism.

In order to illuminate the relationship between institutions and the professions, we can turn to one of the most articulate practitioners of sociological research in law and an early advocate for informal justice, Joel Handler of the University of California at Los Angeles Law School. In his book *The Conditions of Discretion: Autonomy, Community, Bureaucracy*,[69] Handler employs contemporary law and society research, a movement deeply entangled with the law reform enterprise in general and informalism in particular. His work is particularly attentive to the administration of welfare, and in his role as consultant to the Ford Foundation in the 1970s he was one of the most effective American academics in establishing foundation support for ADR.

In a 1988 article, Handler builds a new conception of legal power on a critique of liberalism, focusing on the consequence of law for dependent people.[70] He initiates his discussion of informal justice with "the specter of a litigation crisis" and the calls for "mechanisms, such as community boards, neighborhood justice centers, mediation, and arbitration, that would process disputes outside of or alternative to formal procedures."[71] Handler describes informalism as a response to two impulses: one is a critique of professionalism from the left in the 1960s, and the other is an establishment desire on the part of Chief Justice Burger, large law firms, insurance companies, and the ABA to clear dockets and decide claims "more efficiently, quickly, and cheaply." This polarity might give a careful observer pause, and Handler expresses the "serious concern that the disadvantaged will suffer even more under regimes of informal justice" than they had under the much-maligned formal processes.[72] He calls attention to the record of failure for informal justice in juvenile courts, small claims courts, and housing courts,[73] the inability of informal mechanisms to address the problems of maldistribution in the social structure that manifest themselves in any dispute.

Then, in a style observers of the ADR movement have become familiar with, he goes on to elaborate the alternative process as having new wrinkles, a new informalism, more appealing than before.[74] According to this assessment, informalism may allow the parties to "connect with each other in more humanistic ways than in the formal system," and there is the possibility that "the quality of participation will approach dialogism."[75] As members of a law-school–based movement with a solid antilogical and antiempirical attachment, informalist theorists are able to operate from contradictory positions as if this was a virtue. And, like law, informalism denies its sociological determinants, its class or ethnographic roots.[76]

The informalist movement's material basis involves a telling conjunction of financial interest, careerism, and the intellectual fashion that drives foundation decisions. The NIDR was set up in the 1970s with funds from the Ford Foundation and received substantial support for the next twenty years. Its apparatus is actively involved in professional associations such as the unaffiliated Law and Society Association and the more guild-associated American Bar Foundation. In its academic attachments, NIDR commissions research drawing attention to the issues as movement operatives would have them discussed. In the etiquette of the contemporary academy, the conclusions cannot be stipulated, but it remains perfectly acceptable to set the research agenda and create the setting for its presentation.

The Fund for Research on Dispute Resolution was administered by NIDR under a separate board chaired by Sanford Jaffe and with Handler and Felice Levine, long-time director of the National Science Foundation's Law and Society Program, as members. The fund operated on the edge of the academy, drawing interest in its agenda with a budget of nearly $2 million. Recent grants fuel the ADR movement and provide a form in which academics may cast their work in order to get funding.

In the Harvard Program on Negotiation, the home base of such move-ment figures as Roger Fisher, Sander, and Lawrence Susskind, we have the more fully developed corporate influence over knowledge long bar-gained and managed in private universities. The primary mechanisms are consulting and a special institutional relationship in which the time of university faculty is directly purchased by corporate patrons. Here, the setting is either the corporation itself or the ivy-covered walls where traditional bastions of gentry academicians, like the Harvard Faculty Club, may be rented out to corporate visitors, who pay for the status of dining there under the auspices of the Program on Negotiation.

On the other side, it is hard not to see institutional aspects of Owen Fiss's comment in the *Yale Law Journal*, "Against Settlement."[77] Fiss is a leading advocate of proceduralism, an alternative to informalism, and his work is institutionally based in the scholarship and forms associated with a particular law school. Perhaps not coincidentally, the article begins as a critique of a report by the Harvard Overseers and Derek Bok's call for attention to "the new voluntary mechanisms."[78] Linking the movement to developments central to informalism as a very successful movement in law, such as well-funded institutes, sections of the ABA, and new rules of civil procedure, Fiss holds that the received "account of adjudication and the case for settlement rest on questionable premises."[79]

In such a context of knowledge production it makes little sense to characterize the state as in opposition to economic interests. The state and the economy, in relations like the sections of the ABA or foundation grants to academics, and through the development of the ideological practice of remedy and informalism in law, become mutually constitu-tive. In much the same sense as some of the analytical possibilities dis-cussed in the opening chapter on legal form, we have the intermingling described by Sally Falk Moore and the "interlegality" at the core of Boaventura de Sousa Santos's cartographic analysis of the contemporary state of the law. Santos draws attention to "different legal spaces [as] non-synchronic," resulting in "uneven and unstable mixings of legal codes."[80] These codes reach in and out in cultural space and resonate as layers of meaning through which legality presents itself. The resulting fragmentation, noted by both Stuart Macaulay[81] and Santos,[82] becomes anything but chaotic. In the guise of the informalism examined here, the practices that manifest themselves as a remedial system significantly dull the capacity of law to be wielded against the interests of those it constitutes, however imperceptibly.[83]

101

What Harrington and Merry have called "ideological production," and what Cain and Kulcsar identify as the reasons for the growth of this movement, amount to a complex social and intellectual configuration that masks the interests served by the movement, and in this case its links to the institutional apparatus from which it putatively sets itself apart. The economic support and elite enthusiasm that fuel informalism obviously come from its attractions. Informalism fits nicely into the penetrating modern mechanisms of social control uncovered in all their postmodern ambiguity and seeming innocuousness as against the brutal past by scholars such as Michel Foucault, Dario Melossi, and David Garland.[84] And, as is characteristic of all the movements discussed as part of law's politics, informalism is essentially a legal form. Informalism cries for remedies, for peacemakers and conciliators, who provide a somewhat romanticized analog to the traditional institutions of lawyers and courts. In addition, it constructs the legal formalism of "qualitative interchangeability"[85] in which disputants, like voters and consumers, become atomized in a system that provides for them but which they cannot escape.

The informalist movement, based in the state's institutions, extends the reach of the law by drawing on a conception of its inefficacy and limits. In so doing, it provides microcosmic evidence of the construction of family and personality by law. Here, the ultrarealism of the remedial form commodifies husbands and wives, landlords and tenants into parties to disputes. The family,[86] the schools,[87] and the social welfare bureaucracy,[88] all major instruments of indoctrination to public norms, have either embraced or been depicted as embracing the ideal of a system for resolving disputes. The movement works through conventional institutions, where people can learn the specifics of appropriate degrees of conformity and the propriety of peace. The ultimate power of the state over the demands placed upon its bureaucratic shoulders is in the construction of demand in relation to these institutions. Instituting a new therapeutic discourse, and thus allowing experts to interpret needs in a fashion that functions as the old institutions did, is the characteristic contribution of informalism.[89]

Radical Legal Consciousness
Sex and Rage

Chapter 5

Misogyny is real. Rape is real. Economic discrimination is real. The devaluation of anything female is real. The sexism that defines sex as intercourse (only) and defines intercourse as the male organ (only) is real.

—Andrea Dworkin, "Pornography: The New Terrorism"

Coming from England to America in the seventeenth century must have taken considerable motivation, but the men and women who made the voyage could stand to live with their countrymen no longer. These were intense people, perhaps even angry people. However, their anger must have been largely focused on religious institutions because the political and legal institutions they set up in America drew much from their English experience. The laws of England, the courts, and the lawyers came to dominate the New World. They would also become the subject of resistance. From imperial expansion against Native Americans, through the struggles that united the nation and eliminated slavery, to modern social movements, English institutions have been subjected to attack.

Sometimes these attacks have been accompanied by armed struggle: Native American resistance; the Revolution itself; the Civil War; the radical labor movement; the Weather Underground of the early 1970s. All of these movements took up arms and wielded them with an intensity born of the perception that there was no alternative. In other movements, this intensity has been carried forward by political means. Outrage and radicalism taking form in a struggle against law are the subject of this chapter. As in the other discussions, my focus is on the constitutive function of law. Here the constitutive dimension is in forms that stand in near total opposition to the hegemony that law appears to require. In the early feminist movement against pornography, from which much of the material in this chapter is drawn, but also in the antiabortion movement and in historic struggles like the one over slavery, there is more at stake than simply having the movement circumscribed by the words of the master.[1]

Catharine MacKinnon situates the rage of radical feminism in the critique of liberalism: "Liberal morality cannot deal with illusions that *constitute* reality because its theory of reality, lacking a substantive critique of the distribution of social power, cannot get behind the empirical world."[2] The legal form examined here, radicalism, has a social expression in the rage of its participants. It also takes differentiation as far as it can go. Radical traditions are ones of nearly complete resistance. The form varies from armed resistance through disruption to vandalism and disobedience. The characteristic in each case is an antipathy to the system that results in and is subsequently supported by a blockage of discursive flow. Without the renewal of discourse there is an estrangement that reaches to the core of law's claim to be authoritative.

Consciousness Rising

Perhaps the epitome of outrage toward law derives from abolitionism, the early nineteenth-century struggle against slavery. In this movement, leaders like Frederick Douglass, the black author and activist, William Lloyd Garrison, publisher of *The Liberator*, and John Brown, the radical abolitionist of Harper's Ferry, carried outrage into political practice. In the visage of John Brown, especially in the view of him we get from Thomas Hart Benton's imagist portrait, we have an American enraged. The result is the political mobilization of anger. Of Brown's radicalism, which history has refused to separate from his rage, Frederick Douglass wrote: "He denounced slavery in look and language fierce and bitter; thought that slaveholders had forfeited their right to live; that the slaves had the right to gain their liberty in any way they could; did not believe that moral suasion would ever liberate the slave, or that political action would abolish the system."[3] Brown's raid on the federal arsenal at

Harper's Ferry falls somewhere between the armed resistance of the Civil War itself, which by the conventions of politics we ascribe another status, and the political activity of legal reform.

In politics, where the distribution of power (both active and passive) is the subject, consciousness is a precondition. Spoken of most broadly, to be conscious—or even unconscious—is to be in some mental state in relation to others. The women's movement traditionally has focused on consciousness. As noninstrumental awareness or denial, consciousness is about the forms of politics rather than within them. Like the *courtla* of southern African tribal life, in which the entire tribe discusses a subject until it has been discussed enough,[4] outcomes are affected discursively. Recent scholarship points out how discursive practices operate in ideological struggles where they are not transformative. In contemporary thought, the body as metaphor in politics has been the subject of a good deal of work by women.[5] Most dramatically, the politics of abortion has made the body its subject; it has redefined who and what is inside or outside, and what is on its own.

Cruelty is implicit in domination, as Kate Millett's compelling conclusions on sexual politics demonstrate. Her aim is at the tendency of even the most traumatic social relations to mask the force behind them. Millett calls our attention to the fact that "[w]hen a system of power is thoroughly in command, it has scarcely need to speak itself aloud; when its workings are exposed and questioned, it becomes not only subject to discussion, but even to change."[6] The link between rage and social relations is so embedded in law and systems of power that it is hard to put in words, yet it is an essential quality of the radical legal form.[7]

Consciousness-raising is not about confrontation with the obvious and widely accepted. That is, it is not the "ordinary" response in a system that operates hegemonically. Altered consciousness or ideology is, in fact, counterhegemonic. It counters that which dominates because it comes from seeing the obvious in the not widely accepted. Thus, consciousness is linked with rage, as captured in this 1978 statement by Andrea Dworkin: "The oppressor . . . is the master inventor of justification. He is the magician who, out of thin air, fabricates wondrous, imposing, seemingly irrefutable intellectual reasons which explain why one group must be degraded at the hands of another."[8] For radical feminists opposed to pornography, the state and law are not seen as "on our side."[9] Neither, of course, are law and the state instruments viewed with the liberal's ambivalence, a position to be explored in this chapter. Law is the enemy. Dworkin's was one of the earliest statements in the modern attack on violent pornography, and it demonstrates the "outgroup" quality of the social relations characteristic of this movement.[10]

The literature on social movements from Seymour Martin Lipset to Michael Walzer[11] classifies advocacy of fundamental change as ideologically extreme rather than emotionally intense. In this tradition, a spectrum of political orientations is arrayed as if reflecting the position of the body in space. Susan Sontag has illuminated this spatial relation and called attention to its links with repression:

> Take, for instance, a tenacious metaphor that has shaped (and obscured the understanding of) so much of the political life of this century, the one that distributes, and polarizes, attitudes and social movements according to their relation to a "left" and a "right." . . . It seems . . . that its persistence in discourse about politics to this day comes from a felt aptness to the modern, secular imagination of metaphors drawn from the body's orientation in space—left and right, top and bottom, forward and backward—for describing social conflict, a metaphoric practice that did add something new to the perennial description of society as a kind of body, a well-disciplined body ruled by a "head."[12]

This metaphor has been dominant for the polity since Plato and Aristotle. This is, as Sontag points out, "perhaps because of its usefulness in justifying repression."[13] Not the least reason for this is its capacity to delineate politics as a constrained realm of the possible.

In the case of movement practice, however, we can situate politics by its intensity as well as its place on the political spectrum. Combining the spatial and emotional is tricky, partly because liberalism assumes a connection. This is certainly the case with the militia movement and the antiabortion movement; their radicalism puts them on the political fringe. Yet in constitutive terms the social meaning of a political force is closely tied to its depiction by the dominant interests. One way to see feminists' outrage at pornography's violence and the expression of this outrage in a radical social movement is as a critique of the spectrum and liberalism.

Radicalism as Law's Form

Radicalism, as an ideological form evident in movements against violent pornography, abortion, and discrimination, attacks the same instruments of government appealed to by gay activists—the courts, the judges, and the doctrines of law. Common sense tells us that the "instruments" are the same, only the nature of the response is different. But radicals find the law oppressive. One cannot say that a police officer viewed as a "pig" is really the same institution as the avuncular figure of middle-class socialization. The radical form and the rage that drives these movements come from struggles against the law. Law is associated with despair rather than hope, and it is seen as standing behind oppressive social conditions. This law maintains an inequitable status quo—the inequality of power and wealth, for instance, as gendered relations—while radicals demand a transformation.

The radical legal form in political discourse relies on intense feelings and disquietude. Douglass's characterization of John Brown conveys that emotion, as did the picture of slavery Douglass himself called up. For the women's movement a hundred years later, Millett would summon up a similar rage by her interpretations of the violence and domination in Henry Miller's *Sexus*.[14] The emotion comes from outside of dominant social relations, or at least from outside the institutionalization of those relations as law. As a legal formation, radicalism challenges substantive legal determinations. Drawing on expectations of equality and a shared humanity, it wields these visions in opposition to the status quo.[15] In movements like the opposition to abortion since the 1973 Supreme Court decision in *Roe v. Wade*, a law can be the focus of the rage and radical change in a law can be a strategy. Law in general or a body of law, rather than a particular law, may also be the subject of political unrest. In this sense, the movement plays off the dominant conception of law. The feminist case against pornography and the practices that constitute the movement are a mirror image of the rights claim, in this case, to free expression.

The commentary by Women Against Pornography (WAP) in the late 1970s saw law on the side of the pornographer and proposed that law had in fact fostered the range of pornographic material available. The movement took the liberal successes of the post–World War II period as its terrain. There was general agreement that the laws on pornography were more liberal in the 1970s and 1980s than they had been twenty years or more before, and that the consequence was more pornography. All the while, the movement skirted the edge of censorship and was continually confronted with the challenge of free expression. In the case against pornography, radical feminists argued that in a male-dominated society sexuality involves danger, and that dominant/subordinate power relationships in sex as it is normally practiced perpetuate violence against women.[16] The movement in the early stages identified legal forms with terrorism.

The role, the responsibility, even the nature of law in antipornography discourse can be compared to the forms law takes in other movements. The form evident in the antipornography movement shares with the gay rights claims in the AIDS crisis a belief in the power of appellate doctrine and the compulsion of rights claims grounded in tradition. In the antipornography movement, however, there is much less sense of entitlement than we saw in the gay community.[17] In addition, radical feminists eschew the "sophisticated" cynicism of critical legal studies, with its tendency to minimize the power and responsibility of law. An implicit jurisprudence makes sense out of politics constituted in radical social movements. The feminist position does not simply accept a positive frame of law coming from distant or professionally constituted institutions, though it does take account of those institutions. The position is as sophisticated as the most advanced legal scholarship, which finds tradition, structure, and law where others deny that there is anything but power.

According to Owen Fiss, drawing from Harry Kalven, the Supreme Court has given rise to a free speech tradition in its decisions. Thus, "Free speech is now part of our general culture, and I believe the decisions of the Court implanted that principle in our culture, nurtured it, and gave it much of its present shape."[18] Some kinds of "expression" are not "speech" under the definition of the First Amendment. The modern doctrine comes from *Chaplinsky v. New Hampshire* in 1942. In *Chaplinsky*, a Jehovah's Witness had called a town official a "goddamned racketeer" and a "damned Fascist."[19] Judge Frank Murphy decided that "certain classes of speech never raise constitutional problems" and assumed that this speech could be prevented and punished. "The lewd and the obscene, the profane, the libelous and the insulting or 'fighting words'. . . they are neither essential to any 'exposition of ideas' nor a 'step to truth.'"

The legal history of obscenity begins with legislative involvement; constitutional history is grounded in the court's response. The first U.S. case was *Commonwealth v. Holmes*, an 1821 Massachusetts case involving the 1748 book *Fanny Hill* (*Memoirs of a Woman of Pleasure*), one of the "erotic classics."[20] Most modern pornography prosecution can be traced to the late nineteenth century and the Comstock laws, which set new restraints on the degree of frankness allowed in discussion of sexuality. The history of prosecutions is governed by the Hicklin Rule, first used in 1868, which employed a standard of "whether the market tended to deprave and corrupt the mind of those whose minds are open to such influences" and who might get a hold of the material.

In 1913, Judge Learned Hand rejected the Hicklin test because it forbid all that might corrupt the most corruptible.[21] His protest was echoed by Judge Felix Frankfurter,[22] but *Roth v. United States* (1957) was the clearest reaction. Until 1930, the U.S. Customs Department barred Aristophanes' *Lysistrata*, Balzac's *Droll Stories*, Defoe's *Moll Flanders* and *Roxana*, Flaubert's *Temptation of St. Anthony*, and Voltaire's *Candide*. Early twentieth-century literature that combined politics and eroticism added to the propensity to prosecute these classics. Works such as Tolstoy's *Kreutzer Sonata*, Shaw's *Mrs. Warren's Profession*, Daniel Carson Goodman's *Hagar Revelly*, Theodore Dreiser's *The "Genius"* and Elinor Glyn's *Three Weeks* all contained criticism of the bourgeois politics at the same time that they scandalized this class and its sensibility about sex.

In 1933, a U.S. Court of Appeals substituted for the Hicklin Rule a concern for "obscenity as the dominant effect."[23] The issue of obscenity first came before the Supreme Court in 1948, when the Court affirmed the conviction under a New York obscenity statute for "The Princess with the Golden Hair," part of *Memoirs of Hecate County*, written by Edmund Wilson and published by Doubleday. Judge Jerome Frank, in *United States v. Roth* (1956),[24] wrote an opinion delineating the controversy and appealing to the Supreme Court for a decision, which came the following year. The emergence of the obscenity issue seems to me to be a result of the strength of the First Amendment rather than any particular retrograde tendencies on the part of the public at the time. The year before, the Supreme Court had held in a *per curiam* opinion that a state obscenity statute in Kansas relating to motion pictures was unconstitutional because of vagueness.[25]

The appeal of Judge Frank's decision, *Roth v. United States*, became the key decision on obscenity in constitutional history. Announced in 1957, this was one of Justice William Brennan's earliest opinions, and its logic still governs the debate over pornography. Writing for the Court, Brennan declares, "We hold that obscenity is not within the area of constitutionally protected speech or press." His framework drew from the history of community in America from the Puritans on and the protection in the common law for libel, as well as the newer doctrine of fighting words linked to the states' police power. In Brennan's argument, speech is protected because it is the lifeblood of politics. He begins with the issue of free expression, or "whether obscenity is utterance within the area of protected speech and press."[26] Although Brennan postulates the historical prohibitions against obscene speech, from the care with which he proceeds one senses a concern for expression with more meaning and greater complexity than what we see so often in the contemporary liberal response to the antipornography movement. Brennan held, "The protection given speech and press was fashioned to assure unfettered interchange of ideas for the bringing about of political and social changes desired by the people."[27] Free speech had a purpose, as outlined in the Continental Congress of 1774. According to Brennan, this was "the advancement of truth, science, morality, and arts in general, in its diffusion of liberal sentiments on the administration of government, its ready communication of thoughts between subjects, and its consequential promotion of union among them, whereby oppressive officers are shamed or intimidated, into more honorable and just modes of conducting affairs."[28] Because of all this, a small category of the obscene might be proscribed.

The "obscene" in the opinion refers to "that form of immorality which has relation to sexual impurity and a tendency to incite lustful thoughts." Sex and obscenity are distinguished. Obscene material deals with sex in a manner appealing to prurient interests, that is, it has a tendency to incite lustful thoughts. The obscene is associated with "morbid or lascivious language" and with lust rather than simply sexual excitement. In making this distinction, Brennan makes it clear that he believes that sex is a great and mysterious force and the subject of absorbing interest, while obscenity is a subclass of sex that is offensive to decency. The contribution for which the *Roth* case is most noted is its new test for obscenity. In order to safeguard free expression while enabling the punishment of obscenity, Brennan shifted the standard from the Hicklin Rule's attention to an isolated excerpt and a particularly sensitive person, and focused instead on the average person applying contemporary community standards. In this test, the dominant theme would be taken as a whole and examined with regard to its appeal to the prurient interest.

The "middle years" in obscenity doctrine came to be associated with Justice Potter Stewart's aphorism "I know it when I see it." The distinction in *Roth*, which said that obscenity was by definition utterly without redeeming social values, became a criterion in *Jacobellis v. Ohio* in 1964.[29] Where there are ideas, there is protection. That was the basis of the decision in *Memoirs v. Massachusetts*,[30] another case involving the book *Fanny Hill*. According to Justice Warren Burger (writing in *Miller v. California*), *Memoirs* veered sharply from *Roth*. It was, at least, a restatement. There were three tests: (1) the dominant theme of the material taken as a whole must appeal to a prurient interest in sex; (2) it must be patently offensive by community standards relating to description or representation of sexual matters; and (3) it must be utterly without social value. To be judged obscene, the material had to fail all three tests. Associate Justice Tom Clark dissented because he felt that the "new test" the case introduced—the "utterly without" test—rejected the basic holding of *Roth*, where he had been the deciding vote. Clark believed the test had only two parts, and that social value might even be weighed against offense. Clark's description of *Fanny Hill* makes it seem "dirty." He says it depicts nothing besides the brothels and sees no social value, say, in the various industrial metaphors. He clearly believed it was okay to keep something out of circulation because it caused "genital commotion."

By 1973, the Court had changed. In *Miller v. California*, a new standard distinguished protected from unprotected expression by emphasizing community-based offensiveness, with a focus on hard-core porn—ultimate sexual acts, masturbation, excretory functions, and lewd exhibitions that lack serious literary, artistic, political or scientific value.[31] In *Paris Adult Theater v. Slaton*, a companion case, legitimate state interest in regulating obscenity overcame safeguards against exposure to juveniles and passersby.[32] The quality of life, the "tone of commerce in the great city centers," and public safety (citing the minority report of the commission on obscenity) were considered enough to justify controlling pornography. In dissent, Brennan calls attention to "sensitive adults and juveniles" and zoning in cases such as *Erznoznik v. City of Jacksonville*, which struck down an attempt under nuisance laws to protect citizens from unwilling exposure to offensive material in drive-in movies, and *Young v. American Mini Theatres*, which allowed a Detroit zoning ordinance limiting where adult porn shows could be put on.[33] This is the doctrinal world in which the politics of pornography unfolded.

Dworkin's first speech on the subject of pornography was given in 1977 at the University of Massachusetts, Amherst. It was linked at the time with movements against domestic violence and "female sexual slavery."[34] Concern about pornography became increasingly associated with

111

the condition of women as subjects of male violence. A subsequent speech by Dworkin, spawned by a sit-in at the university over ads for topless clubs in the student newspaper, developed the feminist critique of pornography and lay the foundation for the challenge to liberal idealism. This challenge was important to the intensity of the movement because it examined the "materiality" of speech.

A shift in tactics by some feminists against pornography began to appear in 1983. After an unsuccessful attempt in Minneapolis, activists were able to pass an ordinance in Indianapolis, with the concurrence of the city council, that attacked pornography in a new way. The major aspects of the Indiana ordinance are its "findings" that "Pornography is a discriminatory practice based on sex which denies women equal opportunities in society" and a definition of pornography as "The graphic sexually explicit subordination of women, whether in pictures or in words." As Joel Grossman has argued, "New ordinances attempted to bypass th[e] morass of inscrutable constitutional doctrine by defining pornography as a form of sex discrimination."[35] Certainly, however, the shift in focus toward discrimination and oppression was more than an attempt to bypass a constitutional doctrine. As Donald Downs points out, "Such conflation would undermine the entire edifice of modern First Amendment doctrine and revolutionize the law of equality."[36]

In her opinion in *American Booksellers Association v. Hudnut*, the Indianapolis case, Judge Sarah Evans Barker distinguished the conventional meaning of pornography from the feminist position, taking account of the claims about violence and discrimination as a basis for striking down the ordinance.[37] This brought the new politics back to court, completing the circle of legal struggle but certainly not tying up the movement. By this stage in its evolution, the antipornography campaign had turned its rage toward lawmaking, and it had become a very different sort of movement.[38] The decisions in the courts did very little to address the feminist considerations that have been at the heart of the movement from its inception. The critical relationship of the feminist critique of pornography to the dominant conception of the First Amendment will keep the movement alive.

Dworkin—The Early Rage

Dworkin's University of Massachusetts speech[39] was repeated often on college campuses and was the basis for her remarks at the New York

University Law School forum on the subject. Her remarks begin by associating pornography with mankind's greatest inhumanities. "Slavery, rape, torture, extermination," to Dworkin, are "the substance of life for billions of human beings since the beginning of patriarchal time."[40] Male domination, she points out, has depended on "the law" as an instrument. "The oppressed are encapsulated by the culture, laws, and values of the oppressor. Their behaviors are controlled by laws and traditions based on their presumed inferiority." The effect, to which the movement struggle is addressed, is that women "have burned out of them the militant dignity on which all self-respect is based."[41]

The speech moves in the relentless fashion that exemplifies a social life constituted outside the mainstream. To Dworkin the violence of pornography is "always accompanied by cultural assault," which she describes as "propaganda disguised as principle or knowledge."[42] The result, as a characterization of a people under law, is the form of domination with which she began, women as "an enslaved population—the crop we harvest is children, the fields we work are houses." In this construction of America, "Women are forced into committing sexual acts with men that violate integrity because the universal religion—contempt for women—has as its first commandment that women exist purely as sexual fodder for men."[43]

In the fall of 1978, feminist radicals and law students gathered at New York University to discuss the emerging issue of "violent pornography." The discussion that follows is based on the report of that conference published in the *Review of Law and Social Change*.[44] An explanation of how the conference came about is given by Dean Norman Redlich in his opening remarks. The year before, a feminist student of his, Teresa Hommel, had prepared a discussion of "violent pornography," a new perspective, and the conference had grown out of this interaction.

Dworkin's speech, "Pornography: The New Terrorism," provides the key insights. The ideological practices it advocates are a focus on harm or danger to women and an undifferentiated view of pornography. Recently, activists have called attention to links between pornography and violence. In the context of the feminist case, the attempt to demonstrate that pornography causes violence is reminiscent of the "clear and present danger" logic in constitutional discourse. The logic that there are exceptions to the constitutional right to free speech when there is a possibility of physical harm is so characteristic of the First Amendment tradition that the feminist position appears to be derivative. To the extent that the antipornography movement is focused on harm, it links pornography with the First Amendment tradition.

Dworkin talks both about rape as terror and about the constitutional protection of freedom of expression. Law for her, and for the antipornography movement in its early stages, is a product of patriarchy and the ideological form the problem takes. Law is seen as an epiphenomenon, a rationalization so that "when pornographers are challenged by women," the legal establishment punishes the women "all the while ritualistically claiming to be the legal guardians of 'free speech.'"[45] Much of the substance of the ideology and its significance in social relations draw from the sort of popularly constituted ideology addressed by contemporary legal scholars to show the relevance of High Court materials in the culture.[46] The substance, in fact, is not state law but public mythology about law. This mythology is far more pervasive than law itself and often seems to reach out in various new directions.

The feminist case against pornography paid little attention to the explicit formulations of constitutional law, and in its early years, from about 1977 to 1982, the movement avoided seeking state-supported censorship. Instead, the movement stated a case against domination. Law was spoken by "the oppressor," and he was identified in terms of his perpetuation of "wrongs for his own pleasure or profit."[47] Yet, the movement's practices themselves and subsequent developments suggest that this avoidance may be taken as an influence of doctrine, a tacit recognition of the hegemony of free expression ideology. For years, the split between protected speech and pornography was far more powerful ideologically than what was found in actual legislation or court opinion. Feminists appealed to the mythical First Amendment with the emphasis on pure tolerance commonly placed there.

This popular ideology of free expression, rather than constitutional law on free expression, has been the primary influence on the politics of the feminist antipornography movement. While constitutional law depends on distinctions, movement practice abhorred them. While constitutional doctrine sets standards for determining what is obscene, the conventional public position does not permit a qualitative evaluation of speech. The result is an ideological practice unfamiliar with distinctions and evaluations and different in its impact from state law. While activists in San Francisco and San Diego invoked rights believed to be clearly applicable to the conditions gay men faced at the onset of the AIDS epidemic, this confidence in the specificity of law was not so characteristic of the feminist critique. The consciousness-raising and mobilization characteristic of the early antipornography campaign refused to define the movement in terms of the law. In fact, central to the movement was the denial that law had the doctrinal flexibility to cope with the situation. At the same time, however, there was increasing attention to rape and domestic violence from some of the same quarters within feminism.[48] The fabric of offense for the antipornography movement was all of a piece. Whether it be sexuality in an advertisement for diapers or the brutality of hard-core pornography, law was an agent of domestic terrorism. According to Dworkin, "The violence is always accompanied by cultural assault—propaganda disguised as principle. . . . This propaganda is the glove that covers the fist in any reign of terror."[49]

Books on pornography appearing in the wake of antipornography activism either had to deal with the activism directly or be held accountable. What Jean Elshtain called, somewhat dismissively, "the new porn wars"[50] had changed the intellectual terrain. Movement activists had reason to be concerned that their efforts were providing subject matter and employment for academics and writers, many of whom had little interest in changing the law on pornography. Two books by political scientists interested in constitutional protection for speech and its controversies, Downs's *The New Politics of Pornography* and Richard Randall's *Freedom and Taboo* are noteworthy for what they tell us about the rhetorical reaction to this form of law.[51] Randall's previous book was on censorship, and his interest in pornography goes back awhile. Downs published an important treatment of the free expression controversy in Skokie, Illinois, over Nazis marching in a predominately Jewish community. These are very different books in many respects, but both hold that pornography needs protection.

Randall focuses on the meaning of pornography, viewing sexuality through political theory and vice versa. In this work, obscenity is simply pornography proscribed by law. Randall distinguishes between pornography "as psychological element" and pornography "as social designation."[52] Although he does not refer to Dworkin or MacKinnon, Randall knows the practices of pornography and the law. He describes the modern massage parlor as the missing link in a "behavioral chain" that has prostitution at one end and masturbation at the other. Randall's locutions, like his framework, are familiar. His passage on gratification and perversity, "[n]o external liberty can completely free us from anxiety about the latter, and no social censorship is so complete that it can obliterate the seductive invitation of the former" calls Judge Learned Hand to mind, as does his concluding section, where the discussion of pornography is largely free of judicial terms.[53]

Moving from rights to social control, Randall wants to minimize the sense of inevitability surrounding what he calls "a libertarian obscenity doctrine."[54] This leads him to reassess the tests for obscenity and to ask whether "prurient interest" is simply another way of defining hard-core pornography. Randall holds that a fear of prurience is not a legitimate reason for proscribing pornography; it may not be what it does to the consumer that is the core of the issue, but rather the kind of world the consumer makes us all live in. Or, in Randall's words, pornography "is more straightforwardly understood as being offensive."[55] Similarly, in a nod to the feminist position, Randall finds that vigorous assertions of "the ideals of human sexual relations based on affection and mutual respect . . . may develop a keener sense of social bonds and values."[56] Because the psychosocial world of pornography is more central to his book than the laws on pornography, Randall is less wildly critical of feminists than many of his colleagues in the liberal constitutional law establishment. Indeed, the central focus on what pornography means to the culture makes the book more than simply a formalist liberal response to the threat of censorship. Still, Randall's idea of "the pornography within," like liberalism, dims the prospects for control.

Downs's book is about the radical feminist movement, what he calls the "new politics of pornography." It is a valuable chronicle of the history of the antipornography ordinances in Minneapolis and Indianapolis. The common presence of MacKinnon and Dworkin and the similar, but not precisely identical, conditions in these cities make for a very useful description of the politics of this important issue. We get the local civil liberties unions in each city, with their ties to New York. We see the pace and intensity of local politics, the work that goes into drafting legislation, and the excitement of the process as scores of lifetime politicians, and one novice activist, tackle the problem of pornography. This is not the simple decision of a prosecutor or a cop about what to shut down. It is not the relatively professional politics of zoning and other forms of regulation. It is the politics of local legislation.

Because the movement challenges the traditional left–right spectrum in the United States, attention from political scientists will no doubt expand our vocabulary even if it does not help the movement. Downs does not go as deeply into the history of the pornography issue as Randall does, and consequently his insight into what is new in the politics is less than it might be. That is, although he recognizes the traditional situation of obscenity doctrine in conservative logic, the failure to fully account for the transformative potential of the feminist emphasis on equality leads rather to the more traditional puzzle of radical feminists and conservatives, in Downs's unfortunate conception, "in bed together." His book is about political movements, and his perspective is still tied to the traditional continuum of left and right. While he is not as conscious of this as he might be, the book does help us see the limitations of this particular formulation.

Although Downs's project, being so deeply embroiled in the framework of contemporary legalisms, is not going to appeal to radical feminists, it is meant to draw from their critique. Ultimately, Downs wants to recast the obscenity laws by adding a "prong" to the *Miller* test. Downs proposes adding the issue of "violent obscenity" to the test which requires that obscenity must "appeal to prurient interest, give patent offense, and lack social value." For Downs, "Portrayals of murder, dismemberment, brutality, or violence in the context of obscene acts . . . would be subject to the designation of 'violent pornography.'"[57] Along with the Meese Commission, he would give the written word full protection, but he believes his concern for visual depictions of violence would help in the legitimate task of fostering norms of civility.

MacKinnon criticized Downs in the *New York Times* for not interviewing the antipornography side of the debate and for basing his book on "the favorite fantasies and fabrications" of pornography's defenders.[58] Although this is not technically true, as Downs did interview Charlee Hoyt and Naomi Scheman, supporters of the ordinance in Minneapolis, MacKinnon's point is important. Although Downs reads a great deal of movement literature as well as constitutional law, like most political scientists he takes the perspective of the state. He interviews officials and reads official reports. He does much more with this topic than most political scientists who teach constitutional law, but the perspective he offers is only one side in the debate. As a political scientist, I was pleased with the work that Downs did in bringing the movement into the discipline. But, characteristically, the vantage point is that of dominant interests, in this case the interests of the tolerance community.

Both books distinguish themselves in style from works of advocacy, but they are not really very different. The outcomes are predictable, and in many respects it looks like the framework was largely set up before the inquiry. Things were learned, certainly. Downs has some kind words for radical feminists. Randall is clearly discovering things as he writes about the relationship between anxiety and desire. The thing we are compelled to ask of Randall, given the feminist critique,[59] is what he can tell us about the construction of desire.[60] His insight into the relationship between sexuality and social life is impressive, and reading his book is like having a very fine conversation on a subject that makes face-to-face conversation difficult. On this issue, however, I believe his commitment to liberalism is hard to defend except on the terms liberalism has set for itself. Tolerance rings hollow in light of a number of issues we face, and certainly in light of the radical feminist position. Besides, tolerance as Randall carefully presents it leads to lack of responsibility. Liberals care very little about what the dirty old men are reading in the back room. The new politics of pornography no longer appreciates that kind of tolerance.

The same opportunity to fall back on the "deeper" discussion of political and psychological theory is not available for Downs because his book focuses squarely on the antipornography movement. The book is a systematic treatment of the movement that is valuable for its presentation of the chronology and legal developments. It was unpopular among feminists because, like most law studies in political science, it took the state's perspective. This is unfortunate because Downs is a sensitive and engaged political scientist who has taken the movement more seriously than most colleagues. But when one feels the radicalism of Dworkin in a book like *Intercourse* and wants to recoil from the notion that all men want to do is occupy, violate, invade, and colonize, Downs is little comfort. When I look for qualifiers ("some men,"—I say to my friends), he is also of little help. A book whose cover sports a plain brown wrapper being ripped back to expose a nude statue, and which begins with a quote from Nietzsche, praise from three libertarian male law professors, and acknowledgment to two others, makes "some men" a tougher claim to support.

The disciplining of academic networks is powerful. One wonders about the effect on tenure for one who might have stood against the accepted view of the First Amendment. Some of those who preach tolerance can barely control their own rage at the idea that we might distinguish the feminist position from that of the Nazis or the Klan. The ideology against which radical feminism is arrayed is very powerful indeed, and one finds it in the books mentioned here. It is in Downs's orientation to the state and established institutions. It is in the psychological conception of pornography as inevitable put forth by Randall. It is in the tantalizing covers and the sense that the new and the taboo in the titles will be of interest.

Carol Sternhell's review of Dworkin's books *Ice and Fire* and *Intercourse* suggests a relationship of law to liberal theory, and of liberal theory to consciousness. Sternhell characterizes *Intercourse* as making "a single argument (and it's a doozy)" that "Sexual intercourse should be abolished" because it is "the cause of many of women's problems." Dworkin herself put it this way: "Physically, the woman in intercourse is a space inhabited, a literal territory occupied literally: occupied even if there has been no resistance, no force; even if the occupied person said yes please, yes hurry, yes more." According to Sternhell, the weakness in Dworkin's contribution in both books "is its relentless portrait of Woman Victimized, victimized in essence, victimized as women, victimized without explanation." Dworkin's analysis concludes with the observation that "misogyny is real. Rape is real. Economic discrimination is real. The devaluation of anything female is real. The sexism that defines sex as intercourse (only) and defines intercourse as the male orgasm (only) is real." In saying this, Dworkin, according to Sternhell, "reduces real (I hope changeable) political arrangements to (unchanging) biological design." Sternhell sees Dworkin making the same mistake as a male acquaintance who explained the inevitability of male dominance by analogy to electricity: "The plug goes to the socket; the socket doesn't go to the plug." What she believes the man and Dworkin fail to see is that the analogy is true only when the socket is nailed to a wall, only when "a hole nailed and immobile is the only model of sexuality." Sternhell's countervailing rage is the kind the *New York Times* likes to make available to its readers. The rage and sarcasm are directed at a feminist argument in favor of the sophistication of seeing a world that changes. This is the law's and the society's response to feminist radicalism over pornography; both law and society can change. While true, this is no way to support a movement.

One need not overstate the contributions of French scholars such as Pierre Bourdieu and Michel Foucault to recognize their value in transcending a positivist conventionality.[61] Along with interpretive theorists like Stanley Fish, their approach suggests a new kind of sociology that is attentive to the social foundations of ideas. Sociology of law has long avoided careful inquiry into how communities mutually constitute

119

legal forms. Establishing a sociology of law that captures the forms of law in social relations requires attention to the communities mutually constituting the legal form. The interest is less in the demographics—or at least less centrally in those characteristics of race, sex, age, and national origin that we associate with demography—but more completely in the ideological, social, and material construction of alternative communities.

The alternative for rights movements is to go deeper into American practice, not further away—that is, to draw from the constitutive character of ordinary practice and to conceptualize it in a transformative fashion. This was evident in the work of Charles Reich, Angela Davis, and Malcolm X, and it is now evident in the work of Derrick Bell, Staunton Lynd, and MacKinnon. In her essay "Liberalism and the Death of Feminism," MacKinnon argues that the liberal reaction to the antipornography movement has split feminism.[62] She shows the hegemonic nature of liberalism and its inability to address female inequality in its analysis of social life. At the center of her position is the fact that women inhabit a society organized around men.

The antipornography movement's qualities, aspirations, and radical demands are significant. To those who listen and do not find the equation of law and domination puzzling, the perspective is a powerful force for change. As Dworkin points out, "Strategies of resistance are developing. . . . Some are rude and some are civil. . . . Some disregard male law, break it with militancy and pride."[63] In the end, the demands are not as dramatic as the challenge to law might suggest. Though highly rhetorical, Dworkin's challenge to law, that "[o]thers dare to demand that the law must protect women—even women—from brazen terrorization,"[64] is relatively basic. In fact, this is what law tells us it is doing. In many respects, the social relations built outside this claim are crucial to the sense it makes as a form of law.

Law, Class, and Consciousness

The constitutive approach demands some attention to the class and historical character of the antipornography movement. This means perhaps less attention to the constitutive operations of its ideology. In this respect, the movement has been predominately middle class and rooted in left-liberal feminism. Its movement roots are in the wave of feminism that emerged in the early 1970s and led to such legal transformations as

Roe v. Wade and the introduction of the Equal Rights Amendment. By the late 1970s, when the manifestations of the movement we have focused on become evident, some of those successes were looking less attractive and the careerism of liberal feminism was beginning to show itself to radicals. At this time, a fuller expression of feminist rage was evident in work such as Kathleen Barry's *Female Sexual Slavery*, which went well beyond the comfortable aspirations for equality associated with the Equal Rights Amendment or Simone de Beauvoir's *The Second Sex*.

As the activism conventionally associated with the 1960s began to wane, the antipornography movement was free to go beyond many of the social and ideological characteristics of earlier activists. Women Against Pornography has been influenced by the same counterideological critique that was posed by movement women against left males in the late 1960s—we won't make the coffee, we won't take the minutes— and which was influential at the onset of the women's movement. Thus, elements of left- and right-wing ideology became a part of how Dworkin presented herself, although a "strange bedfellows" angle was a much bigger deal for those outside than within the movement. In the movement, its contribution was at least in part an early impatience with the confines of the traditional political spectrum. Radical men were quite often the worst in their treatment of women.

The movement was closely tied to university and professional settings, with many of its major events situated in middle-class institutions like NYU Law School in the 1970s and Barnard College in 1982. As a key element of feminism, the antipornography movement was linked with other expressions of outrage at the treatment women get in the home, on campus, and in the streets.[65] As the movement's concerns have reached a larger audience, they have inevitably involved a more diverse population. In the battered women's struggle and in the extension of prosecution for rape, the incidents and the use of law have reached members of classes and racial groups that are underrepresented on college campuses.

The feminist case against pornography has subsequently been shaped by debates over what is pornographic, over free expression, and over the nature of legislation as a form of politics. In these considerations, the link between state law and ideology depends on the issue and the group considered. Throughout the debate, and perhaps particularly because it took place in a middle-class environment, the autonomy of the individual has been asserted quite often at the same time that the fallacies of that position—its failure to calculate the degrees of restraint present in the context of expression—have been rampant. As Fiss notes, "The exaltation of autonomy presupposes a world that no longer exists and that is beyond our capacity to recall—a world in which the principle political forum is the street corner. It ignores the manifold ways that the state participates in the construction of all things social and ignores the problem of private censorship."[66] The point is put another way in Jennifer Nedelsky's discussion of the inability of one variation of feminist spirituality to understand that the Bill of Rights is not simply a tool to be used by those outside government to resist, but a tool—indeed, just part of a whole tool box—which the government uses to keep the democratic polity in line.[67]

As the movement shifted toward reliance on the state in late 1983, harm—which liberals like William O. Douglas always contended was the key to justifying restraints on expression—played a central role. On the other hand, legal distinctions between forms of pornography continued to be resisted. When the city of Indianapolis defended its ordinance against violent pornography in court, it conceded that the ordinance would not withstand the standard measure of constitutional authority in *Miller v. California*. Subsequently, the federal courts agreed.

The movement, constituted by its opposition to free speech, could not have existed as it did without notions of law derived from the First Amendment. From the forum at the New York University Law School in the late 1970s, where a new movement against pornography was articulated, to the most recent debates in the left and feminist press, the tension between expression and censorship has been intense.[68] In a politics constituted in this way certain consequences are foreordained, such as who will join on what side and who will already be there. Traditionally, we might have expected feminists and pornographers to share an abhorrence for Victorian moralists, but this was not to be the case. Instead, counterintuitive alliances became part of the public spectacle and heightened attention to the issue of limits on expression.

Radicalism, of the sort that equated state law and terrorism, dominated the feminist case against pornography at the end of the 1970s, before the movement became involved with local ordinances and began to see law as an instrument of reform. To capture the antipornography movement before its turn to law as an instrument of change, I have focused on the 1978 conference at New York University, on Dworkin, and on the early expression of outrage from that period. But the movement continues to grow, in part because of the challenge it presents to conventional wisdom in law.

From its inception, the antipornography movement has been influenced by law. It has operated in a sphere audiences generally associate with legality, illegality, and the Constitution. The movement has also been influenced by one of the generation's most creative legal thinkers. For the last decade, in which the 1960s generation came to maturity in the academy, MacKinnon has been a challenging voice for a new jurisprudence. She has embodied clarity in thought about law at the same time that she has engaged us to think about legal practice in new ways. MacKinnon reshapes, and asks us to rethink, the contours of politics and social life. Such rethinking challenges our notions of mundane and avant-garde, public and private, left and right.

While offering some of the most radical conceptions of practice coming out of the legal academy, MacKinnon has turned the attention of radical activists toward city government and given many caught up in the destruction of property reason to care about the local administration of justice. In drawing attention to the harassment of women in the workplace, MacKinnon has demanded that we take equality and the administrative process seriously. As a theorist of liberal epistemology, particularly idealism in law, MacKinnon has also suggested how we might take ourselves and our work more seriously. Thus, MacKinnon has given feminism its share of legal victories. The cost has been an accusation of "essentialism" by a community concerned with her challenge to liberalism. This charge seems false given the range of her interests and the sensitivity of her political theory. In addition to her work on sexual harassment and pornography, she has developed the seeds of a new legal theory of rape, a conception of abortion engaging to those of us concerned about heavy emphasis on the rhetoric of choice, and a vivid description of the constitutional presumption that equality is less important than free speech. Thus, in law the issue of essentialism is most likely to arise because law on expression most dramatically represents liberal tolerance. The critique of essentialism has, in many respects, been a critique of the constitutive view of law. The limits of both critiques are political as well as epistemological.[69]

The unfavorable reception given by the liberal community to MacKinnon's most recent book, *Only Words*, is understandable in light of liberalism's deep devotion to its contemporary framework. While MacKinnon critiques the real consequences of First Amendment protection, her reviewers cannot conceptualize pornography as anything but another idea in the free marketplace. Calling attention to what pornography does, MacKinnon claims that abuse is protected as speech. Liberals are adamant that the government must champion objectivity, what MacKinnon terms the "'speech you hate' test: the more you disagree with content, the more important it becomes to protect it."[70] The most controversial review of her book demonstrated this perspective and sought to trump the radical feminist position with the traditional speech/action distinction. The images of rape in the review by Carlin Romano victimized and dehumanized MacKinnon in a way that only a male reviewer could.

The liberal free speech position has a problem with distinctions, that is, with a failure to distinguish. This failure is evident in an exchange of letters that took place in Amherst, Massachusetts in December 1989, after feminists broke into a newsstand that sold pornography and vandalized magazines. The exchange was between a local lawyer who was president of the Chamber of Commerce and a college professor supportive of the demonstrators. The newsstand manager was quoted in the *Springfield Union* as equating the feminists who vandalized her bookstore with the Klan (and the Gestapo). The president of the Chamber of Commerce said similar things. The professor responded,

> I've lived in Amherst for fifteen years and teach political science at the University. I think we would know if the KKK was in Amherst. We would know because of what they say and what they do.
>
> As a university professor I fear such puzzling associations because they do so little to advance discussion about either pornography or property. The KKK stands for racism and anti-semitism in America. It stands for brutal repression by a dominant majority. Feminism holds that women have been held back by male domination and it stands for liberation. Those ideas look different to me. Besides the KKK is a male organization.
>
> Amherst is home to many colleges and although we have our heads in the clouds lots of the time, we should be able to recognize the KKK if it comes to town. For one thing they are not going to be our sisters.

The vandalism in Amherst might be described as a violent act against the ACLU theory that says we cannot distinguish between radical feminism and the KKK. This is a theory introduced well into this century and nurtured to extremes in the last decade. My favorite example is Fred Friendly and Martha Elliott's *That Delicate Balance*, a book produced for the television series of the same name, which describes free speech doctrine as "protecting the thought that we hate."

When it fails to distinguish, the ACLU theory denigrates the substantive values of free expression. These are values won in struggle against repression by governments. The value of free expression ought to encourage us to be impatient with those who cannot distinguish between constitutionally protected speech and pornography.

In addition to problems with distinctions, antipornography activism poses fundamental challenges to other aspects of liberalism. The militancy of the movement echoes the outrage of John Brown and the succeeding waves of women's liberation. In all of this, liberalism stands in opposition to the focus and the intensity of the movement. This is evident in the dramatic quality of the coverage of the antipornography vandalism at the Amherst newsstand. It is rare that twenty women from the university constitute a gang, but that was how the women were described. There is no question that women fighting back is news. The vandalism came between murders in Montreal, Canada (done by a man who shouted that feminists had taken too many liberties), and the murder of a female University of Massachusetts student in the local mall parking lot. For those of us who worked at the university all these events had a great impact.

The sanctimonious invocation of the Bill of Rights and freedom of speech by the local Chamber of Commerce president emphasized violence. He condemned the vandalism at the newsroom as "a violent act against freedom of speech." Such theories do not advance the discussion about pornography or property, but rather focus on the process. The conventional view of free speech is puzzling because in most of our life we are taught that what people stand for will determine their place in the community or at least in history. When we learn to distinguish between the Sons of Liberty and George III, the righteousness of the American cause becomes the determining factor and violence a cause for celebration. In calling attention to the assertion that the end cannot justify the means, we confront one of the cornerstones of the ACLU position. The ACLU, one of the groups that claims the end cannot justify the means, has sometimes tried to show that the end is irrelevant. In this context, a value means something and a robust commitment to freedom of expression does not preclude action against pornography.

Radical feminists have been criticized for focusing too narrowly on pornography as a site of feminist struggle.[71] Although the connection between pornography and violence against women is central to the radical argument, some activists doubt that the pornography issue has the capacity to reach out to battered women. From my vantage point, the antipornography movement is one of the most compelling challenges to liberal legalism in existence. The response to strategic concerns ought to be that we need to avoid the many traps of liberalism. There is no problem with focused activism. The demand for "evidence" in this case is a denial of experience.

One of the strengths of the antipornography movement is its challenge to the presumptions of liberalism and the related limits posed for a full understanding of the nature of law. Radical feminism in general, and the movement against pornography in particular, are frontal attacks on liberalism. The frontal quarter to which the attack is often directed makes some men nervous. Specifically, the intensity of the critique of liberal jurisprudence has been very unsettling to the men and women of the civil liberties bar.[72] With regard to the implications of positive theories of law, there must be a place for focused attention that does not accept the premises of state power. Indeed, radical feminism is threatening because of its failure to accept the hegemony of the legal system, not because it sometimes breaks the law.

Given the nature of middle-class politics and politics closely tied to institutions such as universities or to professional communities, the antipornography movement does face challenges to the building of coalitions. But, equally important, the movement faces the challenge of liberalism in developing coalitions with other radical movements. Although central to the pornography issue, the influence of prevailing ideology around speech has been difficult to demonstrate. As noted earlier in the chapter, the Supreme Court has given rise to a "Free Speech Tradition."[73] But it is the vernacular understanding of freedom that has been the terrain for feminist critiques of pornography. Paradoxically, the everyday variety of free speech right is a much less legally sound but, at least among the middle class, a more prevalent conception than what the Supreme Court offers. As Fiss concluded, "Some justices, such as Black and Douglas, made a reputation for themselves by espousing an absolutist position on free speech: No regulation means no regulation."[74] But this has never been a position embraced by the Supreme Court.[75] The Court has always found contrary positions worthy of some attention. The contemporary feminist case against pornography unfolds on this legal and conceptual terrain, which is constituted by the tradition of constitutional thought about the relationship between the First Amendment and obscene or pornographic material.

Many activists in the struggles on the left, such as gay liberation, black and Chicano nationalism, the women's movement, welfare rights, and environmentalism, come out of liberalism. Many participants call themselves liberal because they believe it puts them on the side of social justice and humanity. In some respects they are right. There appears to be a link between these interests and the receptivity to social change associated with liberalism. This receptivity to change at the margins is a feature of liberalism, indeed it is a feature of power in America that makes the system resistant to fundamental change. Liberalism is essential to the system of domination responsible for the conditions of gross inequality that surround us in America. Radical feminism is closer to the tradition of John Brown than Abe Lincoln, closer to Susan B. Anthony than Eleanor Roosevelt, and closer to Malcolm X than Martin Luther King. But radicalism does not deny the appeal of both approaches, whereas liberalism does.

The constitutive approach demands more attention to the class and historical character of belief. In this respect, my sample is the antipornography movement in and around the academy, particularly my own community in what we call the "Pioneer Valley" north of Springfield, Massachusetts, and almost to the Vermont border. The movement here is rooted in the feminism of the "second wave" but reflects developments resulting from twenty years of feminist practice. In this community, the kinds of feminist politics were varied enough to produce subgroups with distinctive identities and political agendas within the larger domain of equality for women. Radical feminism was uncompromising and in many respects shocking to more traditional forms.

In Western Massachusetts, up and down the valley that produced Shay's Rebellion in 1787, radical feminists have created a culture of resistance, one manifestation of which is the antipornography movement. There are many ways to understand this culture. One is to examine lesbian communities and what Janice Raymond calls "GYN/affection."[76] Another is to look to the work of women such as Mary Daly. In addressing "lust," Daly says,

> On the one side, lust and pure lust Name the deadly dispassion that prevails in patriarchy, the life-hating lechery that rapes and kills the objects of its obsession/aggression. Indeed, the usual meaning of lust within the lecherous state of patriarchy is well-known. It means sexual desire of a violent, self-indulgent, character, lechery, lasciviousness. Phallic lust, violent and self-indulgent, levels all life, dismembering spirit/matter, attempting annihilation.[77]

With stories like this and others,[78] collective households, distinctive entertainment, services, and forms of struggle, the community has the cultural presence to support its vision of the law.

While law's "innocence" often covers its responsibility for pain, the most telling critical work has brought domination, pain, law, and society together again. Millett's extraordinary image of the brutality that accompanies oppression calls our attention to one of the most fundamental and little understood truths in American politics—the silence of power. The movements against domestic violence and rape share an ideological structure with the antipornography movement. The struggle is over what women and sexuality are to be.[79] Those who would remain within existing social relations allow law its conventional innocence. Those who would radically change those relations are outraged at law's complicity. Because radical feminism teaches that pornography is not speech but violence, that violence against women is not a "concern" but a crime, and that resistance is not disobedience but self-defense, it is an extraordinary movement. Radicalism in this sense is an explosive foundation for equality; instrumentalism is not.

The radical feminism of MacKinnon and Dworkin has been a challenging voice for a new jurisprudence. They embody clarity in thought about law and engage us to think about legal practice in new ways, reshaping the contours of politics and social life. Although Downs noted that their position on equality might "undermine the entire edifice of modern First Amendment doctrine and revolutionize the law of equality,"[80] the early challenge meant to do even more. Radical feminists challenged law as it constituted the mundane and the avant-garde, the public and the private, the left and the right. While offering very radical conceptions of practice, the movement is democratic in its reconstitution of a political community, and ultimately in its expression of faith in local government. And, because it contains a powerful critique of liberal epistemology, particularly idealism in law, the movement suggests how we might take law more seriously.

The Constitution of Interests
Rethinking Legalism

Chapter 6

Representation as power and power as representation are a sacrament in image and a "movement" in language where, exchanging their effects, the dazzling gaze and the admiring reading consume the radiant body of the monarch.

—Louis Marin,
Portrait of the King

Americans often look too hard for law, and, consequently, we tend to look past it. We expect laws to be tucked away in the inner offices of law firms, in difficult-to-access law libraries, or in obscure professional practices. But law also hides beneath our noses, in social and cultural practices. This law that we don't notice is powerful. As part of the landscape, legal practices determine whose field the farmer plows—his own or that of another—or, just as inconspicuously, mark the boundaries of suburban plots and urban buildings. This legal landscape features zones of pornography, where the movie ratings dip to the bottom of the alphabet, and metropolitan ghettos with black at the center and white at the periphery. Even when we don't notice the law we are in the landscape.

More quiet than the official legal contexts that appear in the chronicles of public life—a trial, a hearing, an execution—features such as rights, realism, remedies, and rage form the legal landscape for various movement activists. Rights are familiar. The other forms begin to complete the picture. In the preceding chapters, we looked at some of these practices and tried to make them "problematic." Sexuality, positivism, disputing, and pornography, as political practices, are linked to distinctive legal forms that constitute participation in the political process. These forms, like the practice of rights, are ways to do things. Legal forms in the practices of distinct communities, such as gays in California appealing to constitutional rights or law professors in Cambridge denying the utility of rights, frame political interests. These legal frames constitute the identities, guide the aspirations, and fuel the interests that define politics in a legal order.

Political interests and the activity that results from them challenge us in the search for law's role in political action. Movement practice in general and these forms in particular are self-conscious. Because they exist in practice, the forms are taken for granted only in a contingent sense, and not in the way that the authority of a stop sign is. The tolerance of drunk driving before mothers organized against it and the progressive nature of free speech before feminists questioned it were both givens that mutated under the gaze of politics. Instrumental strategies appear unfettered. The movement to destroy pornography has been pretty clear about what it wants. The attention we pay to interests—to whether or not they will be satisfied—distracts us from the forms that constitute them, and the self-consciousness of movements, by drawing attention from legal construction, makes that construction particularly significant. This chapter examines legal form as an influence in politics and as a contribution to legal theory.

Intellectuals and Politics

When entrepreneurs and activists of the gay rights movement joined with civil libertarians to oppose closing the baths in San Francisco, this was not a surprising alliance, but an expression of the central role rights—and rights activists—have played in gay life for the last twenty-five years. Gay men in the mid-1980s struggling against AIDS, fear of AIDS, and hostile institutions, saw, in many instances, more promise in law than would be found among some law professors. While bathhouse owners and activists displayed a faith in law as they tried to keep the baths open, the critical legal studies (CLS) movement professed a loss of faith in law. These beliefs about law and what it can do form relationships "in law". The relationships formed to keep the baths open in the early years of the epidemic differed from those that came out of later protests. Relationships that formed deeper in the despair of the epidemic, such as ACT-UP and Queer Nation, were more akin to the radicalism of the Women Against Pornography.

Key players in these developments are the intellectuals who interpret politics with reference to imagined social and cultural possibilities. Various social theorists have tried to situate the ideologies of activists in the social context. In his essay "The Intellectuals," Antonio Gramsci explored the relationship between those who produce ideas and the social classes they serve. He proposed that the "notion of 'the intellectuals' as a distinct social category independent of class is a myth." By intellectuals, Gramsci does not mean simply a group that thinks. He acknowledges that "[a]ll men are potentially intellectuals in the sense of having an intellect and using it" and explores the social uses to which the intellect is put. He divides those who are intellectuals by social function into two groups, the Traditional (or professional) and the Organic. This latter group he calls "the thinking and organizing element of a particular fundamental social class."[1] Lawyers who become involved in fashioning group interests are this sort of intellectual.[2] So are many political activists.

The link between legal form and political activity arises from the way intellectuals articulate the structures of political action. The constitutive quality of law draws intellectuals in. The relations of power, economic and political, are shaped by the intellectuals. Intellectuals interpret law to social movements. Gay activist lawyers, by asserting rights, promise protection while constituting the movement as victims.[3] In doing this, they give law a rhetorical quality that helps to link certain individuals with the struggle and not others. Such is the case with Andrea Dworkin's critique of intercourse, which problematizes traditional sexual relations. In the same movement, Catharine MacKinnon has configured law around new strategies and techniques. In the CLS movement, activist-scholar Duncan Kennedy gave his authority (in this case both personal and institutional) to the doctrine of indeterminacy associated with the critical form in contemporary realism. Stanley Fish, the Milton scholar and theorist of law and literature associated with critical jurisprudence, added his contentious commitment to reason as a gloss on various movements. Since contentious reason is a source of power, Fish has become a star among legal intellectuals.[4]

Academic inquiry elevates some forms, privileging them relative to others, at the same time that it appears to have little political significance.

In the 1950s, a generation of political scientists produced studies that circumscribed mass politics. *Communism, Conformity and Civil Liberties* by Samuel Stouffer was the interpretive key to the civil rights movement and the Vietnam War for a large group of scholars. This study of attitudes influenced civil liberties scholarship after World War II by characterizing democracy and its institutions as likely to be nurtured by elites and threatened by the "masses" of ordinary people, or, in the language of the studies, "the mass public." This research undercut the political authority of the public in matters of fundamental rights. The public was a threat because it had the wrong "opinions." Asked how they felt on matters of policy, ordinary people were seldom a source of knowledge or law. They were marginalized in favor of elites, whose training as doctors in matters of abortion, or lawyers and judges in matters of free expression, gave them special authority.[5]

In attitude studies, the "public" is a political construction that supports a particular view of law. Although not produced by lawyers, this view manifests itself in the bar's interests and in the implications of a marginalized mass public for the institutional life of the law. By valuing experts, whether for their knowledge or opinion, the studies support an orientation to courts. These were the institutions sensitive to fundamental rights and freedoms. In this way, the attitude studies helped to solidify the legal form in matters of civil rights and liberty. The Stouffer study supported values associated with freedom, the marketplace, and the middle class. Other, more progressive values, like equality, which are connected in Western culture to claims of social justice and workers movements, receive less attention. This was accompanied by a turn toward political rights and away from economic rights. This shift in legal orientation is linked to courts through the "Double Standard" in constitutional jurisprudence. Part of constitutional law for the last fifty years, the "Double Standard" justifies judicial review where the political process appears not to be working properly. Subtly, the subject of rights became situated with respect to class, with bad attitudes taking the place of education and personal hygiene[6] as features distinguishing the classes.

By the mid-twentieth century, the ideology of popular intolerance was affecting movement strategies. The civil rights movement, for instance, supported the idea that ordinary folks, at least southern white ones, were a threat to racial progress. In the United States during the late 1960s, from the rednecked supporters of the Ku Klux Klan as a picture of southern bigotry to public initiatives and referenda against fair housing,[7] there was reason to suspect the attitudes held by the American people on issues of equal rights and civil liberties. The Stouffer study and its progeny contributed to the specter of ordinary people threatening basic liberties. By implication, popular institutions, like legislatures, especially state legislatures, were not to be trusted. Learned Hand—the author of the idea that the people had to defend liberty, not the courts—notwithstanding, the late 1950s in America ushered in a period in which only the courts could be trusted with the preservation of rights.

The consequences for gay rights are direct and powerful. The movement was based on the specter of widespread homophobia, and the law was seen as a protective barrier against discrimination. In spite of the role of law in criminalizing homosexual relations and the police repression at the Stonewall Bar itself, the post-Stonewall response, which extended to the bathhouse closings, linked homosexual interests to legal claims in the form of civil rights protection. Realism in law schools tended to leave institutional elitism intact, while informalism turned cynicism about the power of law on its head. With the radical feminist antipornography movement, the perception that the public is an illiberal mass comes full circle. That is, fear of mass politics reinforces the idea that radical opposition to law is reactionary.[8]

Academic intellectuals have had a great deal to say about social movements. The frameworks in sociology and political science are varied and discussion of the appropriate form of social science inquiry into movement politics continues to be lively.[9] For the most part, the concern of movement scholars is simply not for the role of law or legal institutions in the lives of activists. Most of the literature on collective action and the choice to participate in social movements does not amount to the kind of state-centered orientation suggested by Gramsci. In fact, the most common framework extrapolates from a model of individuals characterizing groups on the basis of self-interested individual choice. This framework contributes to the social formulation of liberal institutions, and by isolating individuals and leaving the state unexamined it serves to maintain the hegemony Gramsci revealed.

An exception to this general orientation is the work of Joseph Gusfield and his colleagues working on "new" social movements.[10] Gusfield's own work brought the symbolic dimensions of struggle to the fore to reveal the interweaving of law and politics. In the new social movements literature, scholars have reconceptualized collective action in response to emerging forms of movement practice—such as the peace movement, student movements, anti–nuclear energy protests, minority nationalism, gay rights, animal rights, religious fundamentalism, and women's rights—that seem to lead inexorably to issues of identity.[11] I have suggested in the preceding chapters that movement analysis of identity shows how organization around a form of law influences social relations. The constitutive dimension of law operates on these relations as identities. Thus the gay or radical feminist activist who identifies with the movement and sees him or herself in movement terms is gay or radical at least in part because of law. This may not be as new as some new social movement theorists argue,[12] since there were identity dimensions to the political parties of the nineteenth century, and religious movements like Mormonism are certainly constitutive of identity. It is, nevertheless, a key feature in the constitution of interests.

In addition to this work, Paul Burstein has recently turned his attention to law,[13] and Michael McCann, in *Rights at Work: Pay Equity Reform and the Politics of Legal Mobilization*,[14] has pushed the constitutive frame as an elaboration of Stuart Scheingold's "Myth of Rights."[15] McCann's important book begins with movements, and works, as he says, from the bottom up. It explicitly looks for the influence of law in movement practice and finds law operating much as Scheingold described two decades ago. Drawing on interviews with scores of activists involved in pay equity reform, McCann found law's "most obvious positive contribution" was in movement building. That is, early favorable decisions were used by organizers to mobilize the rank and file.[16] Lawyers were involved here, in ways similar to the civil rights movement,[17] but labor activists played a relatively larger role and held out the promise of the law in order to gain support for demands that in many cases won concessions without the completion of litigation. As McCann puts it, the Supreme Court's *Gunther* ruling[18] and the district court's ruling in AFSCME v. *State of Washington*[19] "cast a long shadow that significantly refigured relations between women workers and employers."[20] Drawing on sociolegal scholarship of the last twenty years, McCann develops and presents this observation in a sophisticated fashion. For instance, he reminds us that law was a constraint as well as an opportunity. "The logics of official antidiscrimination law," he points out, "were not easily refashioned to convey the activists' structural account of systemic wage discrimination."[21] In other words, even at its height the legal opportunity could only be employed within a liberal framework with private property and individual workers at its core.

While technically a rights struggle in the classic sense, the use of rights in pay equity cases, as depicted by McCann, draws attention to social relations in a manner that enables us to extrapolate the constitution of interests to contexts that are not rights based. I share with McCann a belief in the importance of context and believe further that we must read law in the places where movements operate. In each of the movements discussed in this book, intellectuals have articulated a form of law based on relevant institutional life and movement opportunity. In the case of gays defending the baths, the rights claim traces its lineage to the English nobles who demanded autonomy and produced the Magna Carta. In the case of lawyers on the American Bar Association's Committee on Alternative Dispute Resolution, the claims for informalism draw on reformist traditions that also have a noble past. Professors at the Harvard Program on Negotiation depict law by minimizing the role of lawyers and highlighting the principles of informality against a background of distinctly evil traditional legal processes. Here, the mobilization is against law and in opposition to rights.

In addition to the academic intellectual, movements have organic theorists who work to adapt the strategies and maxims of the specific cases to the tenets of the movement and the inclinations of the participants. Sandra Goodman, an antipornography activist in Amherst, has expressed with great insight the challenges to individual women as the movement evolved into a phase unfamiliar to most—that of illegal action. In a statement read to the judge at her trial she said, "This trial is not the struggle that we wish to concentrate on." Similarly, gay rights activists and bathhouse owners situated their claims so as to meet the challenge of keeping bathhouses open in a way that would strengthen rather than debilitate their movement. The institutional advantages of law school movements and alternative dispute resolution (ADR) tie their intermediate strategists more directly to the state. Because both have institutional positions from which to work, intellectuals associated with these movements are able to pursue careers at the same time that they work in the movement. The significance of institutionalization in this form is its link to the state. This link is what makes us think that CLS, law and economics, and ADR lack the tension with established power that we expect of critical or insurgent political movements.

Politics imbricated with law raises issues as to what we call politics[22] and what we call law. Gramsci described law in Italy as ascending while religion diminished in importance. He saw law residing somewhere between science and religion as an instrument of state power, and the state as "an educator" and as "an instrument of rationalization."[23] In order to understand law's function, Gramsci held that law had to be freed from transcendent abstractions and placed in context. These requirements take us, even here near the end of this work, into struggles over politics and epistemology. Conventional discourse makes it particularly hard to get beneath the claims and practices of political movements. The struggles we have with abstractions—ideas about reality beyond convention—are themselves a facet of state power.

Much of the language of class struggle and hegemony is unfamiliar and hence unappealing to Americans. This may account for the enthusiastic reception of Michel Foucault's thesis that contemporary society had developed systems of authority that were beyond law.[24] Yet, class analysis goes back a hundred years, to before the liberal state emerged in its present form with its more subtle rationalizations. The battles of the nineteenth century drew the lines of economic determinism. They related the social to the biological and worked out the scientific foundations of both. For modern social science, the project of social research shows how society produces itself. This involves relating the spontaneous to the rigid by looking at movements to see the law. For example, careers and professional agendas drive the ADR movement. Although ADR has grass-roots rhetoric, and some grass-roots support, the bar associations and the judicial bureaucracy generate interest in the movement and the foundations facilitate its development with their largesse. Here, a rhetoric is appropriated and powerful institutions identify themselves with the common man or woman. The social function of the ADR movement may well be to make things happen without changing class or social relations. The movement against pornography, on the other hand, is truly radical. It exists in opposition to traditional interests, and while it uses law as a vehicle, it does so in an oppositional way.

Some scholars have tried to account for the social relations by which we organize interests. Alain Touraine, who bucked the post-structural trend, is concerned with the "glue" of social relations, the elements of society that hold it together. For Touraine, structure is not something that exists independent of people's activity but is "the property of an activity."[25] Touraine breaks down the rigid structure of interests "outside" the state. Thus, the social structure is the structure of how a group moves, and public life becomes a drama of social action and social relations. In the technical language of this framework, society consists of hierarchized systems of action with at least two components: "historicity," society's capacity to produce the models by which it functions; and "class relations," the processes through which these models become social practices.[26] These concerns reflect the politics of law presented here with reference to legal forms and moving from instrumental to constitutive law.

For American social theory about law, demonstrating the principles in constitutive law began with the early work of CLS scholars. In the late 1970s, the challenge was to show that law was more than words on a page or pronouncements from on high. One response came from labor historian Karl Klare. Drawing from Douglas Hay's *Albion's Fatal Tree* and from his own work, "The Judicial Deradicalization of the Wagner Act," Klare proposed looking at law-making as *praxis*.[27] This picture, merely outlined by Klare, featured prominently in my discussion of legal form in chapter 1. The challenge to fill it in, however, was never taken up by CLS because the movement turned toward realism. Thus, CLS has made it difficult to articulate the role of law in the constitution of interests. Yet, from the beginning of the Enlightenment, law has been in movements and in practice—in lawyers' offices, in the language of equality, in the Iran-Contra hearings, and in contemporary feminism. It has been part of us all along, even as intellectuals, professional and organic, have told us law is theirs.

137

Positivism's Hierarchies

While the public's experience of constitutional rights should be the natural foundation for rights in a democratic system, the dominant classes are very nervous about the public's views on fundamental rights. Social research on attitudes is at the core of this anxiety. Thoughtful people, often progressive people, agonize over what to do about the reactionary attitudes of the working class. They point out a working-class propensity to see welfare as an enemy standing against obvious class interests. The study of law's constitutive force recognizes links between social knowledge and rights as a subject of research, while attitude studies leave the social and cultural sources of feelings unexamined. What people know with reference to legal forms is a source of law. To the extent that welfare is constructed as charity, it becomes a form of wealth. This construction of wealth determines that a salary check paid out, whether from a public or private source, is "mine" while payments from the welfare department are not.[28]

In the United States, the behavioral turn, quantitative methods, and a framework of attitudes had already begun to define the context for civil liberties when the Stouffer study came out. Stouffer's 1954 survey was based on two public opinion polls, one by Gallup and the other by the National Opinion Research Center at the University of Chicago.[29] Stouffer's work is presented as scholarship on people, or "A Cross-section of the Nation." The study has its sources in the intellectual ferment of the period, when the new behavioral science entered the academy, accompanied by a wave of fear about fascism and communism. By 1955, work such as T. W. Adorno's *The Authoritarian Personality*, and the general interest in opinion research, provided the conceptual framework for Stouffer's study. This framework, which recognized the masses as a threat, employed a formulation of opinion or "attitude" research, a way of looking at the world that was oriented toward feelings, the registration of affect, and an accounting of opinion.[30] Forty years after it was written, Stouffer's book provides insight into the construction of mass publics as threatening to fundamental rights. Indeed, the impact of this work and subsequent survey research such as *The American Voter* on political science was to emphasize prediction of a public's propensity to choose on a narrow range of issues.

Stouffer compares elites and masses, directly addressing the political and legal aspects of class.[31] Community leaders become the basis for comparison on matters of toleration. Stouffer describes the middle and working classes as reactionary on civil liberties. Although hopeful that the media and opinion leaders will spread the message of tolerance,[32] he also describes the authoritarian tendencies of older Americans, those with little education, southerners, farmers, and clerical workers, and compares this to the tolerance of college-educated, northern, urban managers. Much of the scholarly work that followed Stouffer operated from within this framework and presented few challenges to his perspective.[33] This is true of the classics of the early 1960s[34] and subsequent work that found an elevated standard of civil liberties in elites as opposed to masses.[35] Reprinting Stouffer's tables in a 1985 article, James L. Gibson and Richard D. Bingham minimize the hysteria of Stouffer's time and hold that the study, put in their framework, "clearly demonstrates the tension between majority rule and democracy."[36]

The critique offered by John Sullivan, James Piereson, and George Marcus, altered the elite/mass dichotomy, substituting a model of democratic decision. These scholars questioned the link between tolerance and democracy characteristic of the Stouffer study and subsequent work in the same tradition.[37] They concluded that the perceived greater tolerance among those who participate in politics and are better educated is related to other factors, and hence "spurious."[38] For them, economic insecurity and a combination of low self-esteem and dogmatism are class based and strongly related to intolerance. Building on these critiques and addressing some of their limits, Jennifer Hochschild's work on equality breaks from traditional attitude research by addressing "beliefs about distributive justice," that is, why Americans do not demand redistribution of wealth. In addition, she addresses the ideological worlds we inhabit but remains attentive to social scientific concerns for validity (in her sample of rich and poor) and the qualities of the lives her respondents lead. Despite these advances, the unit of her analysis is still the individual, presented through the voices of the respondents, and the work is framed in terms of attitudes about policy. Nevertheless, Hochschild reveals the highly developed ideologies concerning capitalism, down to the acceptance of inheritance and the laziness in the rich.[39] People do not like the tax structure, yet they are reluctant to soak the rich. Even at this level of sophistication we can see the elitism in the attitude perspective. When the author points out "confusion" among her respondents,[40] which denigrates their opinions, she is supporting a hierarchy.

One way to transcend the subjectivity that maintains the silences on institutional power is to describe the cultures of power—the law schools, the judicial conferences, the foundations and their agendas. In critical scholarship, for instance, Lance Bennett has suggested drawing more sophisticated research on public values from welfare studies. He notes examples where detailed ethnographic and sociological work portrays the character of laws and institutions governing the poor. In the case of work on welfare, the attention to culture and practice is meant to delineate the institutional nature of legal entitlement.[41] Community power studies, which come from a different intellectual (and political) tradition than the attitude work, have drawn attention to the social relations and material conditions within which the lives of the poor are led. Here, knowledge rather than attitude determines value. In the attention to context, work such as J. Anthony Lukas's *Common Ground* (1985), which looks at the school busing controversy in Boston, Mark E. Kann's *Middle Class Radicalism in Santa Monica* (1986), about rent control and development issues, and Murray Levin's

139

Talk Radio (1987) reveal where class as material condition, access to power, and perception of what is "given" fit into the construction of expectation and the calculus of right.[42] These studies use cultural materials (e.g., the things people say about their lives) and approach them with the sensitivity to the relevance of conceptual and ideological constructions associated with political theory. These materials may also provide a reliable foundation for understanding legal forms. They provide some insight into civil liberties in general, and particularly rich descriptions of property rights as a phenomena in the community. In these cases, the constraints on choice become more evident than the choice that we know as "attitude."

Transcending an instrumental conception of interest is a key to uncovering the politics of form. In his critique of group theory in political science, Mark Kesselman argues that David Truman reduces interests to "subjective attitudes and preferences." Truman, Kesselman observes, failed to "analyze the contingent relationship between subjective preferences and objective interests."[43] Others have made that relationship more central. For instance, Grant McConnell, in *The Decline of Agrarian Democracy*, focused on structural change in the United States through "an objective standard to judge interests," which he suggests made problematic "the relationship between interest and interest group."[44] Over the last generation, public knowledge has been seen increasingly as a source of law in a sociologically sophisticated sense that resides in practice.

Social practices in which legal forms are based are more fundamental than attitude, and they have a claim to authority in matters of fundamental rights. This claim is based on both a common-law tradition that has not yet died out of American practice, and a sociopolitical theory that places popular knowledge at the center of political authority. Constitutional scholars are familiar with the "suspect classifications" of equal protection doctrine (race, sex, alienage, and illegitimacy), the unprotected speech of the First Amendment decisions (obscenity, libel, fighting words), the fundamentals of due process (generally the procedural protection of the Bill of Rights), and the claims to property recognized by the Constitution (ones where there is a legitimate expectation or interest). At this level, there is a connection between judicial claims and public understanding. The public not only receives the distinctions, it is sometimes their source. The impediment, however, is institutional.

Institutional Hegemony

The project on legal formations in politics brings to light the implications of constitutive forms like right, realism, remedy, and rage. By identifying the way movements understand law we may better interpret the hidden forces of hierarchy in liberal capitalist states as they are found in the practice of realism in law schools, in the fear of homosexuality linked to the AIDS epidemic, in the emergence of radical feminism, and in the appeal to the middle ground at the heart of ADR. Having seen how forms of law determine the practice of politics by delineating the possible, we can return to a part of politics too easily overlooked, that is, institutions. Institutions are the most highly conventional and rigid legal form. The institutional delineation of political life is not just in the parameters outside which we cannot reach—the city halls we can't fight or the taxes that are said to be as inevitable as death. More significantly, institutions are in the parameters of the possible that operate to construct politics at its inception by influencing how people bind themselves in movements.

Some studies of politics in which state power takes a constitutive form demonstrate its range and relevance, even if they do not always use the language of constitutive forms. As part of the effort in political science research to "bring the State back in,"[45] scholars have examined the role of state elites in forming working-class consciousness.[46] This move from a "society-centered" explanation for class interests to the state is little known in law studies. As an endeavor that has trouble getting out of the state's own doctrinal constructions, the American study of law seems far removed from a politics explained in terms of "capitalist industrialization."[47] Yet, interest-group scholarship is a manifestation of elites forming working-class consciousness. As interests, the expressions of group needs are sanitized so that they do not look like class or purely economic interests.[48] This is the framework replicated by political science work on law.

In his study of American governmental processes, *Building the New American State*, Stephen Skowronek also makes the state more complex.[49] His construction here is theoretical, historical, and comparative. His subsequent work on the American presidency added the idiosyncrasies of personality and circumstance.[50] Discrete dynamics "of men and their times" are pronounced; general dynamics that define institutions "in time" are obscured. The modern presidency is now understood to change in different contexts, such as international relationships as compared to domestic relationships. The presidency in practice is an expression of Franklin D. Roosevelt and the establishment of the Executive Office in 1939.[51] Skowronek's idea that only the emergent relations matter, and that the submerged do not, misses some of the deeper constitutive dimensions of law, such as constitutional considerations. His conception is that neither the modern nor the constitutional construction of presidential history directly addresses the presidency as an institution operating in a political order, or the president as an actor in political time. In order to focus on institutions, one does not need to obviate the powers of law. One only needs more sophisticated tools for understanding law than those we take from conventional practice.

The Cult of the Court, which I wrote in 1987, focused on the ways reverence for the Supreme Court structures political action in the United States.[52] While institutions reveal the structures of politics imposed by forms of law, some traditional candidates for consideration in the analysis of structures—race, sex, and class (or economic condition)—seem not to be "legal" at all. The constitutive view of law, however, holds that they are. America has moved from a cult of the robe, with its emphasis on special mysteries linked to medieval forms and archaic rituals, to the bureaucratic forms of institution and hierarchy, which constitute a cult of the court. This shift permeates American politics and is changing the way law maintains its empire.

The effect of "entrenchment," or the creation of a Charter of Rights for Canada to supplant an act of the British Parliament as the fundamental organizing institution, has called Canadian scholars to look closely at the impact of judicial institutions on politics. One aspect in the creation of a fundamental legal process with judges and appellate litigation at its center is its effect on the arrangement of powers between different levels of the government in Canada. The effect of the process of entrenchment and the corollary elevation of judges has been to centralize the development of fundamental legal conceptions.[53] Judy Fudge points out that "the entrenchment of a justiciable charter of rights in the Canadian Constitution was not a response to the demands of popular struggle, but was instead an essential element in the central government's response to a popular struggle."[54] Fudge also shows how, in the realm of feminist demands, the Charter has affected political discourse. Feminists in Canada mobilized to include language in the Charter that would protect sex equality. They also provided that Section 28, which guaranteed that the rights and freedoms under the Charter applied equally to women and men, would not be subject to legislative override. But, particularly with respect to the effect of the Charter on the political debate surrounding sexual assault, Fudge holds that "[b]y reconstituting the political discourse in terms of rights, the Charter has polarized and narrowed the debate without challenging prevailing practices." She finds that the Charter hardened the "ideological separation" between public and private by focusing on how the state should respond to sexual violence and drawing feminists "into the state's agenda." The result, she makes clear, is that "the social construction of sexuality and the social relations of power in which sexual practices take place fade into the background."[55]

One of the puzzles in American politics over the last generation has been the propensity for conservatives to stand alone in calling attention to the links among liberal ideology, professional elites, and the courts. Paradoxically, those most resistant to sharing the wealth have emerged as the most suspicious of the elite theory of civil liberties and judicial activism.[56] This relationship requires more careful investigation of the actors and the communities, both social and scholarly, in order to demonstrate the consequences of the political stances taken by judges and jurists for the ideological environment of social movements. The conventional perspective on public attitudes is characteristically liberal in at least two senses. In the Madisonian, untrusting sense, attitude studies are liberal by comparison to the work of neoconservatives like Richard Morgan, whose criticism of "rights production" is directed at "legal intellectuals and interest group advocates."[57] In the neoconservative ideology, rights are not "really" there, and Morgan, like Walter Berns and Christopher Wolfe, criticizes social engineering by lawyers and courts. The attitude perspective is also liberal in the contemporary, everyday sense. In championing rights such as privacy and expression, it is certainly not classically conservative. But in not developing a critique of inequality, the attitude perspective is not very radical either.

Distrust of the public in matters of "civil liberty" correlates with skepticism about institutions closely associated with popular culture (e.g., executives and legislatures) and support for institutions that are more insulated from that culture, such as courts. Public opinion surveys that find respect for the Supreme Court, relative to other national institutions, are an example. This respect, revealed over the last four decades by survey research,[58] reflects the elite orientation of civil liberties liberalism. The Supreme Court's authority in constitutional matters and a similar identification of rights with litigation are the central institutional

143

correlates bearing on legal formations in politics. Support for the Supreme Court appears to be grounded in its special connection to law. The Court is ranked more favorably than Congress or the presidency in about half of the surveys done by political scientists,[59] although there is little evidence that the Supreme Court has a "special place either in the psyche or in the childhood socialization of Americans" or that the outcomes of its decisions "command sweeping generalized approval."[60] Scholars studying these surveys suggest that the Court is ranked more favorably due to the special publics in the legal profession that are attentive to its work and nurture its mystique.

Another institutional dimension in American politics is the attempt to deal with conflicts among elites by elevating the courts. David Barnum did this in his study of the controversy over the Nazis marching in Skokie.[61] Gibson and Bingham are led to the conclusion that "the most democratic thing elites did" in the Skokie case was go to court.[62] They cite Barnum to the effect that a minority of elites in Skokie did "urge that the issue be submitted to the courts and that the decision of the courts be obeyed."[63] This is liberal democracy with a theoretical vengeance. The characteristic democratic institution, by this analysis, becomes the courts, and the characteristic democratic stance becomes resistance to popular will.

The legitimacy of an institution is established in part because people turn toward it and away from other institutions in the political processes. Although legitimacy may not be a zero-sum game,[64] confidence in one institution, such as the picture of the Supreme Court as a body of lawgivers (maintained even in the midst of the most intense controversy), is quite clearly a reflection of the picture of other institutions, such as Congress as a place of deals and self-interest. For the Supreme Court since the New Deal, legitimacy has been "process based." That is, it has depended on an understanding of fundamental rights that justifies judges becoming involved when some action "seems to obstruct political representation and accountability."[65] By this rationale, courts are believed to be superior to legislatures in the protection of fundamental rights. An institutional link between courts and political or process rights has characterized the social "field" of movement politics. The greatest impact of process-based theories is the claim they lay on the protection of basic rights in the Constitution for judges, or, as Laurence Tribe puts it, "the impoverished relevance of the Constitution for everyone except judges."[66]

The aspiration to go "all the way to the Supreme Court," often heard early in litigation, has consequences that are another dimension of ideological impact. This claim entails a consciousness that having reached the Supreme Court one has reached the end of the line. The case of landing rights in the United States for the British-French Concorde Supersonic airplane in the late 1970s exemplifies this institutional authority. When Long Island protesters learned of the Supreme Court's decision to allow the plane to land, their enthusiasm for the struggle diminished dramatically.[67] Certainly, protest does not always cease when the Court makes a decision, but the institutional disposition in that direction has become more marked in the post-war period.[68] Indeed, seeing political possibility in terms of judicial activism has been usurping our understanding of the Constitution as a function of the "institutions, behaviors, and understandings" that form the political culture.[69]

The present inquiry, though it approaches groups from a constitutive perspective, for the most part cuts across the categories of class. Like law, there is a tendency of interest group formulations to relegate economic inequalities to contextual status, one among the many ways in which groups differ. E. P. Thompson's conclusion to *Whigs and Hunters* is a rejoinder to those who think law is simply an outgrowth of class power.[70] Law mediates class relations to the advantage of the rulers *and* imposes inhibitions on the rulers. Law mystifies class rule but is more than mere sham. The defense of the citizen from power's all-inclusive claims, says Thompson, is an unqualified human good. My argument is a little more guarded. In a constitutive perspective, value is less like something institutions are awarded and more like the way the institutions are known.

A consequence of constitutive theory for the study of law in movements has been a different picture of the relations of groups in law from the usual "demographic" approach (i.e., farmers, women, etc.) that is part of a pluralist perspective, and where variety is built from demands and social indicators. The great differences between the groups examined here have not figured prominently in the analysis. That remains to be done as part of the politics of constitutive law. A related consequence has been identification of non-obvious movements and surprising alliances. We have not inquired simply into self-proclaimed "social movements."[71] From the very social and spirited movement of Anglo-Saxon yeoman and their European allies across the North American continent to the most specific concerns about pornography in the latter part of the twentieth century, movements are people acting in concert to pursue interests that are either articulated or articulable. To accept a conventional mythology that treats movements as outsiders seeking to get in is to fall into the trap of pluralism this book has made every effort to avoid. Of course, this framework suggests that some movements move more than others do. The movement for legal abortion was certainly more sedentary after its 1973 success in *Roe v. Wade*, and in the last decade of the twentieth century changes on the Supreme Court that threaten that constitutional protection have motivated descendant pro-choice forces.

In the case of the ADR movement, operation within a professional context and the nature of the claims compel participants to play down their demands and present their interests as the inevitable consequence of how they view the world. Similarly, the attention to conceptual categories suggests non-obvious alliances, like the one that is said to exist between traditional conservatives and feminists on the issue of pornography. Further analysis, however, is less compelling in support of the actual existence of such an alliance. In cases such as this, the ideological drive of liberal thought stops where contrary evidence of social life emerges. Movement identity in a conceptual sense also contributes to how we see strong claims, such as those made by gays faced with the closing of bathhouses and the AIDS epidemic. A strategy that at first seems overblown, or at least not addressed instrumentally to the needs of the moment, is seen on further reflection to be informed by the social facts of gay life during the AIDS crisis, a more reasonable, albeit grand, strategy.

I conclude here with attention to the similar impact of "law's innocence"[72] on the role of law in constituting class, race, and sex, and its role in constituting various political interests.[73] The portrayal of group interests in the previous chapters built on scholarship in the constructivist tradition. Activists were engaged in a debate within the movement at a time of grave crisis for the gay community. Both "realist" movements, those around the politics of the curriculum and those around alternative processes, are entirely professional and very self-conscious about their ideas. Sander, for instance, is not "substantive" in the same sense that other activists, such as those opposing pornography, are. Dworkin was not, in the early years of the antipornography movement, proposing specific ordinances. Yet, the politics in each movement illuminates a constitutive perspective for oppressed groups generally. By calling attention to the relative power of the groups involved we continue the inquiry into the way legal power is hidden.

Ultimately, authority in politics lies in determinations about the way the world is, not simply how people feel about it. The extent to which "interests" have been defined as having feelings or demands rather than knowledge is a powerful agent for maintaining authority relations. For example, when a welfare worker comments concerning a client's mistake, "He says . . . he is on Home Relief . . . I think he means TADC,"[74] he demonstrates that assertions of property rights are subject to correction and refinement by experts, but the authority of the poor to participate in the discussion is substantially diminished by a lack of autonomy and the technical discourse of welfare property. This lack of autonomy leads to characterizing the recipients according to their mental or social health, and their claims on the state become a function of these conditions. The social worker now tends "to lay the blame for waste on 'emotional disturbance,' the 'multiproblem family,' the 'female-centered family,' or the poor man's propensity toward schizophrenia, which reduces our common human squalor to an exotic psychological squalor defined by class."[75] As Douglas Hay, Karl Klare, and others made clear, this involvement, no matter how sympathetic, like the grace of the gentry in the late Middle Ages, reaffirms the hierarchies.[76]

Social service workers teach what property is in a way that gives the workers, and hence the state, control. For instance, in one disability interview observed in Chico, California, in 1988, a man referred to his entitlement in terms of the papers he kept in a little white bank pouch and the people he knew who would handle the papers for him. Already on disability, he was applying for Supplemental Security Income. He did not read or write, but he saw his benefits "in there" (in the pouch) and hoped that, with the case worker's help, the papers might be negotiable for food. Pointing to his papers, he said, "I goofed it up. See the things in there, I don't understand all the words. . . . I see the letters on different cans and boxes and I know what the box is." But his case worker would fix it. "Norma, she's good people," he said. Another man, also in Chico, was trying to get on disability and having a hard time. He brought his life history of pain to the disability process, but described his reaction to the process as "I get this feeling I just want to get in my truck and get up in the mountains and stay." He was taught that the bureaucracy would not make it easy for him. The distinctive feature of the managers is that they gain authority from the state through their positions as experts and officials, and the language of property maintains those relations. Managers of subsidized housing, welfare workers, and legal advocates see themselves as helpers. They understand the expectations, while recipients may know only "the signatures or the forms they need."[77]

The pervasive taken-for-grantedness of property and the way politics is arrayed around it make the public understanding of this constitutional right important and instructive for the discussion of political interests. We can see the manifestations of law in contemporary struggles over housing. Following the "Listeners' Action on Homelessness and Housing" sponsored by radio station WBAI in New York City in 1989, activists proclaimed their movement a success by heralding the numbers of people who marched or were arrested, the coverage and the support among law-makers, all with clear affirmation that the homeless were without property, without entitlement, without legal right to housing.[78] The bias reflecting the hierarchies of attitude scholarship is evident in the language of property. The limited framework of the 1950s, with its distrust of the citizen, constitutes the way we speak about entitlement in the 1990s. In the particularities of entitlement, attitude is an instrument for ignoring expectations.

Looking at groups in terms of how they articulate demands draws attention to their own identity. This may give depth to our understanding of political strategy and to our picture of law. This depth amounts to a critical self-consciousness, and it is not always welcome. But in two respects a degree of self-consciousness is desirable. First, the academy is a source of strength for movements that challenge the exercise of raw power. Power is rationalized in the academy; the arguments and the evidence are lined up. Rather than accede to the academy's claim of innocence, we should note that its complicity is analogous to that of law. Each have their specialties, but scholars and lawyers both work on particular problems, such as abortion or solid waste, at the same time. Second, the attention to the relationships between law and struggle, or law and change, are in the end more supportive that undermining. While an individual gay activist may be reluctant to become the focus of academic inquiry for a number of reasons, not the least of which is the inherent objectification, the movement as a whole thrives on attention from the academic community.

Legal Politics

The politics of law is not simply a reaction to legalism, less formal activity that takes place outside the court or without lawyers. Politics imbricated with law sometimes features its legal trappings, as when Chief Justice Warren Burger gave his keynote speech in St. Paul (see chapter 4), but even then law's role in politics may be difficult to see. In the framework used here, legalism is reconceived as the basis for a politics of law that looks like politics tempered and shaped by legal forms (even where, as in Burger's speech, it is denied). Here, I examine the epistemological debates surrounding race theory and feminism to uncover ways of recognizing the law in politics.

The constitutive dimension of law on race and the way the law masks the construction of race in American politics are evident in Patricia Williams's work on property, as well as Derrick Bell's foreword to the *Harvard Law Review* (examining the 1984 term of the Supreme Court), where he described civil rights as "an inexact euphemism for racial law."[79] The work of both scholars has a mythic quality that reveals the law in parables. Bell draws attention to the absence of major racial issues decided by the Supreme Court in 1984, but instead of the traditional doctrinal discussion, the article is an exchange with the imagined Geneva Crenshaw, a civil rights lawyer in Mississippi who was injured by a racist attack in 1964. The story, though it has all the trappings of a fairy tale, mythic figures, heavenly bodies, and heroic exploits, is full of real but little-known characters, such as William Robert Ming, Jr., who from 1947 to 1953, while at the University of Chicago, was the first black to hold a full-time faculty position at a white law school. With reference to matters of racial law, its lawyers, and their struggles, the story is, to use the demur of Stanley Fish, "embedded in conviction."[80]

Conventional jurisprudence is uncomfortable with conviction, particularly if it is too intense or moves in the wrong direction. Conviction may, in the extreme, threaten the consensus over the rules. This was the case in the civil rights movement when dissenters challenged the premises of *Brown v. Board of Education*. The bodies in these struggles often remain hidden, but conviction has a tendency to call attention to the bodies behind the law. While commitment or conviction may lead jurisprudence to the politics of social relations, the power of critical race theory and feminist jurisprudence is their explicit attention to these relations. We saw in the last chapter how Catharine MacKinnon offers a powerful jurisprudential analysis of the material dimensions of law and the failure of liberalism.[81] In *Feminism Unmodified*, she presents a view of what law is today from the perspective of "gender as a distinct inequality," parallel to race and class inequalities.[82]

149

Here, and with reference to pornography, MacKinnon takes on the politics that defines sex, emphasizing the domination of men and the way treating sex as a "difference rather than a hierarchy" mystifies the power relations.

The force behind MacKinnon's jurisprudence is its explicit attention to the social reality of women's experience. In her introduction to *Feminism Unmodified*, "The Art of the Impossible," she proposes that "women get their class status through their sexual relations."[83] She also argues that gender is a distinct inequality, which also contributes to the social embodiment and expression of race and class inequalities. The gender factor operates in the same way that "the masculinity of money as a form of power takes nothing from its function as capital—though it undermines some models of economics."[84]

MacKinnon's themes epitomize a politics built on the constitutive dimensions of law. Sex is the key to law because "[t]he social relation between the sexes is organized so that men may dominate and this relation is sexual—in fact, is sex." Liberalism, the prevailing ideology behind American law, holds that "gender is basically a difference rather than a hierarchy," which "hides the force behind the description." The same can be said of law in the area of gender relations. The "difference" celebrated in law as neutral is hierarchical when examined in the context of an entire system of laws. Moving from law to social life, she says, "Pornography turns gendered inequality into speech which has made it a right." While liberal convention imagines the need for protected speech in light of a government hostile to sexuality, for MacKinnon the state is hostile to women.

The constitutive relationship between ideas and social life in politics is highlighted in a critique of MacKinnon by Fish.[85] According to Fish, her essays brilliantly exemplify what he calls "the strategy of change." Her method, he says, is to employ her own vocabulary, one "that departs from ordinary (or as she might say 'ideologically frozen') usage in ways that cannot be ignored."[86] For example, the phrase "rape in ordinary circumstances . . . is provocative because in the way of thinking MacKinnon wishes to dislodge, rape is defined as an exceptional and statistically deviant act against a background of mutually agreed upon sexual transactions." Making rape "a constitutive ingredient of everyday heterosexual intercourse, including intercourse in marriage" may not dismantle an entire legal structure, but certain assumptions are undermined when we see the law in a new way.[87]

MacKinnon, notes Fish, posits male and female ways of knowing. The male way of knowing is universalizing and committed to objectivity; it "does not comprehend its own perspectivity, does not recognize . . . that the way it apprehends its world is a form of [the world's] subjugation."[88] In this way, sexual relations become the foundation for epistemology and for law. These observations suggest that "aperspectivity"—the claiming of universality for a partial point of view—may be considered a central feature of the debate brought on by the antipornography movement. But there are other ways, prior to epistemology, in which sexual relations and law are linked. Thus, Fish says that "MacKinnon is not, despite her own pronouncements, exhorting us to a new way of knowing, but to know different things than we currently know (about rape, pornography, etc.) in the same (and only) way we know anything, by having been convinced of it."[89] To Fish, "aperspectivity" is "a name for the condition of believing that what you believe is in fact true, and that is a condition one cannot transcend."[90]

Still, Fish does not provide an account of social relations that counters MacKinnon's. Fish claims that MacKinnon undermines her own position inadvertently in discussing Mary Daly's analysis of suttee, "a practice in which Indian widows are supposed to throw themselves upon their dead husband's funeral pyres in grief."[91] While Daly describes women who practice suttee as "drugged, pushed, browbeaten, or otherwise coerced by the dismal and frightening prospect of widowhood in Indian society," MacKinnon emphasizes that Daly's attention to the surface coercions fails to understand the deeper coercion that leads "some women who are not drugged or pushed to fling themselves on the pyre quite 'freely.'"[92] These, for MacKinnon, "are suttee's deepest victims: women who want to die when their husband dies, who volunteer for self-immolation because they believe their life is over when his is."[93] Although Fish praises the attention MacKinnon gives to will, there is little in his analysis that leads us to see the role of communities in building the steps to the funeral pyres.

To Fish, the power to create the world "is not a matter of epistemology, of the producing of accounts of how we know what we know," but rather "a power that attends successful persuasion . . . a power whose effects are always and necessarily objectifying" because being "under its sway (and everyone is at every moment of his or her life) is to see the world from a point of view."[94] According to Fish, "What is wrong with Indian women from the feminist point of view is not that they are willing

151

(in a precisely non-voluntarist sense) to die for the beliefs that have captured them, but that they have not been captured—constituted, formed,
made into what they are—by the right beliefs."[95] Here Fish cloaks his
radical subjectivity in surface objectivity. He does not distinguish
between the subjective knowing advocated by MacKinnon and the so-
called objective knowing that makes claims of universality. By not
addressing the various sources of coercion, Fish does what the liberals
do and thereby reveals his value to them. He focuses his attention on the
project of indeterminacy while operating at a surface level of conventionality. He is the embodiment of detached reason.[96]

The constitutive project is gaining ground. While its roots are in the
tradition of social scientific studies of law, the seductions in that tradition continue to present hazards. Whether referring back to the positivism of poorly theorized number crunching, or to an equally
problematic highly relativized interpretivism, the framework used in
this book has required a nurturing defense from friends and foes alike.[97]
Some of the ways we have seen victims being made in the process of providing legal rights represent this constitutive approach. Kristin
Bumiller, whose book *The Civil Rights Society* called attention to the role
of civil rights law in constituting victims, has further developed the picture of how law's form manifests itself in politics. Bumiller notes, "The
debate on rape law reform has divided feminists between those who
have faith in the law . . . and those who do not."[98] For those with faith in
the law, the political goal is legislation that does not stereotype the victim. Those who fear the law see its form as inherently responsible for the
oppression of women and do not believe in *reform*. Where rape cases
traditionally turn on consent and link rape to sex, the feminist response
has been attention to rape as an act of domination and violence, that is,
as a crime against women. Law reforms (i.e., the rape shield laws and the
elimination of corroboration requirements) try to mitigate the legal tactics that undermine the victim's credibility. "Real" or prototypical
rape—a woman attacked by a stranger with a lethal weapon on the
street—is not the trial's conception (or at least not the defendant's).
Bumiller argues for a "perspective on the politics of rape that focuses on
the social construction of power relations in rape trials," where, she says
"legal language reinforces existing definitions of rape."[99] The symbolic
dimension of rape is connected to social structure, and certainly to
race.[100] Domination of blacks in the American South through the image
of the black rapist amounts to rape for whites and repression for blacks.

The forms of law in this book draw on these sorts of differences, always with attention to how people organize themselves with reference to the law. The clearest parallel with these epistemological debates is in the antipornography movement, where for a time the law was considered alien territory and radical feminist communities were constituted in opposition to it. In the struggle to keep the baths open in San Francisco, where there was faith in the law, a group of entrepreneurs were drawn to the law and to the belief in legal right that had constituted so much of gay life for the previous twenty years. To guarantee the continuity of their enterprise, these entrepreneurs employed the courts, as well as the sense in the community that rights were something the oppressed could turn to. The ADR movements in law school are both more officially constituted in institutions and less willing to have their institutional positions made explicit.

Contemporary social theory domesticates critique by developing a tone of relativism. Anthropology, of course, has been central to this process because relativism has been its contribution in the twentieth century. Modernism in culture generally—in design, in architecture, in economic structure—has been optimistic and determinative in the fashion pointed out by postmodernists. Modernism in political and social theory, however, has not, at least not in the West. According to anthropologist George Marcus, "[O]ne might look first to the hesitations, misrecognitions, and anxieties articulated in the discourses of problem-solving institutions and their nurturing professional disciplines that are bent on the technical control of an always unruly world."[101] Indeed, mass toxic torts, such as those against asbestos manufacturers, cannot be reduced to the quotidian, but what is postmodern is necessarily the response to such events. That is, how do we interpret the cataclysmic events of the moment (or more accurately for social science, how do we describe the way others have handled these events)? This is what Marcus has done:

> [T]he internal human relations among family members, the face-to-face medium of most anthropological subjects, cannot be understood without also intimately understanding how several different spheres of specialized activity, parallel to, discontinuous in space, and simultaneous in time, with the day-to-day interactions of family members also construct the family and its wealth. Such a human family is tied to its "unseen worlds."[102]

Marcus's sense that forms—some legal and some not—are implicated in the everyday seems right. But the modern may not be juxtaposed against the everyday in the way social theorists have proposed. For Marcus,

"Everyday life is the seat of order in social life, and upon this order is built in human action, the virtues, vices, contingencies, dramas, and themes of life."[103]

In the constitutive analysis of poverty, we face the fact that the poor are who they are because of the law.[104] The law of property is what makes some people poor and some not. Interpretation of that law further imbeds poverty in layers of understanding that mask legal forms. It helps to take the law as given when arguing that people are poor because of lack of effort on their behalf. Many of the richest people in the world are rich through no effort of their own, but this does not matter to the law. People have wealth through property. Family is another source of wealth, but it too is a legal construction. The interesting thing about the "poor" in comparison to the "family"[105] is how different they are as social categories. "Family" is a category self-consciously built and attended to by those in it. We say that we want a family. Whether we succeed or fail, family is our construction. Poverty, however, is a category of others; the conditions described are felt by others as life, not as poverty.

All of the movements discussed in this book result from self-conscious effort to take coherent social action. In studying the aspects of law in social life, I have tried to let movements define themselves while exploring the role of law in that definition. This perspective relies on movements themselves to reveal what the law means to them through public discourse. The social reality of the legal form is based upon self-definition—that is, people within movements addressing each other. This brings us back to the ways law operates in communities. When we see law and are conscious of its commands, the way we see the command in a stop sign, the law operates only on the surface. Law is much more powerful when it operates in society and on our consciousness. Of course, the promise of critical consciousness has been one of the most important claims for movements that would stand outside law.[106] By expanding the reach of law in theory, I suggest that law has always been more expansive in fact than critical commentators have been inclined to acknowledge. Law operates at the level of consciousness when radical activists challenge pornography and become preoccupied with debates on the First Amendment. Law also operates this way when gays aspire to thwart the state because "they have a right," only to become entangled in a politics that pits the movement against public health concerns. Law is in politics when these sorts of things happen, and the politics of these things may be the law's politics in all the imperial respects that the rule of law suggests.

Notes

Notes to Preface

1. Correspondence with the author, spring 1995.
2. David M. Trubek and John Esser, "'Critical Empiricism' in American Legal Studies: Paradox, Program, or Pandora's Box?" *Law and Social Inquiry* 14 (1989): 3–52. But see Christine Harrington and Barbara Yngvesson's response, "Interpretive Sociological Research," *Law and Social Inquiry* 15 (1990): 135.
3. Christine B. Harrington and Sally Engle Merry, "Ideological Production: The Making of Community Mediation," *Law and Society Review* 22 (1988): 709–36.

Notes to Chapter 1

1. I use the terms *law* and *legal phenomena* interchangeably to refer to the bodies of laws and the system of authority that enforces them. I use *the law*, with the definite article, where it is an idiomatic practice, such as "the law on the books" or "the strong arm of the law," and refers to a way of doing things. This use is a jurisprudential convention more common in America than in England and other common law countries.
2. Alexis de Tocqueville, *Democracy in America*, 4th ed. (New York: H. G. Langley, 1845).
3. James Willard Hurst, *The Growth of American Law: The Law Makers* (Boston: Little, Brown, 1950), 3.
4. Alexander Hamilton et al., *The Federalist* (New York: Random House, 1937).
5. See, for instance, Wilson's acceptance speech for his party's nomination, July 7, 1912: "Big business is not dangerous because it is big, but because its bigness is an unwholesome inflation created by privileges and exemptions which it ought not to enjoy." Arthur S. Link, ed. *The Papers of Woodrow Wilson* (Princeton: Princeton University Press, 1966–1994).

6. John Brigham, "Right, Rage and Remedy," *Studies in American Political Development* 2 (1988).

7. Karl Klare, "Law Making as Praxis," *Telos* 40 (1979): 122.

8. Georgia Code Ann. @ 16–6–2 (1984) provides: "(a) A person commits the offense of sodomy when he performs or submits to any sexual act involving the sex organs of one person and the mouth or anus of another. . . .(b) A person convicted of the offense of sodomy shall be punished by imprisonment for not less than one nor more than 20 years."

9. See Klare, "Law Making as Praxis," for a discussion of "praxis," a term from critical theory, which underlies German social science's picture of law.

10. Rogers Smith reiterated this perspective at the American Political Science Association 1992 Annual Meeting, August 29–September 3, 1992, Chicago, Illinois, where he discussed laws in terms of a model that would bring independent and dependent variables together.

11. Lee Epstein, at the meeting cited in note 10, described making law the dependent variable as a new contribution.

12. Indeed, texts themselves may be looked at constitutively, that is, with attention to the practices that give them meaning.

13. Douglas Hay et al., *Albion's Fatal Tree: Crime and Society in Eighteenth-Century England* (New York: Free Press, 1975).

14. Eleanor Flexner, *Century of Struggle: The Women's Rights Movement in the United States* (1959; reprint, Cambridge: Harvard University Press, 1975).

15. See Joseph Schumpeter, *Capitalism, Socialism, and Democracy* (New York: Harper and Row, 1942); Jacques Donzelot, *The Policing of Families* (New York: Random House, 1979); Samuel Bowles and Herbert Gintis, *Schooling in Capitalist America* (New York: Basic Books, 1976).

16. Felix Frankfurter and James M. Landis, *The Business of the Supreme Court* (New York: Macmillan, 1928), 307.

17. Fred Frohock, *The Abortion Controversy* (Westport, Conn.: Greenwood Press, 1983); Kristin Luker, *Abortion and the Politics of Motherhood* (Berkeley: University of California Press, 1984).

18. Phillip Cooper, *Hard Judicial Choices* (London: Oxford University Press, 1988).

19. Ibid., 347.

20. Neal Milner, "Comparative Analysis of Patterns of Compliance with Supreme Court Decisions: Miranda and the Police in Four Communities," *Law and Society Review* 5 (1971): 126; Kenneth M. Dolbeare and Phillip Hammond, *The School Prayer Decisions: From Court Policy to Local Practice* (Chicago: University of Chicago Press, 1971).

21. Charles A. Johnson and Bradley C. Canon, *Judicial Policies: Implementation and Impact* (Washington, D.C.: Congressional Quarterly Press, 1984), 25.

22. Stephen Wasby, *The Impact of the United States Supreme Court* (Homewood, Ill.: Dorsey Press, 1970).

23. Stuart Macaulay, "Non-Contractual Relations in Business: A Preliminary Study," *American Sociological Review* 28 (1963): 55.

24. David M. Engel, "Cases, Conflict, and Accommodation: Patterns of Legal Interaction in a Small Community," *American Bar Foundation Research Journal* 4 (1983), 803–74.

25. See in particular the work of some members of the Amherst Seminar in "Special Issue: Law, Ideology, and Social Research," *Legal Studies Forum* 9 (1985); David Nelken, "Beyond the Study of 'Law and Society'?" *American Bar Foundation Research Journal* 2 (spring 1986): 323–38.

26. See Karen O'Connor, *Women's Organizations' Use of the Courts* (Lexington, Mass.: Lexington Books, 1980), for additional examples.

27. Mary Katzenstein, "Marching Through the Institutions" (paper presented at Amherst College, February 19, 1990).

28. Thurman W. Arnold, *The Symbols of Government* (New Haven: Yale University Press, 1935).

29. Karl Llewellyn, *The Bramble Bush*.

30. Hannah Pitkin, *Wittgenstein and Justice* (Berkeley: University of California Press, 1978).

31. Joseph R. Gusfield, *The Culture of Public Problems: Drinking-Driving and the Symbolic Order* (Chicago: University of Chicago Press, 1981); Murray J. Edelman, *Constructing the Political Spectacle* (Chicago: University of Chicago Press, 1988).

32. Stuart Scheingold, *The Politics of Rights* (New Haven: Yale University Press, 1974), xi.

33. Isaac Balbus, *The Dialectics of Legal Repression* (New York: Russell Sage, 1973); idem, "Commodity Form and Legal Form: An Essay on the 'Relative Autonomy' of the Law," *Law and Society Review* 112

(1977): 571; Zenon Bankowski and Geoff Mungham, *Images of Law* (London: Routledge and Kegan Paul, 1976); Bernard Edelman, *Ownership of the Image: Elements for a Marxist Theory of Law* (London: Routledge and Kegan Paul, 1979).

34. Alan Hunt, *The Sociological Movement in Law* (Philadelphia: Temple University Press, 1978).

35. Gusfield, *Culture of Public Problems*, 141.

36. Ibid., 143.

37. Robert Gordon, "Critical Legal Histories," *Stanford Law Review* 36 (1984): 127.

38. William H. Simon, "Legality, Bureaucracy and Class in the Welfare State," *Yale Law Journal* 92 (1983): 1198; Robert Wiesberg, "Deregulating Death," *Supreme Court Review* (1983): 303.

39. Gordon, "Critical Legal Histories," 121.

40. Owen Fiss, "Free Speech and Social Structure" (unpublished manuscript, 1985).

41. Ibid.

42. Sally Merry, "Concepts of Law and Justice among Working-Class Americans: Ideology as Culture," *Legal Studies Forum* 9 (1985): 67; idem, *Getting Justice and Getting Even* (Chicago: University of Chicago Press, 1990).

43. Johnson and Canon, *Judicial Policies*; Thomas Dalton, *The State Politics of Judicial and Congressional Reform* (Westport, Conn.: Greenwood Press, 1985); see also John Brigham, "Judicial Impact upon Social Practices," *Legal Studies Forum* 9 (1985): 51.

44. 413 U.S. 15 (1973). Joseph F. Kobylka, "A Court-Created Context for Group Litigation: Libertarian Groups and Obscenity," *Journal of Politics* 49 (1987): 1061.

45. Aryeh Neier, *Defending My Enemy* (New York: Dutton, 1979).

46. Richard A. Brisbin, "Antonin Scalia, William Brennan, and the Politics of Expression: A Study of Legal Violence and Repression," *American Political Science Review* 87 (1993): 912–27; see also Brigham, "Judicial Impact"; idem, *Civil Liberties and American Democracy* (Washington, D.C.: Congressional Quarterly Press, 1984).

47. John Griffiths as quoted in Mark Galanter, "Justice in Many Rooms: Courts, Private Ordering, and Indigenous Law," *Journal of Legal Pluralism (and Unofficial Law)* 19 (1981): 48.

48. Ibid.

49. Boaventura de Sousa Santos, "The Law of the Oppressed: The Construction and Reproduction of Legality in Pasargada," *Law and Society Review* 12 (1977): 5.

50. Peter Fitzpatrick, "Marxism and Legal Pluralism," *Australian Journal of Law and Society* 1 (1983): 45–59.

51. See, e.g., Laura Nader and Harry F. Todd, eds., *The Disputing Process: Law in Ten Societies* (New York: Columbia University Press, 1978).

52. Sally Engle Merry, "Legal Pluralism: Review Essay," *Law and Society Review* 5 (1988); see also idem, "Anthropology, Law, and Transitional Processes," *Annual Review of Anthropology* 21 (1992): 357.

53. Brian Z. Tamanaha, "The Folly of the 'Social Scientific' Concept of Legal Pluralism," *Journal of Law and Society* 20 (summer 1993): 192–217.

54. Boaventura de Sousa Santos, *Toward a New Common Sense: Law, Science and Politics in the Paradigmatic Transition* (New York: Routledge, 1995).

55. Merry, "Legal Pluralism," 869; Tamanaha, "Folly of the 'Social Scientific' Concept," 192.

56. Mindie Lazarus-Black and Susan Hirsch, eds., *Contested States: Law, Hegemony, and Resistance* (New York: Routledge, 1994).

57. Antonio Gramsci, "History of the Subaltern Classes: Methodological Criteria," in *Selections from the Prison Notebooks*, ed. and trans. Q. H. Hoare and G. N. Smith. See also Ranajit Guha, "On Some Aspects of the Historiography of Colonial India," *Subaltern Studies: Writings on South Asian History and Society* 1 (1980).

58. According to Kendall Thomas, the subaltern's view tells a story of which constitutional history "has saved all too little of authentic record and tried to forget." For Thomas, writing in the tradition of critical race theory, we should know about the subaltern to set the historical record straight and in order to hear the voices from the grass roots. Kendall Thomas, "Rouge et Noir Reread: A Popular Constitutional History of the Angelo Herndon Case," *Southern California Law Review* 65 (1992): 2665.

59. Rosemary J. Coombe, "The Properties of Culture and the Politics of Possessing Identity: Native Claims in the Cultural Appropriation Controversy," *Canadian Journal of Law and Jurisprudence* 5 (1993).

60. John Opie, *The Law of the Land: Two Hundred Years of American Farmland Policy* (Lincoln: University of Nebraska Press, 1987);

James Willard Hurst, *Law and Markets in United States History* (Madison: University of Wisconsin Press, 1980).

61. Sally Falk Moore, *Law as Process* (Cambridge: Harvard University Press, 1978), 57.

62. Ibid.

63. Ibid.

64. Ibid.

65. Phillip Selznick, "Sociology of Law and Natural Law," *Natural Law Forum* 6 (1961): 84–108.

66. Eugen Ehrlich, *The Fundamental Principles of the Sociology of Law* (Cambridge: Harvard University Press, 1936).

67. Selznick, "Natural Law," 85.

68. Ibid., 100.

69. Balbus, "Commodity Form and Legal Form," 571.

70. Bob Fine, "Law and Class," in Bob Fine et al., eds., *Capitalism and the Rule of Law* (London: Hutchinson, 1979).

71. Adelaide H. Villmoore, "Issues of Conceptualization in the Study of Change in and around Courts: Forms of Law" (paper presented at the Annual Meeting of the Law and Society Association, Toronto, 1982).

72. Doreen McBarnet, "Law and Capital: The Role of Legal Form and Legal Actors," *International Journal of the Sociology of Law* 12 (1984): 231–38.

73. Ibid., 231.

74. Ibid., 232.

75. "The first response of the tax avoider in justifying activities or complaining about measures taken against them, is to invoke the rule of law. Tax avoiders—or avoiders of any law—carefully and deliberately operate in the grey areas of the law, in the no man's land of practices not specifically prohibited by law" (ibid., 236).

76. See Christine B. Harrington, "Creating Gaps and Making Markets," *Law and Policy* 10 (1988): 293–316; Magali Sarfatti Larson, *The Rise of Professionalism: A Sociological Analysis* (Berkeley: University of California Press, 1977).

77. Jennifer Friesen and Ronald K. L. Collins, "Looking Back on *Muller v. Oregon*," *American Bar Association Journal* 69 (1983): 472–79.

78. Clement Vose, "NAACP Strategy in the Covenant Cases," *Western Reserve Law Review* 7 (winter 1955): 101–45; idem, "The National Consumer's League and the Brandeis Brief," *Midwest Journal of Political Science* 1 (1957): 267–90.

79. Theodore L. Becker, ed. *Political Trials* (Indianapolis: Bobbs-Merrill, 1971).
80. Ibid., xi.
81. The five parts of the book are "Political Trials," "Political Trials that Become Political 'Trials,'" "Political 'Trials,'" "'Political' Trials," and "A 'Political Trial.'"
82. Becker, *Political Trials,* xiii.
83. Ibid., 183.
84. Anthony Lewis, *Gideon's Trumpet* (New York: Random House, 1964).
85. Barbara Craig, *Chada: The Story of an Epic Constitutional Struggle* (London: Oxford University Press, 1988).
86. Stanley Fish, "Dennis Martinez and the Uses of Theory," *Yale Law Journal* 96 (1987): 1773–1800.
87. Dick Hebdige, *Subculture: The Meaning of Style* (New York: Methuen, 1979), 128.
88. Louis Althusser, *Lenin and Philosophy* (New York: Monthly Review, 1971), 166.
89. Klare, "Law Making as Practice," 1979.
90. Ibid.
91. The Act, a result of extended working-class struggles, initially represented real gains that were subjected to the needs of capital by the Court's decisions.
92. Douglas Hay, "Property, Authority and the Criminal Law," in Hay et al., *Albion's Fatal Tree.*
93. Gertrude Himmelfarb, *The Idea of Poverty: England in the Early Industrial Age* (New York: Knopf, 1983).
94. Nelken, "Beyond the Study of 'Law and Society'?"
95. Zillah R. Eisenstein, *The Female Body and the Law* (Berkeley: University of California Press, 1988); Catharine MacKinnon, *Feminism Unmodified: Discourses on Life and Law* (Cambridge: Harvard University Press, 1987).
96. One of the challenges to a constitutive view is the "many voices" perspective in some variations of modern liberalism. See Carrie Menkel-Meadow, "Excluded Voices: New Voices in the Legal Profession," *University of Miami Law Review* 42 (1987): 29–53.
97. I have written about practices before and this formulation has an important place in sociology of law scholarship.
98. Elizabeth C. Stanton, "Declaration of Sentiments," in *The First Convention ever Called to Discuss the Civil and Political Rights of*

Women (Seneca Falls, N.Y.: n.p., 1848); See also Flexner, *Century of Struggle.*

99. Gay Health Clinic, "Safe Sex," San Francisco, 1983.

100. Martin Shapiro, *Who Guards the Guardians?* (Atlanta: University of Georgia Press, 1989).

101. Karl Klare, "The Judicial Deradicalization of the Wagner Act and the Origins of Modern Legal Consciousness, 1937–1941," *Minnesota Law Review* 62 (1978): 265; Willliam Forbath, *Law and the Shaping of the American Labor Movement* (Cambridge: Harvard University Press, 1991).

102. Eugene Genovese, *Roll, Jordan, Roll: The World the Slaves Made* (New York: Pantheon Books, 1972); Mark V. Tushnet, *The NAACP's Legal Strategy against Segregated Education, 1925–1950* (Chapel Hill: University of North Carolina Press, 1987).

103. David Silverman and Brian Torode, *The Material Word: Some Theories of Language and Its Limits* (London: Routledge and Kegan Paul, 1980).

104. Ibid., 2.

Notes to Chapter 2

1. Anthony Lewis, *Gideon's Trumpet* (New York: Random House, 1964).

2. For more theoretical discussion sensitive to the constitutive positions advanced here, see Alan Hunt, *Explorations in Law and Society: Toward a Constitutive Theory of Law* (New York: Routledge, 1993); Amy Bartholomew and Alan Hunt, "What's Wrong with Rights?" (paper presented at Rethinking Marxism Conference, Amherst, Massachusetts, December 3–5, 1989).

3. Josh Gamson, "Silence, Death, and the Invisible Enemy: AIDS Activism and Social Movement 'Newness,'" *Social Problems* 36 (1989): 351–67.

4. Michael McCann and Gerald Houseman, *Judging the Constitution: Critical Essays* (Boston: Little, Brown, 1989). This works for equality in the importance of "opportunity." Similarly, Michel Foucault depicted critics of sexuality not as a roadblock to the "power mechanism" of sexual repression but "in fact part of the same historical network as the thing it denounces" (*The History of Sexuality* [New York: Random House, 1978]), 10.

5. This fact about rights is conveyed through stories or "chronicles" by Derrick Bell in his reflection on the civil rights experience in *And We Are Not Saved* (New York: Basic Books, 1987). It is also central to the analysis offered by Catharine MacKinnon in *Feminism Unmodified: Discourses on Life and Law* (Cambridge: Harvard University Press, 1987).

6. Foucault, *Sexuality*.

7. Eve Kosofsky Sedgwick, *The Epistemology of the Closet* (Berkeley: University of California Press, 1990).

8. See Howard Gillman, "The Rights Trump" (paper presented at the American Political Science Association Annual Meeting, Washington, D.C., August 28–September 2, 1991, 1).

9. Critiques of equal protection guarantees are becoming more prominent. See Bell, *And We Are Not Saved*; Kristin Bumiller, *The Civil Rights Society: The Social Construction of Victims* (Baltimore: Johns Hopkins University Press, 1988); Alan Freeman, "Legitimizing Racial Discrimination through Antidiscrimination Law: A Critical Review of Supreme Court Doctrine," *Minnesota Law Review* 62 (1978): 1049–119.

10. Henry Abraham, *Freedom and the Court: Civil Rights and Liberties in the United States*, 4th ed. (Oxford: Oxford University Press, 1982).

11. J. Roland Pennock, "Rights and Citizenship," *News: For Teachers of Political Science* (Washington, D.C.: American Political Science Association, 1981).

12. Tim Kaye, "Natural Law Theory and Legal Positivism: Two Sides of the Same Practical Coin?" *Journal of Law and Society* 14 (1987): 303–20.

13. Pennock, "Rights," 13.

14. Sheldon Wolin, *Politics and Vision* (Cambridge: Harvard University Press, 1960), 27.

15. Earnest Barker, *Church, State and Study* (London: Methuen, 1930), 23.

16. Edward S. Corwin, *The Higher Law Background of American Constitutional Law* (Ithaca: Cornell University Press, 1928), 38.

17. Ibid., 37.

18. Louis Hartz, *The Liberal Tradition in America* (New York: Harcourt, Brace, 1955).

19. Richard Flathman, *The Practice of Rights* (Cambridge: Cambridge University Press, 1976); John Brigham, *Civil Liberties and American Democracy* (Washington, D.C.: Congressional Quarterly Books, 1984).

20. When we say "I have a right to a hearing," we are saying something about the world. Often a claim about a legal part of the world is not so much different from describing the testimony in a hearing we might have attended.

21. The Amherst Seminar, eds., "Special Issue: Law and Ideology," *Law and Society Review* 22 (1988).

22. See Linda C. McClain, "'Atomistic Man' Revisited: Liberalism, Connection, and Feminist Jurisprudence," *Southern California Law Review* 65 (1992): 1171–264.

23. Wesley Hohfeld, *Fundamental Legal Conceptions* (New Haven: Yale University Press, 1919).

24. Flathman, *Practice of Rights*.

25. In this contest, protection for flag burners and defendants did not seem to win many votes.

26. Mari Matsuda, "Looking to the Bottom: Critical Legal Studies and Reparations," *Harvard Civil Rights–Civil Liberties Law Review* 22 (1987): 323; Richard Delgado, "The Ethereal Scholar: Does Critical Legal Studies Have What Minorities Want?" *Harvard Civil Rights–Civil Liberties Law Review* 22 (1987): 301.

27. McClain, "'Atomistic Man' Revisted"; Roberto Alejandro, *Hermeneutics, Citizenship, and the Public Sphere* (Albany: State University of New York Press, 1993); Susan Moller Okin, *Justice, Gender, and the Family* (New York: Basic Books, 1989); see also Charles Taylor, "Atomism," in *Powers, Possessions and Freedom: Essays in Honour of C. B. Macpherson*, ed. Alkis Kontos (Toronto: University of Toronto Press, 1979).

28. See chapter 5 below.

29. Alan Freeman, "Racism, Rights and the Quest for Equality of Opportunity: A Critical Legal Essay," *Harvard Civil Rights–Civil Liberties Law Review* 23 (1988): 295–392.

30. Patricia Williams, "Alchemical Notes: Reconstructing Ideals from Deconstructed Rights," *Harvard Civil Rights–Civil Liberties Law Review* 22 (1987): 401.

31. John Brigham and Christine B. Harrington, "Realism and Its Consequences: An Inquiry into Contemporary Socio-legal Research," *International Journal of the Sociology of Law* 17 (1988): 41–62; Martin Shapiro, *Law and Politics in the Supreme Court* (New York: Free Press, 1964).

32. Sanford Levinson, *Constitutional Faith* (Princeton: Princeton University Press, 1989).

33. William Wiecek, *Equal Justice under Law: Constitutional Development, 1835–1875* (New York: Harper and Row, 1982).

34. John P. Roche, "The Founding Fathers: A Reform Caucus in Action," *American Political Science Review* 55 (1961): 67–68.

35. The women's movement in the United States began at least with the Revolution's rhetoric of equality. It was stimulated and supported in part by efforts to end slavery and grew out of the abolitionist societies formed in the 1830s. Attention to women's education in New England in the mid-1800s was another stimulus. The roots of contemporary feminism can be located in the united front evident in the program put forth by the Grimke sisters, who brought the issue of women's rights to the abolitionist struggle.

36. Eleanor Flexner, *Century of Struggle: The Women's Rights Movement in the United States* (1959; reprint, Cambridge: Harvard University Press, 1975). In 1854 Massachusetts responded to part of the claims and passed the married woman's property act.

37. Arnold Paul, *Conservative Crisis and the Rule of Law, 1887–1895* (Ithaca: Cornell University Press, 1969).

38. A traditional perspective on the mobilization of politics to change law is presented in Richard Kluger, *Simple Justice* (New York: Random House, 1976). For an analysis from within the civil rights movement that sees it at least in part as a construction of the law, see Mark V. Tushnet, *The NAACP's Legal Strategy against Segregated Education, 1925–1950* (Chapel Hill: University of North Carolina Press, 1987).

39. Stuart Scheingold, *The Politics of Rights* (New Haven: Yale University Press, 1974), 83.

40. Squatter claims differ from the hopes of housing activists. We do not hear the homeless challenging property rights because their name says they do not have them. The movement for housing draws instead from sympathy for the plight of those without decent shelter.

41. Kristin Luker, *Abortion and the Politics of Motherhood* (Berkeley: University of California Press, 1984); Faye D. Ginsburg, *Contested Lives: The Abortion Debate in an American Community* (Berkeley: University of California Press, 1989).

42. Claus Offe, "New Social Movements: Challenging the Boundaries of Institutional Politics," *Social Research* 52 (1985): 817–68.

43. Blanca G. Silvestrini, "'The World We Enter When Claiming Rights': Latinos and the Quest for Culture" (paper presented to the Amherst Seminar, Amherst, Massachusetts, 1991), 1.

165

44. Tushnet, *The NAACP's Legal Strategy*; Kluger, *Simple Justice.*
45. See Bell, *And We Are Not Saved*; Williams, "Alchemical Notes."
46. Michael McCann, *Rights at Work: Pay Equity Reform and the Politics of Legal Mobilization* (Chicago: University of Chicago Press, 1994).
47. Bumiller, *Civil Rights Society.*
48. Alan Freeman, "Legitimizing Racial Discrimination through Antidiscrimination Law: A Critical Review of Supreme Court Doctrine," *Minnesota Law Review* 62 (1978): 1049.
49. For instance, Gaetan Dugas, an airline steward, averaged 250 sexual liaisons per year according to Randy Shilts, *And the Band Played On: People, Politics and the AIDS Epidemic* (New York: St. Martin's Press, 1987). A review of Shilts's book in the *New York Times*, October 7, 1987, also summarized the book's findings that "a slow government response, lack of attention from the press and the initial failure of the gay community to accept life style changes" allowed AIDS to rage out of control.
50. Margaret Cruikshank, *The Gay and Lesbian Liberation Movement* (New York: Routledge, 1992).
51. The chronicle of these struggles at the time was presented in "AIDS Media: Counter-Representations," New American Film and Video Series, Whitney Museum of American Art, January 15–February 5, 1989.
52. Bruce Boone, "Gay Language as Political Praxis: The Poetry of Frank O'Hara," *Social Text* 1 (winter 1979): 59–92.
53. Ibid., 76. According to Boone, "[I]f bars, baths, and other institutions brought gays together, that much was certainly to the good. . . . But these same institutions also exploited gay men both financially and sexually. And most important of all, gay men characteristically interiorized the commodity relation thus given as the defining meaning of sexuality itself. Thus promiscuity, self-rejection, and the reification of the sexual experience as a series of 'numbers' or 'tricks' . . . often brought the commodity relation to the center of gay self-experience" (79–80).
54. David F. Greenberg, *The Construction of Homosexuality* (Chicago: University of Chicago Press, 1988), 458.
55. This group, with its alliance of gays and lesbians, seems to be a union in law—an alliance based on the shared situation of minority sexual orientation and the divergent life styles that accompany that orientation.

56. For a discussion of the impact AIDS had on the small designers in the fashion industry, see Melinda Katz, "Law in the Private Sector: Small Designers and Civil Rights" (Honors Thesis, University of Massachusetts, Amherst, 1987).

57. In November 1989, after two decades of effort, Massachusetts became the second state to pass a law prohibiting discrimination against homosexuals in employment, housing, credit, and public accommodation. By that time, eighty municipalities had similar measures. While eleven states had executive orders or civil service rules that barred discrimination, Wisconsin was the only other state with comprehensive legislation. "A Gay Rights Law Is Voted in Massachusetts," *New York Times*, November 1, 1989.

58. A constitutional challenge to Georgia's law against sodomy, the Supreme Court decision was grounded in the privacy doctrines developed in the late 1960s. Justice Byron White distinguished gay rights from those of married persons, holding the latter to be more expansive. *Bowers v. Hardwick* 478 U.S. 186 (1986).

59. John Brigham, *The Cult of the Court* (Philadelphia: Temple University Press, 1987), 214.

60. Shilts, *And the Band Played On,* 352–53; see also Gary Schweikhart, "Shilts Responds to Critics," *Sentinel* 29 (March 1984): 1.

61. In a memorandum entitled "A Strategy for the Remaining Months" circulated in the Reagan Justice Department during the spring of 1988, William Bradford Reynolds urged officials to "polarize the debate" to "keep the debate on our terms." For example, it urged officials to treat AIDS not as a civil rights or privacy issue but "one of public health and safety." Fred Strasser, "Court Faces Challenges," *National Law Journal*, March 21, 1988, 5–7.

62. Katie Leishman, "How San Francisco Coped with AIDS," *Atlantic*, October 1985, 24.

63. Marilyn Thornton Williams, "NYC's Public Baths: A Case Study in Urban Progressive Reform," *Journal of Urban History* 7 (1980): 49–81; Martin Hoffman, *The Gay World: Male Homosexuality and the Social Construction of Evil* (New York: Basic Books, 1968). Hoffman also offers a number of speculations about the transitory nature of gay relationships that have come into disrepute.

64. Shilts, *And the Band Played On,* 19.

65. Ibid., 20.

66. Of the largest gay bathhouse in the world, the Bulldog Baths, Shilts

writes, "Decorated in San Quentin motif . . . 'two-story prison is so incredibly real (real cells, real bars, real toilets . . .) that when you see a guard standing on the second tier looking down at you, you're ready to kneel down'" (ibid., 23).

67. "The sprawling sex palaces reminded Littlejohn of how far the city's sex industry had come since he had moved to S.F. in 1962. His first home in S.F. had been the Embarcadero YMCA, a precursor to the modern bathhouse. After Littlejohn helped organize the city's pioneering gay group, the Society of Individual Rights, in 1964, he had opened one of the city's first private sex clubs. He took some credit as one of the businessmen who introduced a whole generation of gay San Franciscans to the joys of orgy sex" (ibid., 431).

68. Lawrence R. Murphy, *Perverts by Official Order* (New York: Harrington Park Press, 1988).

69. David G. Ostrow, *Biobehavioral Control of AIDS* (New York: Irvington Publishers, 1987), 102.

70. Ibid., 19.

71. Shilts, *And the Band Played On,* 133.

72. Campbell, a former chairman of the board of the National Gay Task Force, carried a great deal of clout in the gay community. Ibid., 180.

73. "Privately, Cleve favored setting up informational pickets outside bathhouses to let patrons know they might be risking their lives in the sex palaces. But even hints toward such action were met with fierce resistance by others who still viewed bathhouses as symbols of the sexual liberation gays had fought so long to gain" (ibid., 180).

74. According to Shilts, describing Paul Volberding's epiphany, "The bathhouses weren't open because the owners didn't understand they were spreading death . . . [they] were open because they were still making money." Shilts, 422.

75. To Foucault sex is repressed because "it is incompatible with a general and intensive work imperative." He says of the "economic factor" that the "essential thing" is recognizing "a discourse in which sex, the proclamation of a new day to come, and the promise of a certain felicity are linked together" (*History of Sexuality*, 6–7).

76. Played by Lily Tomlin in the movie.

77. Shilts, *And the Band Played On,* 154.

78. Michael Callen and Richard Berkowitz, quoted from an article in the *New York Native*, said, "If going to the baths is really a game of

Russian roulette, then the advice must be to throw the gun away, not merely play less often" (ibid., 210).

79. Ibid., 259.

80. Norris G. Lang, "Homophobia and the AIDS Phenomenon," in *Culture and Aids*, ed. Douglas A. Feldman (New York: Praeger, 1991), 177.

81. Shilts, *And the Band Played On*, 305.

82. Ibid., 305, 316, 318.

83. "An owner of a bathhouse took a doctor aside, 'We're both in it for the same thing,' he said. 'Money. We make money at one end when they come to the baths. You make money from them on the other side when they come here.' Paul Volberding [the doctor] was speechless" (ibid., 422).

84. Susan Milstein, "S.F. Goes to Court over Baths," *San Francisco Chronicle*, October 11, 1984.

85. Shilts, *And the Band Played On*, 489.

86. At a conference in Vancouver, British Columbia, in March 1983, the new theories of AIDS transmission were met with insistence by radicals "that all this attention to the U.S. disease would foster homophobia," and anger from gay bathhouse owners "at the local newspaper for running a health page," which they said obsessed about "a handful of sick people in the United States" and that it "was bad for business." Ibid., 247.

87. "The Bay Area Physicians for Human Rights maintained that closure would lead to more cases of AIDS, not fewer. In the end, the only gay group to support Silverman was the Harvey Milk Gay Democratic Club" (ibid., 490).

88. Ibid.

89. By the time the measures were being put in place in San Francisco, "The debate was rapidly growing moot. . . . Only three of the city's eleven bathhouses were still in business" (ibid., 523).

90. Charles C. Hendy, "Other AIDS-Hit Cities Unlikely to Close Sex Clubs," *San Francisco Examiner*, October 14, 1984. Shilts writes, "The right wing was beginning to draw battle lines around issues of promiscuity and bathhouses. Rather than define their own battle lines, many gays adopted these issues as their front line of defense" (*And the Band Played On*, 312).

91. Milstein, "S.F. Goes to Court."

92. Susan Milstein, "Judge Orders Bathhouses in S.F. to Close Temporarily," *San Francisco Chronicle*, October 16, 1984.

93. "Cuomo Panel Proposes Rules to Curb AIDS at Bathhouses," *New York Times*, October 10, 1985.

94. "Bathhouse Curbs Called Help in Coast AIDS Fight," *New York Times*, October 24, 1985.

95. Russell Lewis, "The San Diego Bathhouse Controversy," *Sappho Speaks* (April 1986): 1.

96. The *New York Times* editorialized on November 10, 1985, that although a get-tough policy toward the baths and "other commercial establishments that persist in fostering 'high-risk sexual activity' associated with the spread of AIDS" was "a close call," it was justified due to the failure of voluntary changes in behavior to respond to "this bewildering disease."

97. "Letter to the Editor," *Gayzette*, San Diego, February 7, 1986.

98. Jay M. Kohorn, "Petition for Extraordinary Relief: If the LaRouche AIDS Initiative Had Passed in California," *Review of Law and Social Change* 15 (1986–87): 477–512.

99. "City Shuts a Bathhouse as Site of 'Unsafe Sex,'" *The New York Times*, December 7, 1985.

100. Philip Weiss, "Inside a Bathhouse," *New Republic*, December 2, 1985, 12–13.

101. *New York v. New St. Mark's Baths*, 497 N.Y.S. 2d 979 (1986).

102. Lila Abu-Loghud, "The Romance of Resistance: Tracing Transformations of Power through Bedouin Women," *American Ethnologist* 17, no. 1 (1990): 41–55.

103. Scheingold, *Rights*, 83.

104. Black legal scholars demur. For Patricia Williams, "most blacks have not turned away from the pursuit of rights even if what CLS scholars say about rights—that they are contradictory, indeterminate, reified and marginally decisive in social behavior—is so." Williams, "Alchemical Notes," 404.

105. Thomas L. Haskell, "The Curious Persistence of Rights Talk in the 'Age of Interpretation,'" *Journal of American History* 74 (1987).

106. Ibid., 1.

107. Leo Strauss, *Natural Right and History* (Chicago: University of Chicago Press, 1949), argues that after World War II the United States had the "yoke" of German historicist thought imposed on its tradition of natural right, particularly in the social sciences.

108. "The language of rights now dominates political debate in the United States" (Ronald Dworkin, *Taking Rights Seriously* [Cam-

bridge: Harvard University Press, 1977], 184). Recall the story told by Clifford Geertz about the Englishman in India who, "having been told that the world rested on the back of an elephant which rested in turn on the back of a turtle, asked . . . what did the turtle rest on? Another turtle. And that turtle? 'Ah, Sahib, after that it is turtles all the way down'" (*The Interpretation of Cultures: Selected Essays* [New York: Basic Books, 1973], 28–29).

109. According to Haskell, Nietzsche's response to this conventional observation is a description of rights as "a puffed up form of the will to power" ("Persistence," 15).

110. Ibid., 16.

111. Ibid., 28.

112. Lucinda Furlong, "AIDS Media: Counter-Representations," Whitney Museum of American Art: New American Film and Video Series, 1989, 1; see also Paula A. Treichler, "An Epidemic of Signification," *October* 43 (1987): 31.

113. Simon Watney, *Policing Desire: Pornography, AIDS, and the Media,* 2d ed. (Minneapolis: University of Minnesota Press, 1987).

114. Bumiller, *Civil Rights Society.*

115. One of the reasons may be the very propensity for mystification and innocence associated with rights that I will explore in relation to other movements.

116. Foucault, *Sexuality*, 8–9.

117. Peter Goodrich, *Languages of Law: From Logics of Memory to Nomadic Masks* (London: Weidenfeld and Nicholson, 1990), 108.

118. Ibid., 109–10.

171

Notes to Chapter 3

1. This comment to Derrick Bell was reported by Bell to Bill Rose of the University of Massachusetts at a reception given for Bell at Western New England College School of Law in 1990.

2. Bok had just turned down a tenured faculty appointment for David Trubek, a scholar identified with CLS, and upheld the denial of tenure to Clair Dalton, another "crit."

3. The law and economics movement, along with a more traditional orientation to the thought of the founding generation, provided the basis for Bork's conservatism.

4. Shared practices draw attention to debates in the social sciences

over "neo-institutionalism," in which this study may be placed as a description of the way institutions structure politics. See also Rogers M. Smith, "Political Jurisprudence, the New Institutionalism, and the Future of Public Law," *American Political Science Review* 82 (1988): 89–108; and Susan Burgess, "Beyond Instrumental Politics: The New Institutionalism, Legal Rhetoric, and Judicial Supremacy," *Polity* 25 (spring 1993): 445–59.

5. See Amy Kaplan, *The Social Construction of American Realism* (Chicago: University of Chicago Press, 1988).

6. Yves Dezalay, "From Mediation to Pure Law: Practice and Scholarly Representation within the Legal Sphere," *International Journal of the Sociology of Law* 14 (1986): 89–107.

7. Peter Goodrich, *Languages of Law: From Logics of Memory to Nomadic Masks* (London: Weidenfeld and Nicolson, 1990), 90.

8. In Garry Marshall's film *Pretty Woman*, the kindly manager of a hotel whose job is to mediate between the working-class staff and the upper-class clientele becomes the interpreter of class identifiers for a Los Angeles Cinderella who is elevated from prostitute to lover after her transformation into an acceptable romantic figure.

9. Gary Peller, "The Metaphysics of American Law," *California Law Review* 73 (1985): 1157. See also Pierre Bourdieu, *Outline of a Theory of Practice* (Cambridge: Cambridge University Press, 1977); Barbara Yngvesson, *Virtuous Citizens, Disruptive Subjects* (New York: Routledge, 1993).

10. These rules not only maintain the place of those in the economic elite, they also form and maintain the identity of other groups, whether organized around income (e.g., union members), ethnicity, or sexual orientation, as in the case of the life styles we know as gay or straight.

11. Mary Joe Frug, *Postmodern Legal Feminism* (New York: Routledge, 1992), 111.

12. Ken Emerson, "When Legal Titans Clash," *New York Times Magazine*, April 23, 1990, 25–31.

13. Roland Barthes, *The Eiffel Tower and Other Mythologies*, trans. Richard Howard (New York: Hill and Wang, 1979).

14. Christine B. Harrington, "Creating Gaps and Making Markets," *Law and Policy* 10 (1988): 293–316.

15. Robert Gordon, "'The Ideal and the Actual in the Law': Fantasies and Practices of New York City Lawyers, 1870–1910," in *The New*

High Priests: Lawyers in Post–Civil War America, ed. Gerard W. Gawalt (Westport, Conn.: Greenwood Press, 1984).

16. Robert Gordon, "Lawyers as the American Aristocracy," Holmes Lectures, Harvard Law School, Cambridge, Massachusetts, 1985; idem, "The Ideal and the Actual"; idem, "Legal Thought and Legal Practice in the Age of American Enterprise, 1870–1920," in *Professions and Professional Ideologies in America*, ed. Gerald L. Gelson (Chapel Hill: University of North Carolina Press, 1983).

17. Gordon, "The Ideal and the Actual."

18. Hilary Putnam, *The Many Faces of Realism* (La Salle, Ill.: Open Court, 1987).

19. Emerson, "Legal Titans," 27.

20. Areeda teaches antitrust, and his traditionalism is associated with wealth and power against the challenges of the unwashed descendants of realism.

21. Robert Stevens, *Law School: Legal Education in America from the 1850s to the 1980s* (Chapel Hill: University of North Carolina Press, 1983).

22. Ibid., 73–91.

23. Ibid., 21.

24. Ibid., 20; Burton J. Bledstein, *The Culture of Professionalism* (New York: Norton, 1976); Magali Sarfatti Larson, *The Rise of Professionalism: A Sociological Analysis* (Berkeley: University of California Press, 1977).

25. Stevens, *Law School*, xv.

26. The University of Pennsylvania was at least one exception.

27. Brigham and Harrington, "Realism and Its Consequences: An Inquiry into Contemporary Socio-legal Research," *International Journal of the Sociology of Law* 17 (1988): 41–62.

28. Stevens, *Law School*, 131.

29. Karl Llewellyn, *The Bramble Bush* (New York: Oceana Publications, 1951).

30. Jerome Frank, *Law and the Modern Mind* (New York: Coward-McCann, 1936).

31. Walter F. Murphy and C. Herman Pritchett, *Courts, Judges, and Politics: An Introduction to the Judicial Process* (New York: Random House, 1979), 6. Political scientists, in particular, among social scientists trace their lineage to realism. The work of the judicial behavior movement was an outgrowth of Pound's influence and related to

realism in the law schools. Thus, it is not too surprising that when looking back on their roots political scientists are not as attentive to the development of realism as a legal ideology in its own right.

32. Brigham and Harrington, "Realism and Its Consequences," 55.

33. Harry Stumpf, *American Judicial Politics* (San Diego: Harcourt Brace Jovanovich, 1987), 37. "[T]hese notions have been commonplace in political science since Peltason" (Brigham and Harrington, "Realism," 55).

34. William Twining, *Karl Llewellyn and the Realist Movement* (Norman: University of Oklahoma Press, 1973).

35. The presentation here is a broad sweep that does not adequately engage with important debates generated by scholars such as Twining, Stevens, Kalman, and John Henry Schlegel, whose recent book, *American Legal Realism and Empirical Social Science* (Chapel Hill: University of North Carolina Press, 1995), suggests that we see realism not as a jurisprudence but as a way of life.

36. Jerome Frank, *Courts on Trial* (Princeton: Princeton University Press, 1949).

37. Norman L. Rosenberg has proposed that contemporary realism is in "retreat" from the critical realism of the earlier period. He portrays Anthony Lewis's *Gideon's Trumpet* (New York: Random House, 1964) as a vivid example of a sanitized realism that introduces elements of practice, formerly unseen, to the public. Rosenberg, "Gideon's Trumpet: Sounding the Retreat from Legal Realism," in *Recasting America: Culture and Politics in the Age of Cold War*, ed. Lary May (Chicago: University of Chicago Press, 1989).

38. Bruce Ackerman, *Reconstructing American Law* (Cambridge: Harvard University Press, 1984).

39. Laura Kalman, *Legal Realism at Yale, 1927–1960* (Chapel Hill: University of North Carolina Press, 1986).

40. Peller, "Metaphysics."

41. Brigham and Harrington, "Realism and Its Consequences," 41. Describing this relationship began as a joint project with Harrington, and the consequences for social science research from disputes processing to judicial behavior is tied to that project.

42. Ibid., 42. The philosophical bases of this view have become associated with the relativism and pragmatism of Richard Rorty, *Philosophy and the Mirror of Nature* (Princeton: Princeton University Press, 1979).

43. Brigham and Harrington, "Realism and Its Consequences," 42.

44. David B. Wilkins, "Legal Realism for Lawyers," *Harvard Law Review* 104 (1990): 468–524.

45. Constitutional doctrines announced by these courts, particularly the federal courts of appeal and the Supreme Court, have all but supplanted the text itself, much less public understandings, as sources of law. See John Brigham, *The Cult of the Court* (Philadelphia: Temple University Press, 1987).

46. While the tradition of judicial centralism goes back at least to the early part of this century and is evident in the work of Edward S. Corwin, the source for modern, politically sophisticated attention to the Supreme Court is the work of C. Herman Pritchett. This work led to the legal manifestation of the *behavioral* revolution with its attention to the attitudes of judges. Brigham and Harrington, "Realism and Its Consequences," 46.

47. Schlegel depicts such a narrow slice of academic activity on law that he misses the overriding similarities between realist principles and social research in other parts of the academy.

48. This movement, in the positive tradition, has offered two divergent sorts of insight, hard fact and indeterminate theory. In the last decade theory has been dominant, making law and society more attractive to CLS than law and economics.

49. Roberto M. Unger, *The Critical Legal Studies Movement* (Cambridge: Harvard University Press, 1986).

50. "Mr. Langdell's ideal in the law, the end of all his striving, is the *elegantia juris* or *logical* integrity of the system as a system. He is, perhaps, the greatest living legal theologian." Oliver Wendell Holmes, Jr., "Review of *A Selection of Cases on the Law of Contracts*," *American Law School Review* 233 (1880).

51. "The first principle of legal community is theocratic. It is the attribution of an originary status and authority to the speech of the law. Legal discourse and the texts through which it gains its positive formulations are simply representations of a primary speech that pre-exists and authorizes the legal textual community." Goodrich, *Languages*, 108–9.

52. Unger, *Critical Legal Studies Movement*, 3.

53. Louis Althusser, *Lenin and Philosophy* (New York: Monthly Review Press, 1971).

54. Duncan Kennedy, "Form and Substance in Private Law Adjudication," *Harvard Law Review* 89 (1976): 1685; the constitutive dimensions can

be seen in the work of critical race theorists and feminists, where the movements against sexual harassment and violent pornography and the struggle to preserve antidiscrimination law showed the influence of legal form in some of our most progressive political efforts.

55. David Kairys, ed., *The Politics of Law* (New York: Pantheon, 1982); "Critical Legal Studies Symposium," *Stanford Law Review* 36 (1984); Mark Kelman, *A Guide to Critical Legal Studies* (Cambridge: Harvard University Press, 1987).

56. While there is some attention to the movement in the *Stanford Law Review* symposium, which we will turn to shortly, *The Politics of Law* paid relatively little attention to law and economics.

57. Of 103 index citations to other scholars, 8 are to women, and without the pornography issue and "difference" there would only be one or two.

58. This was not true of the initial CLS conference in Madison, Wisconsin, and the volume edited a few years later by Kairys, himself a practicing Guild lawyer.

59. Sanford Levinson, *Constitutional Faith* (Princeton: Princeton University Press, 1988).

60. David Mamet, *Writing in Restaurants* (New York: Viking, 1986).

61. Levinson, *Constitutional Faith*, 7.

62. Paul Leicester Ford, ed., *Writings of Thomas Jefferson*, vol. 10 (New York: G. P. Putnam's Sons, 1899), 43.

63. Jacob Cooke, ed., *The Federalist* (Cleveland: Meridian Books, 1961), 340.

64. Levinson, *Constitutional Faith*, 155.

65. Ibid., 158.

66. Ibid.

67. Allan C. Hutchinson and Patrick J. Monahan, "Law, Politics and Critical Legal Scholars: The Unfolding Drama of American Legal Thought," *Stanford Law Review* 36 (1984): 199.

68. See, e.g., Richard Epstein, "Judicial Review: Reckoning on Two Kinds of Error," in *Economic Liberties and the Judiciary*, ed. James A. Dorn and Henry G. Manne (Fairfax, Va.: Cato Institute and George Mason University Press, 1987).

69. See, e.g., Richard A. Posner, *Economic Analysis of Law*, 2d ed. (Boston: Little, Brown, 1977).

70. Guido Calabresi and Philip Bobbitt, *Tragic Choices* (New York: Norton, 1978).

71. Richard A. Posner, "A Statistical Study of Antitrust Law Enforcement," *Journal of Law and Economics* 13 (1970): 365–419; idem, *Antitrust Law: An Economic Perspective* (Chicago: University of Chicago Press, 1976).

72. Richard Epstein, *Takings* (Cambridge: Harvard University Press, 1985); Bernard Siegan, *Economic Liberties and the Constitution* (Chicago: University of Chicago Press, 1980); Kate Stith, "Government Interests in Criminal Law," *Albany Law Review* 55 (1992): 679–87.

73. R. H. Coase, "The Problem of Social Cost," *Journal of Law and Economics* 3 (1960): 1.

74. Lewis Kornhauser, "The General Image of Authority," *Stanford Law Review* 36 (1984): 349–89.

75. Mark Kelman, "Choice and Utility," *University of Wisconsin Law Review* (1979): 769; idem, "Consumption Theory, Production Theory, and Ideology in the Coase Theorem," *Southern California Law Review* 52 (1979): 669; Tom Heller, "The Importance of Normative Decision-Making: The Limitations of Legal Economics as a Basis for a Liberal Jurisprudence—As Illustrated by the Regulation of Vacation Home Development," *Southern California Law Review* 53 (1980): 1215; Duncan Kennedy, "Cost-Benefit Analysis of Entitlement Problems: A Critique," *Stanford Law Review* 33 (1981): 387.

76. Kornhauser, "General Image," 352.

77. Brigham and Harrington, "Realism and Its Consequences."

78. Both CLS and law and economics have claimed to be leading the way to a "post-realist" legal scholarship. See Mark Tushnet, "Post-Realist Legal Scholarship," *Wisconsin Law Review* (1980): 1383–1401; Jason Scott Johnston, "Law, Economics, and Post-Realist Explanation," *Law and Society Review* 24 (1990): 1217–54.

79. Posner criticized this move and others like it, arguing that while the methods of economic science simply reflect the true nature of the law, feminism and literary method were unhelpful interlopers into legal discourse. "The Decline of Law as an Autonomous Discipline: 1962–1987," *Harvard Law Review* 100 (1987): 761.

80. Emerson, "Legal Titans," 66. Emerson's article also calls attention to the "lawyer as janitor" metaphor shared by both Kennedy and Charles Fried.

81. The constitutive alternative to legal realism, a modern, relational political economy, allows us to assess the impact and consequences

of realism as a law school ideology. Harrington and Brigham, "Realism and Its Consequences."

82. Austin Sarat and William L. F. Felstiner, "Legal Realism in Lawyer-Client Communications," ABF Working Paper #8723.

83. William L. F. Felstiner and Austin Sarat, "Law and Strategy in the Divorce Lawyer's Office," *Law and Society Review* 20 (1986): 93–134.

84. Ibid., 127.

85. Ibid. In addition, the scholarship continues to promote a "gap" framework in which the ideal, in this case of appellate doctrine, is "preached" and the reality of legal practice is offered as "law as it is experienced" (ibid., 132).

86. Peller, "Metaphysics," 1153.

87. Ibid., 1154. Peller adds, "[T]he present situation is . . . the result of political and existential choices to tame realism and to continue the construction of the metaphysics of liberal authority, the claims to impersonality and impartiality" (ibid., 1260).

88. Ibid., 1263.

89. Ibid., 1265.

90. Brigham and Harrington, "Realism and Its Consequences."

91. Bell, *And We Are Not Saved*, 1.

92. Ibid., 5.

93. Kimberlé Crenshaw, "From Celebration to Tribulation: The Constitution Goes to Trial," *Harvard Law Review* 101 (1988), quoted in Bell, *And We Are Not Saved*, 7.

94. Ibid., 41.

95. Ibid., 60–61.

96. Peter Fitzpatrick, "Racism and the Innocence of Law," *Journal of Law and Society* 14 (1987): 121.

97. Alan Hunt, *Explorations in Law and Society: Toward a Constitutive Theory of Law* (New York: Routledge, 1993).

Notes to Chapter 4

1. Susan Leeson assured me of this quality and described disputes as "always having been around" in commenting on a panel at the Western Political Science Association in Minneapolis, Minnesota, in 1986.

2. Max Gluckman, *The Judicial Process among the Barotse of Northern Rhodesia* (Manchester: Manchester University Press, 1955); P. H.

Gulliver, *Social Control in an African Society* (London: Routledge and Kegan Paul, 1963); Karl Llewellyn and Edward A. Hoebel, *The Cheyenne Way* (Norman: University of Oklahoma Press, 1941).

3. Wilhelm Aubert, "Competition and Dissensus: Two Types of Conflict and of Conflict Resolution," *Journal of Conflict Resolution* 7 (1963): 26.

4. Maureen Cain and Kalman Kulcsar, "Thinking Disputes: An Essay on the Origins of the Dispute Industry," *Law and Society Review* 16 (1981–82): 375–402.

5. The concept of "ideology" is used here after the fashion suggested by Alan Hunt, "The Ideology of Law," *Law and Society Review* 19 (1985): 11, and developed by the Amherst Seminar, "Special Issue: Law and Ideology," *Law and Society Review* 22 (1988).

6. Richard L. Abel, "A Comparative Theory of Dispute Institutions in Society," *Law and Society Review* 8 (1974): 217.

7. Cain and Kulcsar also suggest that in the ideology of disputes the parties are seen as qualitatively identical—like the consumers in the marketplace, they are interchangeable except for quantitative differences, such as more money or more power—and that the conceptual practice of identifying disputes provides a comparative foundation. "Dispute Industry," 380.

8. They are also adhered to in a manner Cain and Kulcsar call ideological idealism.

9. See Richard L. Abel, ed., *Politics of Informal Justice*, vol. 1 (New York: Academic Press, 1982), with the "Special Issue on Dispute Resolution" of the *Law and Society Review* 15 (1980–81) on disputing.

10. Angela Y. Davis, *Women, Race and Class* (New York: Vintage, 1983).

11. Peter Fitzpatrick, *The Mythology of Modern Law* (London: Routledge, 1992).

12. Peter Goodrich, *Languages of Law: From Logics of Memory to Nomadic Masks* (London: Weidenfeld and Nicolson, 1990), 90. Goodrich adds, "Without the interpreters, in other words, justice would have no tongue."

13. Roscoe Pound, "The Causes of Popular Dissatisfaction with the Administration of Justice," *American Bar Association Reports* 29 (1906): 395.

14. My work on these topics draws heavily from Christine B. Harrington, who introduced me to the field and with whom I continue to

share the inquiry into this movement. See her *Shadow Justice* (Westport, Conn.: Greenwood Press, 1985).

15. Roger Fisher and William Ury, *Getting to Yes: Negotiating Agreement without Giving In* (New York: Penguin, 1983).

16. For discussion of practitioner rejection of this theoretical orientation, see Christine B. Harrington, "'Bundles of Input': Negotiating the Nation's First Nuclear Waste Dump—A Profile of Howard Bellman" (paper for the Harvard Program on Negotiation, 1991), reprinted as "Howard Bellman: Using 'Bundles of Input' to Negotiate and Environmental Dispute," in *When Talk Works: Profiles of Mediators*, ed. Deborah Kolb (San Francisco: Jossey-Bass, 1994), 105–47.

17. Harrington, "Bundles of Input," 37.

18. Christine B. Harrington, "Delegalization Reform Movements: A Historical Analysis," in *The Politics of Informal Justice*, vol. 1, ed. Richard L. Abel (New York: Academic Press, 1982).

19. Ibid., 36.

20. Ibid., 39.

21. James Weinstein, *The Corporate Ideal and the Liberal State 1900–1918* (Boston: Beacon Press, 1968).

22. Ibid., xiii.

23. Ibid., 11.

24. Ibid., 18.

25. Ibid., 48.

26. *Ives v. South Buffalo Railroad Co.*, 201 NY 271 (1911).

27. See Leonard D. White, *The City Manager* (Chicago: University of Chicago Press, 1927).

28. Grant McConnell, *Private Power and American Democracy* (New York: Knopf, 1966).

29. Harrington, *Shadow Justice*, 41.

30. Amy Bridges, *A City in the Republic* (Cambridge: Cambridge University Press, 1984).

31. Harrington, *Shadow Justice*, 44.

32. D. Marie Provine, *Judging Credentials: Nonlawyer Judges and the Politics of Professionalism* (Chicago: University of Chicago Press, 1986).

33. Mark Kelman, *A Guide to Critical Legal Studies* (Cambridge: Harvard University Press, 1987); Richard A. Posner, *Antitrust Law: An Economic Perspective* (Chicago: University of Chicago Press, 1976).

34. Kelman, *Guide*, 3.

35. Ibid.

36. Ibid., 247.

37. Nor do the gentry introduced into legal theory by Douglas Hay and E. P. Thompson, because ultimately their grace under the Black Acts is seen as an aspect of legal power and system stability rather than benevolence. Douglas Hay et al., *Albion's Fatal Tree: Crime and Society in Eighteenth-Century England* (New York: Free Press, 1975).

38. Laura Nader described the limitations of what she called "binary thinking" in the law reform literature. See "The Recurrent Dialectic between Legality and Its Alternatives: The Limitations of Binary Thinking," *University of Pennsylvania Law Review* 132 (1984): 621.

39. For an interesting account of this problem and an alternative to the traditional framework pitting informalism against rights, see Craig A. McEwen, Lynn Mather, and Richard J. Maiman, "Lawyers, Mediation, and the Management of Divorce Practice," *Law and Society Review* 28 (1994): 149–86.

40. See Sally Merry and Christine B. Harrington, "Ideological Production," *Law and Society Review* 22 (1988): 709–35.

41. The address was published in *American Bar Association Reports* 29 (1906), 395; an abridged version appeared in *American Bar Association Journal* 57 (1971): 348.

42. Arthur L. Harding, "Professor Pound Makes History," in Harding, ed. *The Administration of Justice in Retrospect*, ed. Arthur L. Harding (Dallas: Southern Methodist University Press, 1957).

43. Roscoe Pound, "The Decadence of Equity," *Columbia Law Review* 5 (1905): 20.

44. *Muller v. Oregon*, 208 U.S. 412 (1908).

45. John Henry Schlegel, *American Legal Realism and Empirical Social Science* (Chapel Hill: University of North Carolina Press, 1995). Schlegel says very little about Pound.

46. Harding, "History," 8.

47. John Wigmore, introduction to *Roscoe Pound . . . The Causes of Popular Dissatisfaction with the Administration of Justice* (Chicago: American Judicature Society, n.d.).

48. Warren Burger, "Agenda for 2000 A.D.—A Need for Systematic Anticipation," *Federal Rules Decisions* 70 (1976): 23–35.

49. Ibid.

50. Pound's example of tinkering was eliminating law Latin and French. Burger's examples included the Administrative Procedure Act and the merger of law and equity.

51. Burger, "Agenda," 32.

52. Ibid.

53. Like Sander's work in general, and that of his colleagues Roger Fisher and Larry Susskind, the speech indicates newer dimensions of informalism. Frank Sander, "Varieties of Dispute Processing," in *Neighborhood Justice*, ed. Malcolm Feeley and Roman Tomasic (New York: Longman, 1982).

54. Harrington, *Shadow Justice*, 52.

55. Christine B. Harrington, "An Overview of the Dispute Resolution Field" (report to the Ford Foundation, May 1986), 4.

56. Robert H. Mnookin and Lewis Kornhauser, "Bargaining in the Shadow of the Law: The Case of Divorce," *Yale Law Journal* 88 (1979): 950.

57. Lon Fuller, "Mediation—Its Forms and Functions," *Southern California Law Review* 44 (1971): 353.

58. Frank Sander, "Successful Techniques for Mediating Family Breakup," *Mediation Quarterly* 2 (1983): 354–63.

59. Ibid., 355.

60. Legal InfoTrac reported reviews in all the major law journals, fourteen in all. See reviews by Simon Roberts, *Modern Law Review* 53 (1990); Barbara Yngvesson, *Law and Social Inquiry* 13 (1988); Sally Engle Merry, *Harvard Law Review* 100 (1987).

61. Sponsors also included the Academy of Family Mediators, American Arbitration Association, ABA Special Committee on Dispute Resolution, American Sociological Association Section on Peace and War to Wayne State University's Center for Peace and Conflict Studies, and Woodbury College's Washington County Mediation Project, for a total of fifty sponsors.

62. Lenore J. Weitzman, Herbert Jacob, and Mary Ann Glendon, "The Divorce Revolution," *New York Times*, November 7, 1985, III 1:3.

63. "Issues to Consider Regarding Mediation of Custody Disputes," Family Law Project Conference on Women and Family Law, New York University, January 16, 1984, 6.

64. For a discussion of some of the scholarship on violence in the context of domestic disputes and feminism, see Jo Dixon, "The Nexus

of Sex, Spousal Violence, and the State," *Law and Society Review* 29 (1995): 359–76.

65. Howard S. Erlanger, Elizabeth Chambliss, and Marygold S. Melli, "Participation and Flexibility in Informal Processes: Cautions from the Divorce Context," *Law and Society Review* 21 (1987): 585.

66. See, e.g., Trina Grillo, "The Mediation Alternative: Process Dangers for Women," *Yale Law Journal* 100 (1991): 1545.

67. Richard A. Posner, "The Ethical Significance of Free Choice: A Reply to Professor West," *Harvard Law Review* 99 (1986): 1431.

68. Harrington, "Bundles of Input," 37.

69. Joel Handler, *The Conditions of Discretion: Autonomy, Community, Bureaucracy* (New York: Russell Sage Foundation, 1986).

70. Joel Handler, "Dependent People, the State, and the Modern/Post Modern Search for a Dialogic Community," *UCLA Law Review* 35 (1988): 999.

71. Ibid., 1031.

72. Ibid.

73. Christine B. Harrington, "Delegalization Reform Movements: A Historical Analysis," in *The Politics of Informal Justice*, ed. Richard L. Abel (New York: Academic Press, 1982).

74. Carrie Menkel-Meadow, "Toward Another View of Legal Negotiation: The Structure of Problem-Solving," *UCLA Law Review* 31 (1984): 754.

75. Handler, "Dependent People," 1033.

76. Pierre Bourdieu, *Distinction: A Social Critique of the Judgement of Taste*, trans. Richard Nice (Cambridge: Harvard University Press, 1984), 3.

77. Owen M. Fiss, "Against Settlement," *Yale Law Journal* 93 (1984): 1073–90.

78. Derek Bok, "A Flawed System," *Harvard Magazine*, May–June 1983, 38.

79. Fiss, "Against Settlement," 1075.

80. Boaventura de Sousa Santos, "Law: A Map of Misreading," in *Toward a New Common Sense* (New York: Routledge, 1995), 473.

81. Stuart Macauley, "Images of Law in Everyday Life: The Lessons of School, Entertainment and Spectator Sports," *Law and Society Review* 21 (1987): 185.

82. Santos, "Map," 473.

83. This point has been driven home in scholarship in the last decade. In Lauren B. Edelman, Howard S. Erlanger, and John Lande,

"Internal Dispute Resolution: The Transformation of Civil Rights in the Workplace," *Law and Society Review* 27 (1993): 497–534, "internal dispute resolution" refers to efforts within firms to deal with rights grievances. The findings are that remedial processes such as these "tend to recast discrimination claims as typical managerial problems . . . [possibly] undermining legal rights by deemphasizing and depoliticizing workplace discrimination."

84. Michel Foucault, *Discipline and Punish: The Birth of the Prison* (New York: Vintage, 1977); David Garland, *Punishment in Modern Society: A Study in Social Theory* (Chicago: University of Chicago Press, 1990); Dario Melossi, *The State of Social Control* (New York: St. Martin's, 1990).

85. Cain and Kulcsar, "Disputes Industry."

86. Youssef Cohen, *The Manipulation of Consent: The State and Working-Class Consciousness in Brazil* (Pittsburgh: University of Pittsburgh Press, 1989), 73.

87. Samuel Bowles and Herbert Gintis, *Schooling in Capitalist America* (New York: Basic Books, 1976).

88. John Brigham, "Bad Attitudes: The Consequences of Survey Research for Constitutional Practice," *Review of Politics* 52 (1990): 582–602.

89. Nancy Fraser is more critical of the struggle between rights and needs discourse. See *Unruly Practices: Power, Discourse, and Gender in Contemporary Social Theory*. (Minneapolis: University of Minnesota Press, 1989).

Notes to Chapter 5

1. In his discussion of the processes of reading the law, Peter Goodrich describes this situation in terms of differentiation: "they speak 'in the name of' the father or of the law, and the sexism or asymmetry of such speech is therefore not a matter of the male gender of representation, or the language—the personal pronouns—of causality, but of the construction of sexuality, of differentiation, as such." Peter Goodrich, *Languages of Law: From Logics of Memory to Nomadic Masks* (London: Weidenfeld and Nicolson, 1990), 287.

2. Catharine MacKinnon, "Not a Moral Issue," in *Feminism Unmodified: Discourses on Life and Law* (Cambridge: Harvard University Press, 1987).

3. W. E. B. Du Bois, *John Brown* (Philadelphia: George W. Jacobs and Co., 1909), 81.
4. John L. Comaroff and Simon Roberts, *Rules and Processes: The Cultural Logic of Dispute in an African Context* (Chicago: University of Chicago Press, 1981).
5. Elizabeth Young-Bruehl, *Mind and the Body Politic* (New York: Routledge, 1989); Zillah Eisenstein, *The Female Body and the Law* (Berkeley: University of California Press, 1988); Susan Sontag, *AIDS and Its Metaphors* (New York: Farrar, Strauss and Giroux, 1989).
6. Kate Millet, *Sexual Politics* (New York: Avon, 1969), 58.
7. The movements against domestic violence and rape share an ideological structure with the antipornography movement and will be developed here in conjunction with the effort to limit access to pornography.
8. Andrea Dworkin, "Pornography: The New Terrorism," in *Letters from a War Zone* (London: Secker and Warburg, 1988), 198.
9. A button at the Lesbian and Gay Pride Rally, Northampton, Massachusetts, May 5, 1990, read: "Pornography is the Theory, Rape is the Practice."
10. In her article "Law, Boundaries, and the Bounded Self" (in *Law and the Order of Culture*, ed. Robert Post [Berkeley: University of California Press, 1991]), Jennifer Nedelsky looks to the feminist author Starhawk as an example of an "alternative framework for thinking about political action and personal psychological transformation" (173). Starhawk's interest in witchcraft and its contribution to women's spirituality reflects the otherness of the community that is central to this discussion of the oppositional force of rage. See Starhawk, *Dreaming the Dark: Magic, Sex, and Politics* (Boston: Beacon Press, 1982).
11. See Egon Bittner, "Radicalism and the Organization of Radical Movements," *American Sociological Review* 28 (1963): 928–40.
12. Sontag, *AIDS*, 6.
13. Ibid.
14. " 'You don't feel in the mood for it, I suppose,' says he, and then he adds: 'that's fine because now I'm going to warm you up a bit.' With that he up and ties her to the bedstead, gags her, and then goes for the razor strop. On the way to the bathroom, he grabs a bottle of mustard from the kitchen. He comes back with the razor strop and he belts the piss out of her. And after that he rubs the

185

mustard into the raw welts. 'That ought to keep you warm for tonight,' he says." Henry Miller, *Sexus* (New York: Grove, 1965), quoted in Millett, *Sexual Politics*, 9.

15. Zillah Eisenstein, *Feminism and Sexual Equality* (New York: Monthly Review Press, 1984).

16. See also J. Vega, "Coercion and Consent: Classical Liberal Concepts in Texts on Sexual Violence," *International Journal of the Sociology of Law* 16 (1988): 75–89.

17. John Brigham, "Right, Rage and Remedy," *Studies in American Political Development* 2 (1987): 303–16.

18. Owen Fiss, "Free Speech and Social Structure" (unpublished manuscript, 1985).

19. *Chaplinsky v. New Hampshire*, 315 U.S. 568 (1942).

20. *Commonwealth v. Holmes*, 17 Mass. 336 (1821). Other "erotic classics" include *The Arabian Nights*, *Tom Jones*, Boccaccio's *Decameron*, Rousseau's *Confessions*, and Ovid's *Art of Love*.

21. *U.S. v. Kennerley*, 209 F. 119 (1913).

22. *Butler v. Michigan*, 352 U.S. 380 (1957).

23. *U.S. v. Ulysses*, 5 F. Supp. 182 (1933).

24. *U.S. v. Roth*, 237 F. 2d 796 (1956).

25. *Holmby Productions v. Vaughan*, 350 U.S. 870 (1955); see also *Winters v. New York*, 333 U.S. 507 (1948), which invalidated part of a New York obscenity statute but did not use the argument of the sort that was to come in *Roth*.

26. *Roth*, 481.

27. Ibid., 484.

28. Ibid.

29. *Jacobellis v. Ohio*, 378 U.S. 184 (1964).

30. 383 US 413 (1966).

31. *Miller v. California*, 413 U.S. 15 (1973).

32. *Paris Adult Theater v. Slaton*, 413 U.S. 49 (1973).

33. *Erznoznik v. City of Jacksonville*, 43 LW 4809 (1975); *Young v. American Mini Theatres*, 427 US 50 (1976).

34. See Kathleen Barry, *Female Sexual Slavery* (Englewood Cliffs, N.J.: Prentice-Hall, 1979).

35. Joel Grossman, "The First Amendment and the New Anti-Pornography Statutes," *News for Teachers of Political Science* 45 (1985): 16.

36. Donald Downs, *The New Politics of Pornography* (Chicago: University of Chicago Press, 1989), 155.

37. *American Booksellers Association v. Hudnut*, 58 F. Supp. 1316 (1984).
38. A proposed ordinance for Cambridge, Massachusetts, modeled after the Minneapolis and Indianapolis ordinances, was defeated in November 1985 by a vote of 13,031 to 9,419.
39. Dworkin, "Pornography."
40. Ibid., 198.
41. Ibid.
42. Ibid., 199.
43. Ibid., 200.
44. "Colloquium, Violent Pornography: Degradation of Women versus Right of Free Speech," *New York University Review of Law and Social Change* 8 (1978–79).
45. Dworkin, "Pornography," 218.
46. Mark Kessler, "Legal Discourse and Political Intolerance: The Ideology of Clear and Present Danger," *Law and Society Review* 27 (1993): 559–98.
47. Dworkin, "Pornography," 215.
48. See Judy Fudge, "The Effect of Entrenching a Bill of Rights upon Political Discourse: Feminist Demands and Sexual Violence in Canada," *International Journal of the Sociology of Law* 17 (1989): 445–63.
49. Dworkin, "Pornography," 216.
50. Jean Elshtain, "The New Porn Wars," *Nation*, June 25, 1984, 15–20.
51. Donald Downs, *The New Politics of Pornography* (Chicago: University of Chicago Press, 1989); Richard Randall, *Freedom and Taboo* (Berkeley: University of California Press, 1989).
52. Randall, *Freedom and Taboo*, 5.
53. Ibid., 265.
54. Ibid., 228.
55. Ibid., 241.
56. Ibid., 133–34.
57. Downs, *New Politics*, 195.
58. MacKinnon's letter was in response to a review by Franklin E. Zimring that appeared in the *New York Times*, January 28, 1990.
59. That is, if we are to get beyond the censorship issue.
60. During the question period after a speech in Amherst in February 1990, MacKinnon answered the "perennial first question" about lesbian pornography with an extraordinary discussion of the

images constructed by the pornographer. This is something Randall tells us about.

61. Pierre Bourdieu, "The Force of Law: Toward a Sociology of the Juridical Field," *Hastings Law Journal* 38 (1987): 201.

62. Catharine MacKinnon, "Liberalism and the Death of Feminism," in *The Sexual Liberals and the Attack on Feminism*, ed. Dorchen Leidholdt and Janice G. Raymond (New York: Pergamon Press, 1990).

63. Dworkin, "Pornography," 201.

64. Ibid., 201.

65. Susan Brownmiller, *Against Our Will: Men, Women and Rape* (New York: Penguin, 1975).

66. Fiss, "Free Speech," 26.

67. Nedelsky, "Boundaries," 174.

68. Carole S. Vance, *Pleasure and Danger: Exploring Female Sexuality* (Boston: Routledge and Kegan Paul, 1984); Ann Ferguson, "The Sex Debate in the Women's Movement: A Socialist-Feminist View" (unpublished manuscript, 1980); see also idem, *Blood at the Root: Motherhood, Sexuality and Male Dominance* (London: Pandora, 1989).

69. The constitutive relationship between ideas and social life in politics is brought out in the critique of MacKinnon discussed in the next chapter. Stanley Fish, "Going Down the Anti-Formalist Road," paper presented to the Amherst Seminar on Legal Ideology, February 24, 1989, and reprinted in *Doing What Comes Naturally: Change, Rhetoric, and the Practice of Theory in Literary and Legal Studies* (Durham, N.C.: Duke University Press, 1989).

70. "You can tell you are being principled by the degree to which you abhor what you allow." Catharine MacKinnon, *Only Words* (Cambridge: Harvard University Press, 1993), 75.

71. As part of a tactical discussion titled "Beyond Pornography," Jessica LaMontagne criticized the antipornography movement in the journal *Left Field*, March 1990, published by graduate students at the University of Massachusetts, Amherst.

72. Brief Amici Curiae of Feminist Anti-Censorship Task Force et al., in *American Booksellers v. Hudnut, Journal of Law Reform* 21 (1988): 69; see also Dorchen Leidholt and Janice G. Raymond, *The Sexual Liberals and the Attack on Feminism* (New York: Pergamon Press, 1990).

73. Fiss, "Free Speech," 1.

74. Ibid., 21.

75. Ibid.

76. Janice Raymond, *A Passion for Friends* (Boston: Beacon Press, 1986).

77. Mary Daly, "Be-Witching: Re-Calling the Archimagical Powers of Women," in Leidholdt and Raymond, *Sexual Liberals*, 212.

78. For example, "The man-dated world is clockocracy—the society that is dead set by the clocks and calendars of fathered time. It is marked by measurements that tick off women's Lifetimes/Lifelines in tidy tidbits. Clockocracy is marked by male-ordered monotony that breaks Biorhythms, preparing the way for the fullness of fathered time, that is, doomsday." Ibid., 219.

79. See Kristin Luker, *Abortion and the Politics of Motherhood* (Berkeley: University of California Press, 1984).

80. Downs, *New Politics*, 155.

Notes to Chapter 6

1. Antonio Gramsci, "The Intellectuals," in *Selections from the Prison Notebooks* (New York: International Publishers, 1971).

2. Magali Sarfatti Larson, *The Rise of Professionalism: A Sociological Analysis* (Berkeley: University of California Press, 1977).

3. Kristin Bumiller, *The Civil Rights Society: The Social Construction of Victims* (Baltimore: Johns Hopkins University Press, 1988).

4. For the link between reason and intellectual influence, see Gramsci, *Notebooks*, 257–64.

5. John Brigham, "Bad Attitudes: The Consequences of Survey Research for Constitutional Practice," *Review of Politics* 52 (1990): 582–602.

6. Hygienics was an earlier movement to make cleanliness a standard of social acceptability.

7. California's initiative against the Rumford Fair Housing statute was later overturned by the U.S. Supreme Court.

8. Subsequent to the period under study, the militia movement linked to the bombing of a federal building in Oklahoma City in 1995 further supported this sense of rage.

9. See Sidney Tarrow, *Power in Movement: Social Movements, Collective Action and Politics* (Cambridge: Cambridge University Press, 1994).

10. Enrique Laraña, Hank Johnston, and Joseph R. Gusfield, *New Social Movements: From Ideology to Identity* (Philadelphia: Temple University Press, 1994).

11. Ibid., 3.
12. Ibid., 8.
13. Paul Burstein, "Legal Mobilization as a Social Movement Tactic: The Struggle for Equal Employment Opportunity," *American Journal of Sociology* 96 (1991): 1201–25.
14. Michael McCann, *Rights at Work: Pay Equity Reform and the Politics of Legal Mobilization* (Chicago: University of Chicago Press, 1994).
15. Stuart Scheingold, *The Politics of Rights* (New Haven: Yale University Press, 1974).
16. McCann, *Rights at Work*, 279.
17. Mark Tushnet, *The NAACP's Legal Strategy against Segregated Education, 1925–1950* (Chapel Hill: University of North Carolina Press, 1987).
18. *County of Washington, Oregon v. Gunther*, 452 U.S. 161 (1982).
19. *AFSCME v. State of Washington*, 770 F. 2d 1401 (9th Cir. 1985) rev'g 578 F. Supp. 846 (D. Wash. 1983).
20. McCann, *Rights at Work*, 285.
21. Ibid.
22. Gramsci argued that political science declined when "[p]olitics became synonymous with parliamentary politics." He proposed a "science of the State," the State being "the entire complex of practical and theoretical activities with which the ruling class not only justifies and maintains its dominance, but manages to win the active consent of those over whom it rules." Gramsci, *Notebooks*, 243–53.
23. Gramsci describes Machiavelli as asserting the "necessity for the State to be ruled by law, by fixed principles, which virtuous citizens can follow in certainty of not being destroyed by the blows of blind fate." By this mechanism, the Italian medieval bourgeoisie might "pass from the corporate to the political phase" by freeing itself from "the medieval cosmopolitan conception represented by the Pope, the clergy and also by the lay intellectuals." Gramsci, *Notebooks*, 257–64.
24. Michel Foucault, *Discipline and Punish: The Birth of the Prison* (New York: Vintage, 1979); but see Alan Hunt, *Explorations in Law and Society: Toward a Constitutive Theory of Law* (New York: Routledge, 1993).
25. "One sees better the nature of state bureaucracy in its relation to movements than in its own terms." Alain Touraine, *The Voice and*

the Eye: An Analysis of Social Movements (Cambridge: Cambridge University Press, 1981), 26.

26. Ibid., 25–29.
27. Karl Klare, "Law Making as Praxis," *Telos* 40 (1979): 122.
28. See John Brigham, *Property and the Politics of Entitlement* (Philadelphia: Temple University Press, 1990).
29. Samuel Stouffer, *Communism, Conformity, and Civil Liberties* (New York: Doubleday, 1955), 15.
30. The attitude framework parallels the constrained choices epitomized by voting in most Western societies.
31. Stouffer, *Communism*, 274.
32. Ibid., 236.
33. But see Benjamin Ginsberg, *The Captive Public: How Mass Opinion Promotes State Power* (New York: Basic Books, 1986).
34. See Herbert McClosky, "Consensus and Ideology in American Politics," *American Political Science Review* 58 (1964): 361–82.
35. Alida Brill and Herbert McClosky, *Dimensions of Tolerance: What Americans Believe about Civil Liberties* (New York: Russell Sage, 1983).
36. James L. Gibson and Richard D. Bingham, "Skokie, Nazis, and the Elitist Theory of Democracy," *Western Political Quarterly* 33 (1985): 12.
37. John Sullivan, James Pierson, and George Marcus, *Political Tolerance and American Democracy* (Chicago: University of Chicago Press, 1982). For these authors, "Though one may by definition link tolerance and democracy, as a practical matter the two may be at odds" (8).
38. Ibid., 251.
39. Jennifer Hochschild, *Political Tolerance and American Democracy* (Chicago: University of Chicago Press, 1982), 29.
40. Ibid., 150.
41. W. Lance Bennett, *Public Opinion in American Politics* (New York: Harcourt, Brace, Jovanovich, 1980), 124; Frances Fox Piven and Richard A. Cloward, *Regulating the Poor: The Functions of Public Welfare* (New York: Vintage, 1971), 169.
42. J. Anthony Lukas, *Common Ground* (New York: Knopf, 1985); Mark E. Kann, *Middle Class Radicalism in Santa Monica* (Philadelphia: Temple University Press, 1986); Murray Levin, *Talk Radio* (Lexington, Mass.: Lexington Books, 1987).

191

43. Mark Kesselman, "Conflictual Evolution of American Political Science," in *Public Values and Private Power in American Politics*, ed J. David Greenstone (Chicago: University of Chicago Press, 1982), 39.
44. Ibid.
45. Peter B. Evans, Dietrich Rueschemeyer, and Theda Skocpol, *Bringing the State Back In* (New York: Cambridge University Press, 1985).
46. Youssef Cohen, *The Manipulation of Consent: The State and Working-Class Consciousness in Brazil* (Pittsburgh: University of Pittsburgh Press, 1989).
47. Ibid., 9.
48. See Kann, *Middle Class Radicalism*, for an unusual perspective on this point.
49. Stephen Skowronek, *Building the New American State* (Cambridge: Cambridge University Press, 1982).
50. Stephen Skowronek, *The Politics Presidents Make: Leadership from John Adams to George Bush* (Cambridge: Harvard University Press, 1994).
51. Ibid.
52. John Brigham, *The Cult of the Court* (Philadelphia: Temple University Press, 1987), 208–17.
53. Michael Mandel, *The Charter of Rights and the Legalization of Politics in Canada* (Toronto: Wall and Thompson, 1989).
54. Judy Fudge, "The Effect of Entrenching a Bill of Rights upon Political Discourse: Feminist Demands and Sexual Violence in Canada," *International Journal of the Sociology of Law* 17 (1989): 446.
55. Ibid., 458–59.
56. Richard Morgan, *Disabling America* (New York: Basic Books, 1984).
57. Ibid., 5.
58. David Adamany and Joel Grossman, "Support for the Supreme Court as a National Policy Maker," *Law and Policy* 5 (1983): 405–37.
59. Ibid., 409.
60. Ibid., 434.
61. David Barnum, "Decision Making in a Constitutional Democracy," *Journal of Politics* 47 (1982): 480–508.
62. Gibson and Bingham, "Skokie," 191.
63. Ibid.
64. Joel Grossman pointed this out to me in comments on an earlier draft of this chapter.
65. Laurence Tribe, *American Constitutional Law*, 2d ed. (New York: Foundation Press, 1988), 1063.

66. Ibid., 1080.

67. Brigham, *Cult*, 214.

68. See also Charles A. Johnson and Bradley C. Canon, *Judicial Policies: Implementation and Impact* (Washington, D.C.: Congressional Quarterly Press, 1984), for attention to the authoritative populations of "interpreters and implementers" who link elite positions to the Supreme Court.

69. Robert Nagel, *Constitutional Cultures* (Berkeley: University of California Press, 1989), 1.

70. E. P. Thompson, *Whigs and Hunters*. New York: Vintage Books, 1975.

71. James Willard Hurst, *Law and Markets in United States History* (Madison: University of Wisconsin Press, 1980). See discussion in chapter 1 above.

72. See Peter Fitzpatrick, "Racism and the Innocence of Law," *Journal of Law and Society* 14 (1987): 119–32.

73. See Allen Feldman, *Formations of Violence: The Narrative of the Body and Political Terror in Northern Ireland* (Chicago: University of Chicago Press, 1991); Michael J. Piore, *Birds of Passage: Migrant Labor and Industrial Societies* (Cambridge: Cambridge University Press, 1979).

74. Richard M. Elman, *The Poorhouse State: The American Way of Life on Public Assistance* (New York: Pantheon, 1966), 77.

75. Ibid., 11.

76. "Praxis" was described in terms of the seeming irrationality of the legal system in the late Middle Ages. An account by Douglas Hay, interpreting attempts to put the legal system on a more secure footing by making punishment sure and efficient, points out the advantage of the pardons, the grace controlled by the gentry, as an affirmation of their hegemony. Douglas Hay et al., *Albion's Fatal Tree: Crime and Society in Eighteenth-Century England* (New York: Free Press, 1975).

77. Interviews conducted by the author at Chico Legal Internship Center, Chico, Calif., July 1988.

78. Flyer dated February 2, 1989, "Listeners Action on Homelessness and Housing," on file with the author.

79. Patricia J. Williams, *Notes of a Law Professor* (Cambridge: Harvard University Press, 1991); Derrick Bell, "Foreword: The Civil Rights Chronicles," *Harvard Law Review* (1985): 4–83.

193

80. Stanley Fish, *Doing What Comes Naturally: Change, Rhetoric, and the Practice of Theory in Literary and Legal Studies* (Durham, N.C.: Duke University Press, 1989).

81. Catharine MacKinnon, *Feminism Unmodified: Discourses on Life and Law* (Cambridge: Harvard University Press, 1987), intro., chaps. 3, 7, 11.

82. Ibid., 2.

83. Ibid., 3.

84. Ibid., 2.

85. Stanley Fish, "Going Down the Anti-Formalist Road" (paper presented to the Amherst Seminar on Legal Ideology, February 24, 1989; published as the introduction to *Doing What Comes Naturally*.

86. Ibid, 17.

87. Ibid.

88. Catharine MacKinnon, "Feminism, Marxism, Method, and the State: An Agenda for Theory," *Signs* 7, no. 3 (spring 1982): 24.

89. Fish, "Going Down," 21.

90. Ibid., 28.

91. MacKinnon, *Signs*, 25.

92. Fish, "Going Down," 19.

93. MacKinnon, *Signs*, 23.

94. Fish, "Going Down," 19.

95. Ibid., 32.

96. Fish's critique, though supportive, does suggest the more volatile reception of MacKinnon's book *Only Words* (Cambridge: Harvard University Press, 1993), where the predictably unfavorable response of the press, once heightened by a provocative metaphorical use of rape by Carlin Romano in the *Nation*, became a cause for the antipornography movement to rally around.

97. For a discussion of the platform from which I have sought to take off with this constitutive frame, see David M. Trubek, "Where the Action Is: Critical Legal Studies and Empiricism," *Stanford Law Review* 36 (1984): 575; and David M. Trubek and John Esser, "'Critical Empiricism' in American Legal Studies: Paradox, Program, or Pandora's Box?" *Law and Social Inquiry* 14 (1989): 3.

98. Kristin Bumiller, "The Social Construction of Rape in Criminal Trials" (paper presented at the Conference on Legal Ideology and Social Relations, Amherst, Massachusetts, 1987).

99. Ibid.

100. Angela Y. Davis, *Women, Race and Class* (New York: Vintage, 1983).

101. George Marcus said, "[I]t is precisely the reliance of social theory on certain assumptions about a domain conceived as everyday life that has made it inadequate to do its job of encompassing, of domesticating for intellectual consumption, late twentieth century realities as social processes." George Marcus, "Mass Toxic Torts and the End of Everyday Life" (paper presented to the Amherst Seminar, February 2, 1990).

102. Ibid.

103. See also Fredric Jameson, "Regarding Postmodernism—A Conversation with Fredric Jameson (Anders Stephanson)," *Social Text* 17 (1987): 29–54; George E. Marcus and Michael Fischer, *Anthropology as Cultural Critique* (Chicago: University of Chicago Press, 1986).

104. Piven and Cloward, *Regulating the Poor*; Charles Reich, "The New Property," *Yale Law Journal* 74 (1964): 1245.

105. Jacques Donzelot, *The Policing of Families* (New York: Random House, 1979).

106. See David Theo Goldberg, "The Prison-House of Modern Law," *Law and Society Review* 29 (1995): 541–52.

Bibliography

Books and Articles

Abel, Richard L. "A Comparative Theory of Dispute Institutions in Society." *Law and Society Review* 8 (1974): 217.

———, ed. *The Politics of Informal Justice*, vol. 1. New York: Academic Press, 1982.

Abraham, Henry. *Freedom and the Court: Civil Rights and Liberties in the United States*. 4th ed. Oxford: Oxford University Press, 1982.

Abu-Loghud, Lila. "The Romance of Resistance: Tracing Transformations of Power through Bedouin Women." *American Ethnologist* 17 (1990): 41–55.

Ackerman, Bruce. *Reconstructing American Law*. Cambridge: Harvard University Press, 1984.

Adamany, David, and Joel Grossman. "Support for the Supreme Court as a National Policy Maker." *Law and Policy* 5 (1983): 405–37.

Alejandro, Roberto. *Hermeneutics, Citizenship, and the Public Sphere*. Albany: State University of New York Press, 1993.

Althusser, Louis. *Lenin and Philosophy*. New York: Monthly Review, 1971.

Amherst Seminar, eds. "Special Issue: Law and Ideology." *Law and Society Review* 22 (1988).

———. "Special Issue: Law, Ideology and Social Research." *Legal Studies Forum* 9 (1985).

Arnold, Thurman W. *The Symbols of Government*. New Haven: Yale University Press, 1935.

Aubert, Wilhelm. "Competition and Dissensus: Two Types of Conflict and of Conflict Resolution." *Journal of Conflict Resolution* 7 (1963): 26.

Balbus, Isaac. "Commodity Form and Legal Form: An Essay on the 'Relative Autonomy' of the Law." *Law and Society Review* 112 (1977): 571.

———. *The Dialectics of Legal Repression*. New York: Russell Sage, 1973.

Bankowski, Zenon, and Geoff Mungham. *Images of Law*. London: Routledge and Kegan Paul, 1976.

Barker, Earnest. *Church, State and Study*. London: Methuen, 1930.

Barry, Kathleen. *Female Sexual Slavery*. Englewood, Cliffs, N.J.: Prentice-Hall, 1979.

Barthes, Roland. *The Eiffel Tower and Other Mythologies*. Translated by Richard Howard. New York: Hill and Wang, 1979.

Bartholomew, Amy, and Alan Hunt. "What's Wrong with Rights?" Paper presented at Rethinking Marxism Conference, Amherst, Massachusetts, 1989.

Becker, Theodore L., ed. *Political Trials*. Indianapolis: Bobbs-Merrill, 1971.

Bell, Derrick. *And We Are Not Saved*. New York: Basic Books, 1987.

———. "Foreword: The Civil Rights Chronicles." *Harvard Law Review* 99 (1985): 4–83.

———. *Voices From the Bottom of the Well*. New York: Basic Books, 1992.

Bennett, W. Lance. *Public Opinion in American Politics*. New York: Harcourt Brace, Jovanovich, 1980.

Bittner, Egon. "Radicalism and the Organization of Radical Movements." *American Sociological Review* 28 (1963): 928–40.

Blackstone's Commentaries. 1771. Reprint, Philadelphia: J. B. Lippincott, 1900.

Bledstein, Burton J. *The Culture of Professionalism*. New York: Norton, 1976.

Bok, Derek. "A Flawed System." *Harvard Magazine*, May–June 1983, 38.

Boone, Bruce. "Gay Language as Political Praxis: The Poetry of Frank O'Hara." *Social Text* (winter 1979): 59–92.

Bourdieu, Pierre. *Distinction: A Social Critique of the Judgement of Taste*. Translated by Richard Nice. Cambridge: Harvard University Press, 1984.

———. "The Force of Law: Toward a Sociology of the Juridical Field." *Hastings Law Journal* 38 (1987): 201.

———. *Outline of a Theory of Practice*. Cambridge: Cambridge University Press, 1977.

Bowles, Samuel, and Herbert Gintis. *Schooling in Capitalist America*. New York: Basic Books, 1976.

Brest, Paul, and Ann Vandenberg. "Politics, Feminism, and the Constitution: The Anti-Pornography Movement in Minneapolis." *Stanford Law Review* 39 (1987): 607–61.

Bridges, Amy. *A City in the Republic*. Cambridge: Cambridge University Press, 1984.

Brigham, John. "Bad Attitudes: The Consequences of Survey Research for Constitutional Practice." *Review of Politics* 52 (1990): 582–602.

———. *Civil Liberties and American Democracy*. Washington, D.C.: Congressional Quarterly Books, 1984.

———. *The Cult of the Court*. Philadelphia: Temple University Press, 1987.

———. "Judicial Impact upon Social Practices." *Legal Studies Forum* 9 (1985): 47–58.

———. *Property and the Politics of Entitlement*. Philadelphia: Temple University Press, 1990.

———. "Right, Rage and Remedy." In *Studies in American Political Development*. Edited by Karen Orren and Stephen Skowronek. New Haven: Yale University Press, 1988.

Brigham, John, and Christine B. Harrington. "Realism and Its Consequences: An Inquiry into Contemporary Socio-legal Research." *International Journal of the Sociology of Law* 17 (1988): 41–62.

Brill, Alida, and Herbert McClosky. *Dimensions of Tolerance: What Americans Believe about Civil Liberties*. New York: Russell Sage, 1983.

Brisbin, Richard A. "Antonin Scalia, William Brennan, and the Politics of Expression: A Study of Legal Violence and Repression." *American Political Science Review* 87 (1993): 912–26.

Brownmiller, Susan. *Against Our Will: Men, Women and Rape*. New York: Penguin, 1975.

Bumiller, Kristin. *The Civil Rights Society: The Social Construction of Victims*. Baltimore: Johns Hopkins University Press, 1988.

———. "The Social Construction of Rape in Criminal Trials." Paper presented at the Conference on Legal Ideology and Social Relations, Amherst, Massachusetts, 1987.

———. "Victims in the Shadow of the Law: A Critique of the Model of Legal Protection." *Signs* 12 (1987): 421–39.

Burger, Warren. "Agenda for 2000 A.D.—A Need for Systematic Anticipation." *Federal Rules Decisions* 70 (1976): 23–35.

Burgess, Susan. "Beyond Instrumental Politics: The New Institutionalism, Legal Rhetoric, and Judicial Supremacy." *Polity* 25 (spring 1993): 445–59.

Burstein, Paul. "Legal Mobilization as a Social Movement Tactic: The Struggle for Equal Employment Opportunity." *American Journal of Sociology* 96 (1991): 1201–25.

Cain, Maureen, and Kalman Kulcsar. "Thinking Disputes: An Essay on the Origins of the Dispute Industry." *Law and Society Review* 16 (1981–82): 375–402.

199

Calabresi, Guido, and Philip Bobbitt, *Tragic Choices*. New York: Norton, 1978.

Carrington, Paul. "Of Time and the River." *Journal of Legal Education* 34 (1984): 222.

Clark, Robert. "Tenure at Harvard Law School Examined." *Boston Globe Magazine*, October 30, 1990, 21: 4.

Coase, R. H. "The Problem of Social Cost." *Journal of Law and Economics* 3 (1960): 1.

Cohen, Youssef. *The Manipulation of Consent: The State and Working-Class Consciousness in Brazil*. Pittsburgh: University of Pittsburgh Press, 1989.

"Colloquium: Violent Pornography: Degradation of Women versus Right of Free Speech." *New York University Review of Law and Social Change* 8 (1978–79).

Comaroff, John L., and Simon Roberts. *Rules and Processes: The Cultural Logic of Dispute in an African Context*. Chicago: University of Chicago Press, 1981.

Cooke, Jacob, ed. *The Federalist*. Cleveland: Meridian Books, 1961.

Coombe, Rosemary J. "The Properties of Culture and the Politics of Possessing Identity: Native Claims in the Cultural Appropriation Controversy." *Canadian Journal of Law and Jurisprudence* 6 (1993): 249–85.

Cooper, Phillip. *Hard Judicial Choices*. London: Oxford University Press, 1988.

Corwin, Edward S. *The Higher Law Background of American Constitutional Law*. Ithaca, N.Y.: Cornell University Press, 1928.

Craig, Barbara. *Chada: The Story of an Epic Constitutional Struggle*. London: Oxford University Press, 1988.

"Critical Legal Studies Symposium." *Stanford Law Review* 36 (1984).

Cruikshank, Margaret. *The Gay and Lesbian Liberation Movement*. New York: Routledge, 1992.

Dalton, Thomas. *The State Politics of Judicial and Congressional Reform*. Westport, Conn.: Greenwood Press, 1985.

Davis, Angela Y. *Women, Race and Class*. New York: Vintage, 1983.

Delgado, Richard. "The Ethereal Scholar: Does Critical Legal Studies Have What Minorities Want?" *Harvard Civil Rights–Civil Liberties Law Review* 22 (1987): 301.

de Tocqueville, Alexis. *Democracy in America*. 4th ed. New York: H. G. Langley, 1845.

Dezalay, Yves. "From Mediation to Pure Law: Practice and Scholarly Representation within the Legal Sphere." *International Journal of the Sociology of Law* 14 (1986): 89–107.

Dixon, Jo. "The Nexus of Sex, Spousal Violence, and the State," *Law and Society Review* 29 (1995): 359–76.

Dolbeare, Kenneth M., and Phillip Hammond. *The School Prayer Decisions: From Court Policy to Local Practice.* Chicago: University of Chicago Press, 1971.

Donzelot, Jacques. *The Policing of Families.* New York: Random House, 1979.

Downs, Donald. *The New Politics of Pornography.* Chicago: University of Chicago Press, 1989.

Du Bois, W. E. B. *John Brown.* Philadelphia: George W. Jacobs, 1909.

Dworkin, Andrea. "Pornography: The New Terrorism." In *Letters from a War Zone.* London: Secker and Warburg, 1979.

Dworkin, Ronald. *Law's Empire.* Cambridge: Harvard University Press, 1986.

———. *Taking Rights Seriously.* Cambridge: Harvard University Press, 1977.

Edelman, Bernard. *Ownership of the Image: Elements for a Marxist Theory of Law.* London: Routledge and Kegan Paul, 1979.

Edelman, Lauren B., Howard S. Erlanger, and John Lande. "Internal Dispute Resolution: The Transformation of Civil Rights in the Workplace." *Law and Society Review* 27 (1993): 497–534.

Edelman, Murray J. *Constructing the Political Spectacle.* Chicago: University of Chicago Press, 1988.

Ehrlich, Eugen. *The Fundamental Principles of the Sociology of Law.* Cambridge: Cambridge University Press, 1936.

Eisenstein, Zillah R. *The Female Body and the Law.* Berkeley: University of California Press, 1988.

———. *Feminism and Sexual Equality.* New York: Monthly Review Press, 1984.

Elman, Richard M. *The Poorhouse State: The American Way of Life on Public Assistance.* New York: Pantheon, 1966.

Elshtain, Jean. "The New Porn Wars," *Nation,* June 25, 1984, 15–20.

Emerson, Ken. "When Legal Titans Clash." *New York Times Magazine,* April 23, 1990, 25–31.

Engel, David M. "Cases, Conflict, and Accommodation: Patterns of Legal Interaction in a Small Community." *American Bar Foundation Research Journal* 4 (1983): 803–7.

Epstein, Richard. *Takings.* Cambridge: Harvard University Press, 1985.

———. "Judicial Review: Reckoning on Two Kinds of Error." In *Eco-*

nomic Liberties and the Judiciary. Edited by James A. Dorne and Henry G. Manne. Fairfax, Virginia: Cato Institute and George Mason University Press, 1987.

Erlanger, Howard S., Elizabeth Chambliss, and Marygold S. Melli. "Participation and Flexibility in Informal Processes: Cautions from the Divorce Context." *Law and Society Review* 21 (1987): 585.

Evans, Peter B., Dietrich Rueschemeyer, and Theda Skocpol. *Bringing the State Back In.* New York: Cambridge University Press, 1985.

Feldman, Allen. *Formations of Violence: The Narrative of the Body and Political Terror in Northern Ireland.* Chicago: University of Chicago Press, 1991.

Felstiner, William L. F., and Austin Sarat. "Law and Strategy in the Divorce Lawyer's Office." *Law and Society Review* 20 (1986): 93–134.

Felstiner, William L. F., and Austin Sarat. "Legal Realism in Lawyer-Client Communications," ABF Working Paper #8723.

Ferguson, Ann. *Blood at the Root: Motherhood, Sexuality and Male Dominance.* London: Pandora, 1989.

———. "The Sex Debate in the Women's Movement: A Socialist-Feminist View." Unpublished manuscript, 1980.

Fine, Bob, et al., eds. *Capitalism and the Rule of Law.* London: Hutchinson, 1979.

Fish, Stanley. "Dennis Martinez and the Uses of Theory." *Yale Law Journal* 96 (1987): 1773–1800.

———. *Doing What Comes Naturally: Change, Rhetoric, and the Practice of Theory in Literary and Legal Studies.* Durham, N.C.: Duke University Press, 1989.

Fisher, Roger, and William Ury. *Getting to Yes: Negotiating Agreement without Giving In.* New York: Penguin, 1983.

Fiss, Owen. "Against Settlement." *Yale Law Journal* 93 (1984): 1073–90.

———. "Free Speech and Social Structure." Unpublished manuscript, 1985.

Fitzpatrick, Peter. "Law and Societies." *Osgoode Hall Law Journal* 22 (1984): 115–38.

———. "Marxism and Legal Pluralism." *Australian Journal of Law and Society* 1 (1983): 45–59.

———. *The Mythology of Modern Law.* London: Routledge, 1992.

———. "Racism and the Innocence of Law." *Journal of Law and Society* 14 (1987): 119–32.

Flathman, Richard. *The Practice of Rights.* Cambridge: Cambridge University Press, 1976.

Flexner, Eleanor. *Century of Struggle: The Women's Rights Movement in the United States.* 1959. Reprint, Cambridge: Harvard University Press, 1975.

Forbath, William. *Law and the Shaping of the American Labor Movement.* Cambridge: Harvard University Press, 1991.

Ford, Paul Leicester, ed. *Writings of Thomas Jefferson,* vol. 10. New York: G. P. Putnam's Sons, 1899.

Foucault, Michel. *The Archaelogy of Knowledge and the Discourse on Language.* New York: Harper and Row, 1976.

———. *Dicipline and Punish: The Birth of the Prison.* New York: Vintage, 1977.

———. *The History of Sexuality.* New York: Random House, 1978.

Frank, Jerome. *Courts on Trial.* Princeton: Princeton University Press, 1949.

———. *Law and the Modern Mind.* New York: Coward-McCann, 1936.

Frankfurter, Felix, and James M. Landis. *The Business of the Supreme Court.* New York: Macmillan, 1928.

Fraser, Nancy. *Unruly Practices: Power, Discourse, and Gender in Contemporary Social Theory.* Minneapolis: University of Minnesota Press, 1989.

Freeman, Alan. "Legitimizing Racial Discrimination through Antidiscrimination Law: A Critical Review of Supreme Court Doctrine." *Minnesota Law Review* 62 (1978): 1049.

———. "Racism, Rights and the Quest for Equality of Opportunity: A Critical Legal Essay." *Harvard Civil Rights–Civil Liberties Law Review* 23 (1988): 295–392.

Friesen, Jennifer and Ronald K. L. Collins. "Looking Back on *Muller v. Oregon.*" *American Bar Association Research Journal* 69 (1983): 472–79.

Frohock, Fred. *The Abortion Controversy.* Westport, Conn.: Greenwood Press, 1983.

Frug, Mary Joe. *Postmodern Legal Feminism.* New York: Routledge, 1992.

Fudge, Judy. "The Effect of Entrenching a Bill of Rights upon Political Discourse: Feminist Demands and Sexual Violence in Canada." *International Journal of the Sociology of Law* 17 (1989): 445–63.

Fuller, Lon. "Mediation—Its Forms and Functions." *Southern California Law Review* 44 (1971): 305–39.

Furlong, Lucinda. "AIDS Media: Counter-Representations." Whitney Museum of American Art: New American Film and Video Series, 1989.

203

Galanter, Mark. "Justice in Many Rooms: Courts, Private Ordering, and Indigenous Law." *Journal of Legal Pluralism (and Unofficial Law)* 19 (1981): 48.

Gamson, Josh. "Silence, Death, and the Invisible Enemy: AIDS Activism and Social Movement 'Newness.'" *Social Problems* 36 (1989): 351–67.

Garland, David. *Punishment and Modern Society: A Study in Social Theory*. Chicago: University of Chicago Press, 1990.

Gay Health Clinic. "Safe Sex." San Francisco, 1983.

Geertz, Clifford. *The Interpretation of Cultures: Selected Essays*. New York: Basic, 1973.

Genovese, Eugene. *Roll, Jordan, Roll: The World the Slaves Made*. New York: Pantheon, 1972.

Gibson, James L., and Richard D. Bingham. "Skokie, Nazis, and the Elitist Theory of Democracy." *Western Political Quarterly* 33 (1985): 12.

Gillman, Howard. "The Rights Trump." Paper presented at American Political Science Association Annual Meeting, August 28–September 2, 1991, Washington, D.C.

Ginsberg, Benjamin. *The Captive Public: How Mass Opinion Promotes State Power*. New York: Basic, 1986.

Ginsberg, Faye D. *Contested Lives: The Abortion Debate in an American Community*. Berkeley: University of California Press, 1989.

Glassburg, David. "The Public Bath Movement in America." *American Studies* 20 (fall 1979): 5–20.

Gluckman, Max. *The Judicial Process among the Barotse of Northern Rhodesia*. Manchester: Manchester University Press, 1955.

Goldberg, David Theo. "The Prison House of Modern Law." *Law and Society Review* 29 (1995): 541–52.

Goldberg, Stephen B., Eric D. Green, and Frank E. A. Sander. *Dispute Resolution*. Boston: Little, Brown, 1985.

Goodrich, Peter. *Languages of Law: From Logics of Memory to Nomadic Masks*. London: Weidenfeld and Nicolson, 1990.

Gordon, Robert. "Critical Legal Histories." *Stanford Law Review* 36 (1984): 127.

———. "'The Ideal and the Actual in the Law': Fantasies and Practices of New York City Lawyers, 1870–1910." In *The New High Priests: Lawyers in Post–Civil War America*. Edited by Gerard W. Gawalt. Westport, Conn.: Greenwood Press, 1984.

———. "Lawyers as the American Aristocracy." Holmes Lectures, Harvard Law School, Cambridge, Massachusetts, 1985.

————. "Legal Thought and Legal Practice in the Age of American Enterprise, 1870–1920." In *Professions and Professional Ideologies in America*. Edited by Gerald L. Gelson. Chapel Hill: University of North Carolina Press, 1983.

Gramsci, Antonio. *Selections from the Prison Notebooks*. New York: International Publishers, 1971.

Greenberg, David F. *The Construction of Homosexuality*. Chicago: University of Chicago Press, 1988.

Grillo, Trina. "The Mediation Alternative: Process Dangers for Women." *Yale Law Journal* 100 (1991): 1545.

Grossman, Joel. "The First Amendment and the New Anti-Pornography Statutes." *News for Teachers of Political Science* 45 (1985): 16.

Guha, Ranajit. "On Some Aspects of the Historiography of Colonial India." *Subaltern Studies: Writings on South Asian History and Society* 1 (1980).

Gulliver, P. H. *Social Control in an African Society*. London: Routledge and Kegan Paul, 1963.

Gusfield, Joseph R. *The Culture of Public Problems: Drinking-Driving and the Symbolic Order*. Chicago: University of Chicago Press, 1981.

————. *Symbolic Crusade: Status Politics and the American Temperance Movement*. Champaign: University of Illinois Press, 1966.

Hamilton, Alexander, et al. *The Federalist*. New York: Random House, 1937.

Handler, Joel. *The Conditions of Discretion: Autonomy, Community, Bureaucracy*. New York: Russell Sage, 1986.

————. "Dependent People, the State, and the Modern/Post Modern Search for a Dialogic Community." *UCLA Law Review* 35 (1988): 999.

————. *Social Movements and the Legal System*. New York: Academic Press, 1978.

Handler, Joel, Ellen Hollingsworth, and Howard Erlanger. *Lawyers and the Pursuit of Legal Rights*. New York: Academic Press, 1978.

Harding, Arthur L. "Professor Makes History." In *The Administration of Justice in Retrospect*. Edited by Arthur L. Harding. Dallas: Southern Methodist University Press, 1957.

Harrington, Christine B. "Bundles of Input: Negotiating the Nation's First Nuclear Waste Dump—A Profile of Howard Bellman." Paper presented to the Harvard Program on Negotiation, May 17, 1991.

————. "Creating Gaps and Making Markets." *Law and Policy* 10 (1988): 296–316.

205

————. "Delegalization Reform Movements: A Historical Analysis." In *The Politics of Informal Justice*. New York: Academic Press, 1982.

————. "Regulatory Reform: Creating Gaps and Making Markets." *Law and Policy* 10 (1988): 293.

————. *Shadow Justice*. Westport, Conn.: Greenwood Press, 1985.

Harrington, Christine B., and Sally Engle Merry. "Ideological Production: The Making of Community Mediation." *Law and Society Review* 22 (1988): 709–36.

Harrington, Christine B., and Barbara Yngvesson. "Interpretive Sociolegal Research." *Law and Social Inquiry* 15 (1990): 135.

Hartz, Louis. *The Liberal Tradition in America*. New York: Harcourt, Brace, 1955.

Haskell, Thomas L. "The Curious Persistence of Rights Talk in the 'Age of Interpretation.'" *Journal of American History* 74 (1987): 984–1012.

Hay, Douglas, et al. *Albion's Fatal Tree: Crime and Society in Eighteenth-Century England*. New York: Free Press, 1975.

Hebdige, Dick. *Subculture: The Meaning of Style*. New York: Methuen, 1979.

Heller, Tom. "The Importance of Normative Decision-Making: The Limitations of Legal Economics as a Basis for a Liberal Jurisprudence—As Illustrated by the Regulation of Vacation Home Development." *Southern California Law Review* 53 (1980): 1215.

Hendy, Charles C. "Other AIDS-Hit Cities Unlikely to Close Sex Clubs." *San Francisco Examiner*, October 14, 1984.

Himmelfarb, Gertrude. *The Idea of Poverty: England in the Early Industrial Age*. New York: Knopf, 1983.

Hochschild, Jennifer. *Political Tolerance and American Democracy*. Chicago: University of Chicago Press, 1982.

Hoffman, Martin. *The Gay World: Male Homosexuality and the Social Construction of Evil*. New York: Basic, 1968.

Hohfeld, Wesley. *Fundamental Legal Conceptions*. New Haven: Yale University Press, 1919.

Holmes, Oliver Wendell, Jr. "Review of *A Selection of Cases on the Law of Contracts*." In *American Law School Review* (1880): 233.

Hunt, Alan. *Explorations in Law and Society: Toward a Constitutive Theory of Law*. New York: Routledge, 1993.

————. "The Ideology of Law." *Law and Society Review* 19 (1985): 11.

————. *The Sociological Movement in Law*. Philadelphia: Temple University Press, 1978.

Hurst, James Willard. *The Growth of American Law: The Law Makers.* Boston: Little, Brown, 1950.

———. *Law and Markets in United States History.* Madison: University of Wisconsin Press, 1980.

Hutchison, Allan C., and Patrick J. Monahan. "Law, Politics and Critical Legal Scholars: The Unfolding Drama of American Legal Thought." *Stanford Law Review* 36 (1984): 199.

Jameson, Fredric. "Regarding Postmodernism—A Conversation with Fredric Jameson (Anders Stephanson)." *Social Text* 17 (1987): 29–54.

Johnson, Charles A., and Bradley C. Canon. *Judicial Policies: Implementation and Impact.* Washington, D.C.: Congressional Quarterly Press, 1984.

Johnson, Jason Scott. "Law, Economics, and Post-Realist Explanation." *Law and Society Review* 24 (1990): 1217–54.

Kairys, David, ed. *The Politics of Law.* New York: Pantheon, 1982.

Kalman, Laura. *Legal Realism at Yale, 1927–1960.* Chapel Hill: University of North Carolina Press, 1986.

Kann, Mark. *Middle Class Radicalism in Santa Monica.* Philadelphia: Temple University Press, 1986.

Kaplan, Amy. *The Social Construction of American Realism.* Chicago: University of Chicago Press, 1988.

Katz, Melinda. "Law in the Private Sector: Small Designers and Civil Rights." Honors Thesis, University of Massachusetts, Amherst, 1987.

Katzenstein, Mary. "Marching through the Institutions." Paper presented at Amherst College, February 19, 1990.

Kaye, Tim. "Natural Law Theory and Legal Positivism: Two Sides of the Same Practical Coin?" *Journal of Law and Society* 14 (1987): 303–20.

Kelman, Mark. "Choice and Utility." *University of Wisconsin Law Review* (1979): 769.

———. "Consumption Theory, Production Theory, and Ideology in the Coase Theorem." *Southern California Law Review* 52 (1979): 669.

———. *A Guide to Critical Legal Studies.* Cambridge: Harvard University Press, 1987.

Kennedy, Duncan. "Cost-Benefit Analysis of Entitlement Problems: A Critique." *Stanford Law Review* 33 (1981): 387.

———. "Form and Substance in Private Law Adjudication." *Harvard Law Review* 89 (1976): 1685.

Kesselman, Mark. "Conflictual Evolution of American Political Science." In *Public Values and Private Power in American Politics*, ed. J. David Greestone. New York: Cambridge University Press, 1982.

Kerruish, Valerie. *Jurisprudence as Ideology*. London: Routledge, 1991.

Kessler, Mark. "Legal Discourse and Political Intolerance: The Ideology of Clear and Present Danger," *Law and Society Review* 27 (1993): 559–98.

Klare, Karl. "The Judicial Deradicalization of the Wagner Act and the Origins of Modern Legal Consciousness, 1937–1941." *Minnesota Law Review* 62 (1978): 265.

———. "Law Making as Praxis." *Telos* 40 (1979): 122.

Kluger, Richard. *Simple Justice*. New York: Random House, 1976.

Kobylka, Joseph F. "A Court-Created Context for Group Litigation: Libertarian Groups and Obscenity." *Journal of Politics* 49 (1987): 1061.

Kohorn, Jay M. "Petition for Extraordinary Relief: If the LaRouche AIDS Initiative Had Passed in California." *Review of Law and Social Change* 15 (1986–87): 477–512.

Kornhauser, Lewis. "The General Image of Authority." *Stanford Law Review* 36 (1984): 349–89.

LaMontagne, Jessica. "Beyond Pornography." *Left Field*, March 1990, 1–3.

Lang, Norris G. "Homophobia and the AIDS Phenomenon." In *Culture and Aids*. Edited by Douglas A. Feldman. New York: Praeger, 1991.

Laraña, Enrique, Hank Johnston, and Joseph R. Gusfield. *New Social Movements: From Ideology to Identity*. Philadelphia: Temple University Press, 1994.

Larson, Magali Sarfatti. *The Rise of Professionalism: A Sociological Analysis*. Berkeley: University of California Press, 1977.

Lazarus-Black, Mindie, and Susan Hirsch, eds. *Contested States: Law, Hegemony, and Resistance*. New York: Routledge, 1994.

Leeson, Susan. "Comments," Panel on Social Movements, Western Political Science Association, Eugene, Oregon, 1986.

Leidholdt, Dorchen, and Janice G. Raymond, eds. *The Sexual Liberals and the Attack on Feminism*. New York: Pergamon Press, 1990.

Leishman, Katie. "How San Francisco Coped with AIDS." *Atlantic*, October 1985, 18–41.

Levin, Murray. *Talk Radio*. Lexington, Mass.: Lexington Books, 1987.

Levinson, Sanford. *Constitutional Faith*. Princeton: Princeton University Press, 1989.

Lewis, Anthony. *Gideon's Trumpet*. New York: Random House, 1964.

Lewis, Russell. "The San Diego Bathhouse Controversy." *Sappho Speaks*, April 1986, 1–3.

Llewellyn, Karl. *The Bramble Bush*. New York: Oceana Publications, 1951.

Llewellyn, Karl, and Edward A. Hoebel. *The Cheyenne Way*. Norman: University of Okalahoma Press, 1941.

Lukas, J. Anthony. *Common Ground*. New York: Knopf, 1985.

Luker, Kristin. *Abortion and the Politics of Motherhood*. Berkeley: University of California Press, 1984.

McBarnet, Doreen. "Law and Capital: The Role of Legal Form and Legal Actors." *International Journal of the Sociology of Law* 12 (1984): 321–28.

McCann, Michael. *Rights at Work: Pay Equity Reform and the Politics of Legal Mobilization*. Chicago: University of Chicago Press, 1994.

McCann, Michael, and Gerald Houseman. *Judging the Constitution: Critical Essays*. Boston: Little, Brown, 1989.

Macaulay, Stuart. "Images of Law in Everyday Life: The Lessons of School, Entertainment and Spectator Sports." *Law and Society Review* 21 (1987): 185.

———. "Non-Contractual Relations in Business: A Preliminary Study." *American Sociological Review* 28 (1963): 55.

McClain, Linda C. "'Atomistic Man' Revisited: Liberalism, Connection, and Feminist Jurisprudence." *Southern California Law Review* 65 (1992): 1171–1264.

McClosky, Herbert. "Consensus and Ideology in American Politics." *American Political Science Review* 58 (1964): 361–82.

McConnell, Grant. *Private Power and American Democracy*. New York: Knopf, 1966.

McCourt, Kathleen. *Working-Class Women and Grass-Roots Politics*. Bloomington: Indiana University Press, 1977.

McEwen, Craig A., Lynn Mather, and Richard J. Maiman. "Lawyers, Mediation, and the Management of Divorce Practice." *Law and Society Review* 28 (1994): 149–86.

MacKinnon, Catharine. "Feminism, Marxism, Method, and the State: An Agenda for Theory." *Signs* 7, no. 3 (spring 1982): 24.

———. *Feminism Unmodified: Discourses on Life and Law*. Cambridge: Harvard University Press, 1987.

———. *Only Words*. Cambridge: Harvard University Press, 1993.

Mamet, David. *Writing in Restaurants*. New York: Viking, 1986.

Mandel, Michael. *The Charter of Rights and the Legalization of Politics in Canada*. Toronto: Wall and Thompson, 1989.

Marcus, George. "Mass Toxic Torts and the End of Everyday Life." Paper presented to the Amherst Seminar, February 2, 1990.

Marcus, George, and Michael Fischer. *Anthropology as Cultural Critique.* Chicago: University of Chicago Press, 1986.

Marin, Louis. *Portrait of the King.* London: Macmillan, 1988.

Matsuda, Mari. "Looking to the Bottom: Critical Legal Studies and Reparations." *Harvard Civil Rights—Civil Liberties Law Review* 22 (1987): 323.

Melossi, Dario. *The State of Social Control.* New York: St. Martin's, 1990.

Menkel-Meadow, Carrie. "Excluded Voices: New Voices in the Legal Profession." *University of Miami Law Review* 42 (1987): 29–53.

———. "Toward Another View of Legal Negotiation: The Structure of Problem-Solving." *UCLA Law Review* 31 (1984): 754.

Merry, Sally. "Anthropology, Law, and Transitional Processes," *Annual Review of Anthropology* 21 (1992): 357.

———. "Concepts of Law and Justice among Working-Class Americans: Ideology as Culture." *Legal Studies Forum* 9 (1985): 59–71.

———. *Getting Justice and Getting Even.* Chicago: University of Chicago Press, 1990.

———. "Legal Pluralism: Review Essay." *Law and Society Review* 5 (1988): 869–96.

Merry, Sally, and Christine B. Harrington. "Ideological Production." *Law and Society Review* 22 (1988): 709–35.

Millett, Kate. *Sexual Politics.* New York: Avon, 1969.

Milner, Neal. "Comparative Analysis of Patterns of Compliance with Supreme Court Decisions: *Miranda* and the Police in Four Communities." *Law and Society Review* 5 (1971): 126.

———. "The Denigration of Rights and the Persistence of Rights Talk." *Law and Social Inquiry* 14 (1989).

———. "The Dilemmas of Legal Mobilization." *Law and Policy* 8 (1986).

Milstein, Susan. "Judge Orders Bathhouses in S.F. to Close Temporarily." *San Francisco Chronicle,* October 16, 1984.

Mnookin, Robert H., and Lewis Kornhauser. "Bargaining in the Shadow of the Law: The Case of Divorce." *Yale Law Journal* 88 (1979): 950.

Mohr, Richard D. *Gays/Justice: A Study of Ethics, Society and Law.* New York: Columbia University Press, 1988.

Moore, Sally Falk. *Law as Process.* Cambridge: Harvard University Press, 1978.

Morgan, Richard. *Disabling America.* New York: Basic, 1984.

Murphy, Lawrence R. *Perverts by Official Order.* New York: Harrington Park Press, 1988.

Murphy, Walter F., and C. Herman Pritchett. *Courts, Judges, and Politics: An Introduction to the Judicial Process.* New York: Random House, 1979.

Nader, Laura. "The Recurrent Dialectic between Legality and Its Alternatives: The Limitations of Binary Thinking." *University of Pennsylvania Law Review* 132 (1984): 621.

Nader, Laura, and Harry F. Todd, eds. *The Disputing Process: Law in Ten Societies.* New York: Columbia University Press, 1978.

Nagel, Robert. *Constitutional Cultures.* Berkeley: University of California Press, 1989.

New York Times. "Bathhouse Curbs Called Help in Coast AIDS Fight." October 24, 1985.

———. "City Shuts a Bathhouse as Site of 'Unsafe Sex.'" December 7, 1985.

———. "Cuomo Panel Proposes Rules to Curb AIDS at Bathhouses." October 10, 1985.

Nedelsky, Jennifer. "Law, Boundaries, and the Bounded Self." In *Law and the Order of Culture.* Edited by Robert Post. Berkeley: University of California Press, 1991.

Neier, Aryeh. *Defending My Enemy.* New York: Dutton, 1979.

Nelken, David. "Beyond the Study of 'Law and Society'?" *American Bar Foundation Journal* 2 (spring 1986): 323–38.

O'Connor, Karen. *Women's Organizations' Use of the Courts.* Lexington, Mass.: Lexington Books, 1980.

Offe, Claus. "New Social Movements: Challenging the Boundaries of Institutional Politics." *Social Research* 52 (1985): 817–68.

Okin, Susan Moller. *Justice, Gender, and the Family.* New York: Basic, 1989.

Opie, John. *The Law of the Land: Two Hundred Years of American Farmland Policy.* Lincoln: University of Nebraska Press, 1987.

Ostrow, David G. *Biobehavioral Control of AIDS.* New York: Irvington Publishers, 1987.

Paul, Arnold. *Conservative Crisis and the Rule of Law, 1887–1895.* Ithaca, N.Y.: Cornell University Press, 1969.

Peller, Gary. "The Metaphysics of American Law." *California Law Review* 73 (1985): 1151–1290.

Pennock, J. Roland. "Rights and Citizenship." *News: For Teachers of Political Science.* Washington, D.C.: American Political Science Association, 1981.

211

Piore, Michael J. *Birds of Passage: Migrant Labor and Industrial Societies.* Cambridge: Cambridge University Press, 1979.

Pitkin, Hannah. *Wittgenstein and Justice.* Berkeley: University of California Press, 1978.

Piven, Frances Fox, and Richard A. Cloward. *Regulating the Poor: The Functions of Public Welfare.* New York: Vintage, 1971.

Posner, Richard A. *Antitrust Law: An Economic Perspective.* Chicago: University of Chicago Press, 1976.

————. "The Decline of Law as an Autonomous Discipline, 1962–1987." *Harvard Law Review* 100 (1987): 761.

————. *Economic Analysis of Law.* 2d ed. Boston: Little, Brown, 1977.

————. "The Ethical Signifigance of Free Choice: A Reply to Professor West." *Harvard Law Review* 99 (1986): 1431.

————. "A Statistical Study of Antitrust Law Enforcement." *Journal of Law and Economics* 13 (1970): 365–419.

————. "The Decadence of Equity." *Columbia Law Review* 5 (1905): 20.

Pound, Roscoe. "The Causes of Popular Dissatisfaction with the Administration of Justice." *American Bar Association Report* 29 (1906): 395.

Provine, D. Marie. *Judging Credentials: Nonlawyer Judges and the Politics of Professionalism.* Chicago: University of Chicago Press, 1986.

Putnam, Hilary. *The Many Faces of Realism.* LaSalle, Ill.: Open Court, 1987.

Randall, Richard. *Freedom and Taboo.* Berkeley: University of California Press, 1989.

Raymond, Janice. *A Passion for Friends.* Boston: Beacon, 1986.

Report of the Commission on Obscenity and Pornography. New York: Random House, 1970.

Reich, Charles. "The New Property." *Yale Law Journal* 74 (1964): 1245.

Roche, John P. "The Founding Fathers: A Reform Caucus in Action." *American Political Science Review* 55 (1961): 67–68.

Rorty, Richard. *Philosophy and the Mirror of Nature.* Princeton: Princeton University Press, 1979.

Rosenberg, Norman L. "Gideon's Trumpet: Sounding the Retreat from Legal Realism." In *Recasting America: Culture and Politics in the Age of the Cold War.* Edited by Lary May. Chicago: University of Chicago Press, 1989.

Sander, Frank E. A. "Family Mediation: Problems and Prospects." Keynote Address at the First American Bar Association Conference on Alternative Means of Family Dispute Resolution, June 1982.

———. "Successful Techniques for Mediating Family Break Up." *Mediation Quarterly* 2 (1983): 354–63.

———. "Varieties of Dispute Processing." In *Neighborhood Justice*. Edited by Malcolm Feeley and Roman Tomasic. New York: Longman, 1982.

Santos, Boaventura de Sousa. "The Law of the Oppressed: The Construction and Reproduction of Legality in Pasargada." *Law and Society Review* 12 (1977): 5.

———. *Toward a New Common Sense: Law, Science and Politics in the Paradigmatic Transition.* New York: Routledge, 1995.

Sarat, Austin, and William L. F. Felstiner. "Law and Social Relations: Vocabularies of Motive in Lawyer-Client Interaction. *Law and Society Review* 22 (1988): 737–769.

Scheingold, Stuart. *The Politics of Rights.* New Haven: Yale University Press, 1974.

Schlegel, John Henry. *American Legal Realism and Empirical Social Science.* Chapel Hill: University of North Carolina Press, 1995.

Schneider, Elizabeth. "The Dialectic of Rights and Politics: Perspectives from the Women's Movement." *New York University Law Review* 61 (1986): 589–652

Schumpeter, Joseph. *Capitalism, Socialism, and Democracy.* New York: Harper and Row, 1942.

Schweikhart, Gary. "Shilts Responds to Critics." *Sentinel* 29 (March 1984): 1.

Sedgwick, Eve Kosofsky. *The Epistemology of the Closet.* Berkeley: University of California Press, 1990.

Selznick, Phillip. "Sociology of Law and Natural Law." *Natural Law Forum* 6 (1961): 84–108.

Shapiro, Martin. *Law and Politics in the Supreme Court.* New York: Free Press, 1964.

———. *Who Guards the Guardians?* Atlanta: University of Georgia Press, 1989.

Shilts, Randy. *And the Band Played On: People, Politics and the AIDS Epidemic.* New York: St. Martin's, 1987.

Siegan, Bernard. *Economic Liberties and the Constitution.* Chicago: University of Chicago Press, 1980.

Silverman, David, and Brian Torode. *The Material Word: Some Theories of Language and Its Limits.* London: Routledge and Kegan Paul, 1980.

Silvestrini, Blanca G. "'The World We Enter When Claiming Rights': Latinos and the Quest for Culture." Paper presented to the Amherst Seminar, Amherst, Massachusetts, April 15, 1991.

213

Simon, William H. "Legality, Bureaucracy and Class in the Welfare State." *Yale Law Journal* 92 (1983): 1198.

Skowronek, Stephen. *Building the New American State*. Cambridge: Cambridge University Press, 1982.

———. "Notes on the Presidency in the Political Order." *Studies in American Political Development*. New Haven: Yale University Press, 1986.

———. *The Politics Presidents Make: Leadership from John Adams to George Bush*. Cambridge: Harvard University Press, 1994.

Smith, Rogers M. "Political Jurisprudence, the New Institutionalism, and the Future of Public Law." *American Political Science Review* 82 (1988): 89–108.

Sontag, Susan. AIDS and Its Metaphors. New York: Farrar, Straus and Giroux, 1988.

Stanton, Elizabeth C. "Declaration of Sentiments." In *The First Convention Ever Called to Discuss the Civil and Political Rights of Women*. Seneca Falls, N.Y.: n.p., 1848.

Starhawk. *Dreaming the Dark: Magic, Sex, and Politics*. Boston: Beacon, 1982.

Sternhell, Carol. "Review of Andrea Dworkin, *Ice and Fire, Intercourse*." *New York Times Book Review*, May 3, 1987.

Stevens, Robert. *Law School: Legal Education in America from the 1850s to the 1980s*. Chapel Hill: University of North Carolina Press, 1983.

Stith, Kate. "Government Interests in Criminal Law." *Albany Law Review* 55 (1992): 679–87.

Stouffer, Samuel. *Communism, Conformity, and Civil Liberties*. New York: Doubleday, 1955.

Strauss, Leo. *Natural Right and History*. Chicago: University of Chicago Press, 1949.

Stumpf, Harry. *American Judicial Politics*. San Diego: Harcourt, Brace, Jovanovich, 1987.

Sullivan, John, James Piereson, and George Marcus. *Political Tolerance and American Democracy*. Chicago: University of Chicago Press, 1982.

"Symposium: The Proposed Minneapolis Pornography Ordinance: Porn Regulation v. Civil Rights or Porn Regulation as Civil Rights." *William Mitchell Law Review* 11 (1985): 39.

Tamanaha, Brian Z. "The Folly of the 'Social Scientific' Concept of Legal Pluralism." *Journal of Law and Society* 20 (summer 1993): 192–217.

Tarrow, Sidney. *Power in Movement: Social Movements, Collective Action and Politics*. Cambridge: Cambridge University Press, 1994.

Taylor, Charles. "Atomism." In *Powers, Possessions and Freedom: Essays in Honour of C. B. Macpherson*. Edited by Alkis Kontos. Toronto: University of Toronto Press, 1979.

Thomas, Kendall. "Rouge et Noir Reread: A Popular Constitutional History of the Angelo Herndon Case." *Southern California Law Review* 65 (1992): 2665.

Thompson, E. P. *Whigs and Hunters*. New York: Vintage Books, 1975.

Touraine, Alain. *The Voice in the Eye*. 1979.

Treichler, Paula A. "An Epidemic of Signification." *October* 43 (1987): 31.

Tribe, Laurence. *American Constitutional Law*. 2d ed. New York: Foundation Press, 1988.

Trubek, David M. "Where the Action Is: Critical Legal Studies and Empiricism." *Stanford Law Review* 36 (1984): 575.

Trubek, David M., and John Esser. "'Critical Empiricism' in American Legal Studies: Paradox, Program, or Pandora's Box?" *Law and Social Inquiry* 14 (1989): 3–52.

Tushnet, Mark V. *The NAACP's Legal Strategy against Segregated Education, 1925–1950*. Chapel Hill: University of North Carolina Press, 1987.

———. "Post-Realist Legal Scholarship." *Wisconsin Law Review* (1980): 1383–1401.

Twining, William. *Karl Llewellyn and the Realist Movement*. Norman: University of Oklahoma Press, 1973.

Unger, Roberto M. *The Critical Legal Studies Movement*. Cambridge: Harvard University Press, 1986.

Vance, Carole S. *Pleasure and Danger: Exploring Female Sexuality*. Boston: Routledge and Kegan Paul, 1984.

Vega, J. "Coercion and Consent: Classical Liberal Concepts in Texts on Sexual Violence." *International Journal of the Sociology of Law* 16 (1988): 75–89.

Villmoare, Adelaide H. "Issues of Conceptualization in the Study of Change in and around Courts: Forms of Law." Paper presented at the Annual Meeting of the Law and Society Association, Toronto, 1982.

Vose, Clement. "NAACP Strategy in the Covenant Cases." *Western Reserve Law Review* 6 (winter 1955): 101–45.

———. "The National Consumer's League and the Brandeis Brief." *Midwest Journal of Political Science* 1 (1957): 267–90.

Wasby, Stephen. *The Impact of the United States Supreme Court*. Homewood, Ill.: Dorsey Press, 1970.

Watney, Simon. *Policing Desire: Pornography, AIDS, and the Media.* 2d ed. Minneapolis: University of Minnesota Press, 1987.

———. *Shattered Mirrors: Our Search for Identity and Community in the AIDS Era.* Cambridge: Harvard University Press, 1989.

Weinstein, James. *The Corporate Ideal and the Liberal State, 1900–1918.* Boston: Beacon, 1968.

Weiss, Philip. "Inside a Bathhouse." *New Republic*, December 2, 1985, 12–13.

Weitzman, Lenore J., Herbert Jacob, and Mary Ann Glendon. "The Divorce Revolution." *New York Times*, November 7, 1985, III 1:3.

White, Leonard D. *The City Manager.* Chicago: University of Chicago Press, 1927.

Wiesberg, Robert. "Deregulating Death." *Supreme Court Review* (1983): 305.

Wigmore, John. *Introduction to Roscoe Pound: The Causes of Popular Dissatisfaction with the Administration of Justice.* Chicago: American Judicature Society, n.d.

Wilkins, David B. "Legal Realism for Lawyers." *Harvard Law Review* 104 (1990): 468–524.

Williams, Marilyn Thornton. "NYC's Public Baths: A Case Study in Urban Progressive Reform." *Journal of Urban History* 7 (1980): 49–81.

Williams, Patricia J. "Alchemical Notes: Reconstructing Ideals from Deconstructed Rights." *Harvard Civil Rights–Civil Liberties Law Review* 22 (1987): 401–33.

———. *Notes of a Law Professor.* Cambridge: Harvard University Press, 1991.

Wolin, Sheldon. *Politics and Vision.* Cambridge: Harvard University Press, 1960.

Yngvesson, Barbara. *Virtuous Citizens, Disruptive Subjects.* New York: Routledge, 1993.

Young-Bruehl, Elizabeth. *Mind and the Body Politic.* New York: Routledge, 1989.

Cases

AFSCME v. State of Washington, 770 F. 2d 1401 (9th Cir. 1985), rev'g 578 F. Supp. 846 (D. Wash. 1983).

American Booksellers Association v. Hudnut, 58 F. Supp. 1316 (1984).

Bowers v. Hardwick, 478 U.S. 186 (1986).

Brown v. Board of Education, 347 U.S. 483 (1954).

Butler v. Michigan, 352 U.S. 380 (1957).

Chaplinsky v. New Hampshire, 315 U.S. 568 (1942).

Commonwealth v. Holmes, 17 Mass. 336 (1821).

Colton v. Kentucky, 407 U.S. 104 (1972).

Erznoznik v. City of Jacksonville, 43 LW 4809 (1975).

Holmby Productions v. Vaughan, 350 U.S. 870 (1955).

Ives v. South Buffalo Railroad Co., 201 N.Y. 271 (1911).

Jacobellis V. Ohio, 378 U.S. 184 (1964).

Miller v. California, 413 U.S. 15 (1973).

Memoirs v. Massachusetts, 383 U.S. 413 (1966).

Muller v. Oregon, 208 U.S. 412 (1908).

Near v. Minnesota, 283 U.S. 697 (1931).

New York v. New St. Marks Baths, 497 N.Y.S. 2d 979 (1986).

Paris Adult Theater v. Slaton, 413 U.S. 49 (1973).

Roe v. Wade, 410 U.S. 113 (1973).

United States v. Kennerley, 209 F. 119 (1913).

United States v. Roth, 237 F. 2d 796 (1956).

United States v. Ulysses, 5 F. Supp. 182 (1933).

Winters v. New York, 333 U.S. 507 (1948).

Young v. American Mini Theatres, 427 U.S. 50 (1976).

Index

www.ingramcontent.com/pod-product-compliance
Lightning Source LLC
Chambersburg PA
CBHW032132020426

42334CB00016B/1132

* 9 7 8 0 8 1 4 7 1 2 8 6 3 *